Lost Tribes Found

Lost Tribes Found

Israelite Indians and Religious Nationalism in Early America

Matthew W. Dougherty

UNIVERSITY OF OKLAHOMA PRESS : NORMAN

Library of Congress Cataloging-in-Publication Data

Names: Dougherty, Matthew W., author.
Title: Lost tribes found : Israelite Indians and religious nationalism in early
    America / Matthew W. Dougherty.
Description: Norman : University of Oklahoma Press, [2021] |
    Includes bibliographical references and index. | Summary: "Studies
    early American religious nationalism through the lens of settler and
    Indigenous narratives claiming that Native Americans were 'Israelites'
    or 'Jews'"—Provided by publisher.
Identifiers: LCCN 2020051255 | ISBN 978-0-8061-6888-3 (hardcover)
Subjects: LCSH: Nationalism—Religious aspects—Christianity. |
    Indians—Relations with Jews. | Lost tribes of Israel. | Indians of North
    America—Origin. | Indians of North America—Religion. | Manifest
    Destiny. | Nationalism—United States—History—19th century. |
    Christianity and politics—United States—History. | United States—
    Religion—19th century.
Classification: LCC BR525 .D59 2021 | DDC 261.2/299709034—dc23
LC record available at https://lccn.loc.gov/2020051255

To Joanna:
Etiam, contra mundum.

Contents

Acknowledgments

The most delightful part of writing this book has been the generosity I have encountered from the people who helped me along the way. It is my pleasure to acknowledge them in print.

At the University of Oklahoma Press, I was fortunate to work with a wonderful editorial team. Alessandra Jacobi Tamulevich, Steven B. Baker, and Eva Silverfine all helped guide this project to publication. I am grateful also to my reviewers, David Koffman and Tisa Wenger, for their insightful critiques of the manuscript, which enriched the final project immensely.

This project would not have been possible without generous financial support. The Graduate School of the University of North Carolina (UNC) at Chapel Hill funded both my initial dissertation research and a year-long research fellowship to support my writing. The UNC–Chapel Hill Department of Religious Studies, the Carolina Center for Jewish Studies, and the American Jewish Historical Society all helped fund an extended research trip. The William L. Clements Library of the University of Michigan funded a two-month research fellowship that deepened the arguments on expansion here. While at Queen's University, I was fortunate to hold a postdoctoral fellowship supported by the family of Flora Jane Baker that allowed me to devote myself to preparing this book for publication. Queen's University and the Helmerich Center for American Research supported a crucial extended research trip to Oklahoma.

This project began life as a paper for David Hempton at Harvard Divinity School. It blossomed with the encouragement and patient guidance of my doctoral adviser at UNC, Laurie Maffly-Kipp. She read draft after draft, helped me to keep my eye on what was most interesting and vital in this work, and kept me going through more than one moment of despair. I am also grateful for the continuing support of the members of my doctoral committee. Kathleen DuVal, Jonathan Boyarin, Brandon Bayne, and Kathryn Burns all read drafts and helped me reflect on my thoughts as this project changed and grew throughout the dissertation process. I am fortunate to have had them as mentors and teachers.

The faculty of the School of Religion at Queen's University gave me a home while I transformed the dissertation into a book. I am especially grateful to my postdoctoral supervisor, Pamela Dickey Young, who supported me along the way and helped me to slow down and think about how to reframe my research. Shobhana Xavier, Sharday Mosurinjohn, and Richard Ascough all gave advice, feedback, and support. I could not have asked for a better community.

Other scholars gave generously of their time to critique some or all of this project. Stan Thayne and Sonia Hazard responded to a last-minute call for help with generous comments that enriched this book. At UNC–Chapel Hill, I benefitted from working alongside the members of the American Indian and Indigenous Studies colloquium, the Triangle Religions in the Americas Colloquium, and the Diálogo de Saberes for Interdisciplinary Pathways of Knowledge Production Working Group. In Toronto, I benefitted from the insight of the History of Indigenous Peoples Network at York University. Jessie Embry and two anonymous reviewers at the *Journal of Mormon History* helped me refine my arguments in chapter 2 and deepened my understanding of early Mormon communities.

My research allowed me to collaborate with many wonderful archivists. I am thankful for assistance from the staff of the American Jewish Historical Society, the Princeton University Rare Books and Special Collections, the Houghton Library at Harvard University, the Congregational Library and Archives, the William L. Clements Library, the Helmerich Center for American Research, the Department of Special Collections at the University of Tulsa, the Oklahoma History Collection, the Western History Collection at the University of Oklahoma, the Special Collections of John Vaughan Library at Northeastern State University, and the Church History Library of the Church of Jesus Christ of Latter-day Saints. Special thanks go to the Houghton Library of Harvard University for permission to quote from the American Board of Commissioners for Foreign Missions Papers.

I wish to especially thank the historians, archivists, and community members who helped me navigate difficult historical terrain during my research trip to Oklahoma. Julie Reed generously shared her knowledge of Cherokee history and provided guidance on how to find Cherokee records. Renee Harvey and Natalie Panther at the Helmerich Center were unflaggingly supportive. Jerrid Miller of the Cherokee Heritage Center Archives gave helpful advice and cautions on writing Cherokee history. The congregants of Park Hill Presbyterian Church in Tahlequah, Oklahoma, kindly welcomed me at their worship service. Shirley Pettengill shared a wealth of local historical knowledge and took the time to show me key historical sites.

My family supported me throughout the doctoral process and through an international move. I am particularly grateful to my parents, Susan and Thomas Dougherty, my brother, Jeffrey Dougherty, and to Helen Palmer, Joshua Rifkin, Marc Sacks, and Naomi Sacks. Finally, my deepest thanks go to Joanna Rifkin, my partner in all things, who walked with me all along the way.

Introduction

"We Rule All the Indians"

In the winter of 1644, the frozen canals and icy streets of Amsterdam's Jewish Quarter hummed with an incredible tale. A Jewish traveler named Aaron Levi had arrived that September from New Grenada (now Colombia), where he claimed to have found the lost tribes of Israel hidden in the mountains of the Cordillera Central. According to Jewish and Christian legend, these tribes had been missing since the Assyrian conquest of Israel in 740 BCE. For the Jews of Amsterdam, who were largely descended from Sephardim who fled Spanish territories for the newly independent Netherlands, Levi's discovery seemed to herald the imminent return of the Messiah and the end of the Spanish Empire.[1]

Levi claimed that, while traveling from Quito to Cartagena de Indias under the assumed name of Antonio de Montezinos, he had worked with an Indigenous man named Francisco who alluded to "an unknown people" who would help throw off Spanish rule. Levi paid scant attention to Francisco's story at the time but soon had the opportunity to mull it over when the Office of the Inquisition in Cartagena imprisoned him. Reports had come to them that one "Antonio Montessinos" in the area was secretly practicing Judaism, and Levi was a prime suspect.[2] Being Jewish was not in itself a crime, but Levi was a converso, a descendant

1

of Jews forced to convert to Catholicism, and could be guilty of heresy under church law if he practiced Jewish traditions. Heresy, in a worst-case scenario, was punishable by death.[3] While anxiously awaiting his trial, Levi came to suspect that Francisco's story might have something to it. He was reciting the morning blessings (*birchot hashachar*) in his cell one day when his mind wandered, and he said to himself: "The Hebrews are Indians; then coming to himself again, he . . . added; can the Hebrews be Indians?"[4] The idea was not so far-fetched as it may seem. Spanish Catholic authors had debated whether Indigenous peoples were Hebrews or Israelites since at least the late sixteenth century, and it is not hard to imagine that Levi had heard of such theories.[5] He swore to find out if his intuition were true should he ever be released. Eighteen months later, he made good on this vow when the Inquisition freed him after failing to confirm that he was the "Montessinos" named in the report.[6]

Finding Francisco, Levi revealed to him that he was Jewish and obtained his guidance to travel into the mountains to meet, as Francisco said, other "Israelites" like him. After an arduous journey, the two met a tribe of bearded, pale people who spoke an Indigenous language and a smattering of Hebrew, including the Shema Yisrael, a central confession of faith. With Francisco translating, the men of the tribe explained that they were Israelites who now wished to contact their long-lost brethren in Europe. Through a secret alliance with Indigenous leaders, of whom Francisco was one, they would soon deliver the Jews of Europe from Spanish tyranny. As Francisco reassured Levi, "Be secure, for we rule all the Indians. After we have finished a business which we have with the wicked Spaniards, we will bring you out of your bondage."[7] This message is what stirred the Jewish quarter of Amsterdam. An army of Indigenous Americans and lost Israelites was an unlikely source of deliverance but a thrilling one.

To Levi, and to the Jews of Amsterdam, this story promised that the Israelites of America would transform their political world by overturning what they saw as an oppressive empire. Over a century and a half later, Levi's account touched off a sequence of events in the early United States that led both settlers and Indigenous people to again use stories about Israelite Indians to think about empire. Their stories interpreted early American politics, and especially the crucial question of expansion, using the histories, theologies, and eschatological expectations surrounding the idea of Israel. Some found, as Levi did, that the identification between Israelites and Indigenous people could be used to argue against imperial power. For others, this same identification promised that it was Christian settlers who, in truth, ruled "all the Indians."

Levi's story eventually came to influence the early United States because of one of his contemporaries, the famous rabbi Menasseh Ben Israel. Ben Israel, who lived in Amsterdam and met Levi several times, had correspondents among puritan thinkers allied with Cromwell's government in England. He knew they would be eager to hear a story promising that God would defeat their Catholic enemies in Spain. Hoping to secure their support for reopening England to Jewish settlement, in 1650 Ben Israel publicized and commented on Levi's story in his book Esperança de Israel (The Hope of Israel). This work emphasized that the Israelites of America were the allies of Indigenous peoples, not their relatives, likely because Ben Israel feared that associating Israelites too closely with Indigenous peoples would lower the status of Jews in the eyes of English Christians. English speakers, however, did not pick up on this subtlety. They read an error-filled translation of Ben Israel's book that seemed to say that Indigenous people were Israelites.[8]

This misunderstanding of Levi's story quickly became important among more radical English-speaking Protestants. It briefly ignited in some puritans a passion for the idea that the Indigenous nations of New England, such as the Wampanoag, Massachusett, and Narragansett, might also be Israelites. If they were, then God might be about to begin the prophesied conversion of the Jews in North America, making the puritan colonies vital to the redemption of the world and the second coming of Christ. Enthusiasm for the idea in puritan circles, however, did not long outlast the English Civil War. When the brutality of King Philip's War (1675–78) turned New England settlers' opinions against the "praying Indians" who had converted to Christianity, such millennial hopes seemed to die a quiet death.[9] But the idea had been planted, and in the religious hothouse of the early United States it flowered vibrantly.[10] In this book, I explore that flowering.

Stories about Israelite Indians roused intense emotions amid the religious innovation, rapid territorial expansion, and stark racial hierarchies of the early United States. The fear, hope, excitement, pride, love, awe, and pity they roused in their audiences allowed them to gain an amount of traction that is now surprising. More than that, the feelings they evoked became entangled with multiple nationalisms that reimagined or opposed the United States' growing empire. Although they were never the dominant way of talking about that empire, examining these stories shows the inseparability of religious and political feelings for a wide cast of actors in this period, including Indigenous activists, Protestant reformers, early Mormons, and American Jews.

Religious Nationalisms and the Imperial State

According to one account—familiar from countless high school textbooks—the story of religious nationalism in America is simple. It begins with English settlements in the Massachusetts Bay and Plymouth colonies, where radical Protestant settlers regarded themselves as a chosen people in a binding covenant with God to create a righteous society. This concept of chosen-ness transferred to the young American nation, where mid-nineteenth-century Americans used it to argue that it was White Christians' "manifest destiny" to rule the entirety of the North American continent. From there, it was a short step to believing that God had chosen America to bring Christianity and democracy beyond the continent, leading to imperialist interventions abroad from the Spanish–American War, to Vietnam, to the wars in Iraq and Afghanistan.[11]

Like most simple accounts, this story about the perennial significance of manifest destiny conceals historical complexity. Historians of American religions have shown that the collusion between American religion and nationalism began not at Plymouth Rock but during and after the Revolution, when colonists first began to imagine themselves as a nation distinct from Britain. White Americans in the first half of the nineteenth century, far from cohering around the idea that theirs was a chosen nation, differed sharply on how and whether Christianity and the state should have anything to do with one another. Not one but multiple religious nationalisms emerged from these disagreements, varying by specific regional and religious culture. In the decades after the Revolution, for example, Virginia elites strove to separate religion from government, northeastern Congregationalists sought to extend their ideas of covenant to the whole nation, and frontier Methodists exalted the poor and politically dispossessed even as they acquiesced to racial hierarchy.[12] Still more religious nationalisms come into view if we consider that White Americans were not the only ones invested in the nation's political order. Indigenous religious leaders adapted traditional ceremonies and stories to imagine new futures for their nations and form new coalitions.[13] Black Americans used Christian language to find humanity in inhumane conditions and to envision political independence for themselves.[14]

Not all these nationalisms had equal access to state power, however. In the latter half of the century, the United States brought state governments, Indigenous nations, and overseas colonies into an extensive empire. As recent histories of religion in America have shown, this empire's inequalities shaped the relationship between majoritarian White Protestantism and all other religions. The colonial relationships that made up American empire determined the meaning of "religious freedom" by restricting its protections to religions that supported the state and the racial hierarchy on which it depended. Christian benevolent organizations, which were standard-bearers of the idea that God had a mission for America, over time saw less and less daylight between what they believed to be God's purposes and the extension of American rule. Religious ideas that questioned this empire, especially those emerging from racialized communities, remain outside our histories of American religious nationalism in part because the state considered them not to be religions at all or, at best, to be forms of "bad religion" such as sects, cults, or fanaticism.[15]

Scholars studying the role of religion in this imperial transformation have focused on the legal and political structures of American empire. I focus instead on the shared emotional life of religion and nationalism in specific communities. Telling stories about Israelite Indians allowed members of those communities to express their sense of American empire and invoke religious ideas to envision its transformation. I attend, in this way, to the shared emotional life of religion and nationalism and to how U.S. colonialism shaped that emotional life.

Speculative Histories: Jewish Indians in Euro-American Thought and Politics

When Levi told his story, he participated in a much longer tradition of European speculation about the origins and nature of the Indigenous peoples of the Americas. Scholars studying this tradition have offered several explanations for why, from the early sixteenth to the nineteenth centuries, Europeans persistently identified Indigenous people with Israelites. Perhaps the most common explanation is ignorance. As the argument goes, finding unknown peoples in the "New World" astounded Europeans. Naturally, they turned to the Bible for an explanation, and the legend of the lost tribes of Israel was a convenient way to fit Indigenous people into biblical narratives. Doing so not only made Indigenous people understandable but justified biblical inerrancy against skeptics who used their existence to question the Bible's account of humanity.[16]

Neither the need to fit Indigenous people into a pre-existing mental framework nor the need to support the Bible explains, however, why Europeans turned specifically to the legend of the lost tribes of Israel. As early as the publication of Gregorio García's *Origen de los Indios* in 1607, Europeans had already speculated that Indigenous people might be descended from nomadic central or east Asian peoples, from Phoenicians, or from the mysterious Ophir son of Joktan mentioned in Genesis.[17] All these explanations gave Europeans ways to categorize Indigenous peoples that fit into biblical histories, so why turn to Israel? In the most sophisticated version of this argument, Zvi Ben-Dor Benite offers one answer: that the mystery surrounding the lost tribes of Israel was itself the point. Precisely because they were lost, they inspired searches along the edges of colonial expansion and gave both Jews and Christians hope for what might result should they be found.[18]

This explanation, however, does not give enough weight to how classifying peoples was, for Europeans, a technique of governance. From the Middle Ages through the early modern period, Europeans divided humans into "lineages" and "nations"—the terms in Latin were *gentes* and *nationes*—that shared common descent, language, customs, and style of dress. European monarchs often governed several such "nations" and treated each differently by, for example, allowing them some measure of self-governance or granting specific legal privileges. As European states became colonial empires, they governed subjugated peoples by categorizing them according to their lineages and nations as well as their "nature," that is, their supposed physical and psychological traits.[19] Between the sixteenth and nineteenth centuries, these ways of categorizing people gradually hardened into what we now call race. Increasingly, a person's body alone, not markers of cultural identity, language, or class, determined the scope of their rights and legal personhood. In the early United States, race became the primary way of determining who was a citizen with rights, who was a foreigner to the body politic, and who was a commodity to be bought and sold.[20]

Understanding how Israelite Indian stories interacted with the politics of human classification requires attention to their specific contexts. The most sophisticated such explorations have concentrated on the Spanish discussions about Israelite Indians that inspired Levi. Jonathan Boyarin has argued that comparisons between Indigenous peoples and Jews allowed Spanish imperial officials to import the means of governance and surveillance developed for conversos to Indigenous peoples. In the process, they expressed their suspicion of Indigenous peoples' loyalty to the church and the state in terms of their long-standing association between the presence of Jews in the body politic and the presence of sin in individual Christians. For Boyarin, comparisons between Jews and Indians were signs of the formation in the Spanish Empire of an incorporating society, that is, a society that wished to extend its rule over and assimilate "others" but also to keep those others at arms' length. Jews, to early modern Spanish Christians, were the paradigmatic example of the person who was subject yet alien to the nation.[21]

This dynamic does not entirely hold in the early American context. Most of the people covered in this book did not envision the incorporation of Indigenous people into White Christian society. Instead, following the dominant tendency of the American way of doing colonialism, they insisted on the impossibility of racially distinct people belonging to the same society without tight legal controls to ensure their separation. This attitude underwrote not only slavery and wars against Indigenous nations but most nineteenth-century attempts to end the "problem" of racial difference benevolently, such as the colonization movement to deport free Black Americans to Africa.[22] This is one reason why they stressed the Israelite, rather than Jewish, identity of Indigenous people. Jews, for Europeans, were internal others to be monitored and controlled. Israel, in nineteenth-century understandings of the Bible, was a nation of people with an independent existence who remained separate from the surrounding nations. Following this understanding, most Israelite Indian stories told in the early United States implied that Indigenous people would remain distinct from Whites.

In this book, I examine how, in the context of early American expansion, identifications between Israelites and Indigenous people briefly served some political purposes, leading to a sudden profusion of such narratives over the space of a few crucial decades.[23] Hence, it is not a history of a single "Jewish Indian theory" winding through different communities but of a set of interrelated stories that linked Indigenous peoples with ancient Israel.[24] Focusing, like studies of Israelite Indian stories in the Spanish Empire, on the use of these narratives in a colonial context, I demonstrate their entanglement with American expansion.[25]

Empire, Religion, Emotion

What does empire feel like? In early America, this question asks how individual people experienced the titanic changes accompanying the extension of White settlement and U.S. power over the continent.[26] When I say that Israelite Indian stories were about religious nationalism, I mean that both settler and Indigenous people turned to practices they understood as religious to cultivate, shape, and transform their feelings about political collectives. In making this argument, I use three concepts—empire, religion, and emotion or affect—that have their own bodies of literature giving them more technical meanings than they have in everyday speech. Understanding those meanings in some detail will make this analysis easier to follow.

Here, the term "empire" refers to a set of strategies for rule, not a specific form of government. Imperial states divide their subjects into legally and politically distinct categories by sorting them according to markers—such as race, geographic location, religion, or language—that the state selects as significant. Members of these categories are not equal. Instead, empires characteristically allow some populations to rule over others, sometimes creating complex hierarchies and internal oppositions. The condition created by this relationship, referred to as colonialism, can take many forms, from the extraction of resources to the elimination and displacement of a subjugated group by settlers.[27]

In this sense, the nineteenth-century United States was an empire. Popular histories often explain the ironic contrast between the democratic ideals and brutal racial inequalities of early America as a sign that Americans only imperfectly realized the intentions of the Revolutionary founders. However, America's racial caste system did not contradict but instead supported the liberties extended to White citizens. Nineteenth-century justifications for the idea that all White men were equal, regardless of social or economic rank, depended on the elevation of White men above Black people, Indigenous peoples, and White women.[28] The broader economic opportunities available to White men in the United States compared with Europe similarly depended on an economy driven by the unfree labor of enslaved people and the low-cost land appropriated from Indigenous peoples.[29] Hence, both the political and economic orders of the United States depended on a fundamental imperial move: the creation of separate categories of person—in this case, "races"—and of different legal systems to govern them. The brutality this caused was not a sign that American values fell short but a sign that the political order was working as intended to ensure maximum freedom for the only category of people included in the body politic, namely White people. It is this reality that I mean when I speak here of American empire, imperialism, and colonialism.

Although I consider only one empire here, that of the United States, I consider multiple nations.[30] I use the term "nation" for political communities that imagined themselves as autonomous, bounded, and unified by a structuring commonality such as language, religion, or ethnicity. Nationhood, I argue, was about collective imagination and practice as much as it was about official legal recognition. Nations manifested themselves in rituals such as parades, banners, festivals, and diplomacy. These rituals, and the emotions accompanying them, made concrete and visible an abstract political entity. The United States itself was, of course, such a nation, but so were many self-conscious groups that the United States did not legally recognize or which it considered subject to itself.[31] Many of those groups used practices they understood as religious to make their political autonomy seem more concrete.

This view of empire and nationhood informs how I name people in this book. I use the names of specific Indigenous nations when applicable, preferring the name most widely in use among descendant groups when speaking English. When this name is substantially different from a name most readers will recognize, I place the better-known term in parentheses in the first instance. When speaking about the first peoples of North America in general, I use the term "Indigenous peoples" rather than "American Indians." Using the term Indigenous has, for my purposes, the advantage of more clearly distinguishing between actual Indigenous peoples and the images of them as "Indians" or "Israelite Indians" in the imaginations and legal systems of non-Indigenous people. I use "Indian" and, in the Mormon context, "Lamanite," only to discuss these fictions or the names of policies, such as Indian removal. "Native American" would have done similar work but is not common in contemporary Indigenous communities or outside the borders of the United States. Since those borders artificially cut off some Indigenous peoples from members of their nations living in Canada or Mexico, where the terms "Indigenous" and "*indígena*" are common, I have chosen the term that has broader hemispheric currency and, I hope, better signals my awareness of the historical contingency of those borders and of their imposition on the First Peoples of the continent.

When speaking of non-Indigenous people, I make use of the terms "settler," "White," and "Black." "White" was, and is, a political category designating a racial caste, not simply a marker of European descent. White Americans in the nineteenth century did not always consider European Jews, for example, to belong to their race and rarely recognized people of mixed African and European descent as "White." When I use the term, it is because I am making a generalization about people belonging to that caste. The related term "settler" refers to all people who lived in North America and benefitted from what students of empire call "settler colonialism," or a colonial system that seeks to eliminate local populations and claim their lands.[32] I do not use the term, however, to refer to those people whose ancestors arrived involuntarily in North America from Africa, since they were rarely able to access the economic and political benefits of settlement. For them, I use the terms Black people or Black Americans. I capitalize both "White" and "Black" to emphasize that both are socially constructed categories with their own histories, not neutral markers of difference.

These same imperial histories shape the concept "religion." The ideas that religion is a universal human practice, that it is separate from other domains of life such as politics and economics, and that it is a matter first and foremost of belief all emerge from colonial politics. Although the word "religion" and its cognates existed in Europe before the beginning of European imperialism, it was only as European empires sought to understand and rule new populations that the term developed these meanings. Through the description and comparison of the religions they attributed to subject peoples, colonizing empires isolated and discussed certain practices as "religious," placed those practices under missionary control, and created boundaries between subject populations understood as religiously distinct. The colonial origins of the term, however, did not stop subject peoples from using it to give legal sanction to certain traditions and practices.[33]

American empire participated in this construction of religion, and in turn the construction of religion helped constitute American empire. As historians of Christianity in the United States have long recognized, the moves to disestablish state churches and guarantee "freedom of religion" between 1791 and 1818 paradoxically initiated a massive rise in Christian affiliation and church attendance. For some, this transformation shows that in this period American Christianity was "democratizing," that is, adapting to and encouraging the assumptions that undergirded republican government.[34] For others, it demonstrates the extension of social control, as White Protestants responded to disestablishment by reshaping Americans' attitudes toward and practices of religion in their own image.[35] Both interpretations illuminate different aspects of the construction of religion in the expanding American empire. Over the first half of the nineteenth century, the way that Americans talked about and regulated "religion"—a category given new legal force by the First Amendment to the Constitution—changed in ways that both encouraged adaptation to republican politics and disciplined religions into more Protestant shapes. By midcentury, this process of adaptation and discipline cohered into what scholars now term "secularism."

Secularism, in this sense, was not religion's opposite but a set of practices White Americans used to relate politics and government to religion. American secularism endorsed the idea that true religion came from individuals making reasonable choices driven by their inborn common sense, just as did the American state. In both cases, White Americans assumed that only they could make the proper religious and political choices unaided and that others would have to be controlled through legal and educational regimes to make them choose correctly. Secularism, in short, insisted that true religion endorsed both the republican freedoms that America's empire extended to White citizens and the exclusion of non-White people from full personhood. Things that looked like religions but did endorse these practices it classified as "superstition," "fanaticism," or simply no kind of religion at all. This close analogy between the state and majoritarian Protestantism, over time, constrained voices that used Protestant discourses to critique the United States.[36] While building on the insights of work on American secularism, here I attend to these other voices, which related Christianity to the American state in ways not easily captured by the logic of secularism. These minority perspectives, which now might seem strange or insignificant, allow us to mark more precisely the growing entanglement of religion, secularism, and the American state over the nineteenth century.

My analysis relies, finally, on thinking about emotion. It is common to think of emotions as subjective experiences arising from an authentic, inner self. However, I draw on work that treats emotions as practices. By practices, I mean both the choices people make to navigate their cultural contexts and the habitual responses they have from long formation in those contexts. These choices and responses are strategic in that they allow people to maneuver through their social worlds, not necessarily in the sense that they are conscious plans. Hence, I do not assume that the emotions I describe were either wholly sincere or wholly pretense but strive to leave my analysis in the middle space between those poles.[37]

Although the term "practice" may call to mind bodily movements as in ritual, performance, or everyday comportment, the emotions I consider here were practiced in writing and preserved in textual archives. Reading emotions in written sources takes interpretation. When the authors of my sources reported on their own or others emotions, spoke about the nature and desirability of different emotions, or used emotional language and emotionally significant symbols to appeal to their audiences, they did not do so with complete fidelity to what they or others may have felt. Instead, they wrote what was expected or encouraged in their contexts, denied or left out what was not, and failed to record much that seemed irrelevant or uninteresting. With this patchiness in mind, I attempt to uncover feelings in my sources by attending to the specific communities that shaped their authors, their audiences, and the circumstances of their creation.

Specific political and religious communities shaped how my sources recorded emotions three main ways. First, they required or enabled participation in practices that shaped emotional responses, such as parades, singing, worship, and daily prayer. When these practices "worked" as they were supposed to—and they did not always—they evoked specific feelings such as awe, reverence, pride in one's nation, or fear of God. Second, communities influenced how people described and communicated their emotions. A nineteenth-century Methodist, for example, might have named an intense, negative feeling as "conviction of sin" and communicated it through sighs, tears, and trembling in a revival. In the process of defining this emotion to themselves and communicating this emotion, they shaped their inner life to match what they believed "conviction of sin" felt and looked like. Third, communities created categories of feeling such as "benevolence," "sympathy," and "longing" to taxonomize and control their members' emotions. As discussed later in this book, for example, evangelical reformers believed that the American citizenry would need careful regulation and education to cultivate the highest forms of benevolence and conduct themselves for the good of the nation. Revivalist evangelicals, on the other hand, emphasized that Americans could become truly moral only by undergoing authentic transports of sorrow and joy in conversion and emerging remade as Christians. In both cases, these religious communities scrutinized and disciplined their members' practice and expression of emotion to encourage them to hew closer to these norms.[38]

In each chapter, I analyze the specific practices that evoked emotions, repertoires of expressing and talking about emotion, and ways of categorizing or evaluating emotions in the communities that shaped the authors and audiences of my sources. With these practices in mind, I seek to understand the emotions these writers and readers invested in the concepts of "Israel" and "the Indians" to reconstruct the significance that associating those concepts together might have had for them. I take this approach because, in each case I examine, these stories were less disciplined theories meant to be defended and justified than enthusiastic feats of association and imagination. Evangelicals trained to associate "Israel" with their concern for the reform of society and their hope for its future flourishing on earth felt anticipation, wonder, and some anxiety at the idea that the Indigenous peoples oppressed by the United States might, in fact, be Israelites. Mormons who saw the Israelites of their new scripture as mirrors of their excitement at the dawning of a new age and their growing anger with the United States looked for signs of those feelings in the Indigenous people they encountered. Some Jewish and Indigenous activists found in these stories reasons for pride in themselves and hope for their communities. As my discussions of their reception make clear, these narratives' popularity and significance lay not in the weight of their arguments but in their ability to make suggestive links and to lodge the identification of Israelite with Indians in the minds even of those who never quite found the idea convincing.[39]

These three concepts—empire, religion, and emotion—are vital to how early Americans used Israelite Indian stories. As I show, comparisons of Indigenous peoples to Israelites or Jews often articulated forms of religious nationalism in the context of an expansive U.S. empire. These nationalisms claimed that

God had chosen some populations—American Jews, Indigenous peoples, Mormons, or White settlers—to have territory and political sovereignty. These nationalisms were effective precisely because of their entanglement with religion and its regulation. They constructed Indigenous religions by identifying some practices and traditions as revealed by the God of Israel and made appeals to the practices of specific religious communities. They drew on the feelings that the communities discussed here cultivated about "Israel" and "Israelites" and encouraged the transfer of those feelings into new visions of the place of Indigenous peoples in the American political order.

Plan of the Book

This book opens and closes with analyses of Israelite Indian stories in the context of national politics in the early United States. The first chapter analyzes how these stories emerged in and helped shape a national evangelical culture that supported missions to Indigenous peoples. The final chapter, similarly, discusses religious nationalism on a country-wide scale to explain the decline in use of Israelite Indian stories after 1830. In the intervening chapters, I explore more local and specific conversations that invoked Israelite Indian stories.

In chapter 1 I discuss how the stories Levi introduced to Anglophone America went through a renaissance in the early United States. Working largely from seventeenth- and eighteenth-century British sources, early American evangelicals from the 1790s through the 1820s transformed these stories and used them to support the idea that the United States must missionize Indigenous peoples in order to expand across the continent without losing the favor of God. With these stories, they sought to evoke sympathy for Indigenous people and anxiety lest God punish the nation for their persecution of his chosen people. At the same time, their versions of Israelite Indian stories depicted Indigenous people as inferiors to be pitied and suggested that, once Indigenous peoples converted to Christianity, they would joyfully leave the continent in White hands and "return" to Palestine.

Early Mormons extended and elaborated these ideas. As I show in chapter 2, between 1830 and 1847, Mormons understood themselves to be living in an age of millennial transformation, when God's purposes for the "Lamanites," or Israelite Indians, would be revealed. By encountering Lamanites in worship and recounting Lamanite histories, early Mormons cultivated the love for their new religion and wonder at living in an age of revelations that knit them together as a community. By discussing prophecies about an army of Israelite Indians or "Lamanites" that would soon destroy the United States to make room for God's kingdom of Zion, they transferred their anger at the United States onto Lamanites and schooled themselves to patience. Because of this complex of feelings, the nationalism that bound Mormons together immediately before and after the death of Joseph Smith reached for both imagined Lamanites and actual Indigenous allies to help spark the creation of Zion.

In chapter 3 I analyze two intellectuals who used Israelite Indian narratives to engage with the ascendant White supremacy and populist political rhetoric of the 1830s. One, the prominent Jewish newspaper editor Mordecai Noah, used these narratives to strengthen American Jews' claims to American citizenship and western territory. The other, the Pequot activist and preacher William Apess, used them to argue for the humanity of Indigenous people and to envision an "Israel" of independent Indigenous Christians. For both men, these narratives allowed them to enlist the sympathy of evangelical reformers on behalf of their communities. They also attempted to use them, however, to evoke the pride and hope that might nurture new Jewish or Indigenous nationalisms.

I focus in chapter 4 on a small group of Christian Cherokees who drew on missionary stories of Israelite Indians to identify their ancestors with the people described in the Bible. Their narratives argued that the Christian God had given the Cherokees their land, in part because they wanted to enlist missionary sympathies against the state and federal governments then pressuring the Cherokee Nation to give up its territory. More, their narratives argued against missionary descriptions of Cherokee ceremonies as heathenism by claiming that it was Christian Cherokees, not White pastors, who understood the ceremonies' true meaning. Although the Cherokees who told these stories had reason to hope that they would help start a broader reform in their society, the genocidal Trail of Tears and the disarray that followed prevented their narratives from being published and distributed in the new Cherokee Nation.

Finally, in chapter 5 I return to a national focus to analyze the eclipse of Israelite Indian stories in American life. I track the rise of American secularism, a then-new way of relating religion to the state, and its effects on the articulation of religious nationalisms, including the much-discussed concept of "manifest destiny." In the process, I show how new versions of Israelite Indian stories arose in the 1830s and 1840s that muted their emotional appeals to blend more seamlessly with the practices of secularism. At the same time, a new literature arose that emphasized both the danger and the inevitability of frontier settlers' thirst for violence. Only the state and Christianity working in concord, they implied, could restrain this violence. By the beginning of the Civil War, these new ways of relating feelings about religion and about the American state had supplanted older Israelite Indian narratives.

An army of Israelites and Indigenous people never materialized to liberate Jews in the Spanish Empire. Levi, however, went to his death in Recife swearing to the truth of his story. Whatever he experienced or did not experience in the mountains, the story he told had become a vision of Jewish nationhood and liberation from Spanish colonialism that he was unwilling to surrender.[40]

Similarly, many of the nationalisms discussed in this book did not have the results their creators hoped. They do, however, expand our ideas of who possessed religious nationalisms in the early United States and, in the ways they deployed the concepts of "a promised land" and "a chosen people," help place discussions of religion and politics in this era within the concrete realities of land and legal personhood crucial to American empire.

1

Friends of Zion

During the first few years after her marriage in 1819, Lydia Howard Sigourney returned often to the library that dominated the north wing of her grand home in Hartford, Connecticut. Soon, she would become one of the most acclaimed poets in America, a mentor to both John Greenleaf Whittier and Harriet Beecher Stowe. Now, though, she had to steal time in her library between caring for three young stepchildren. Her collection was extensive: the will her husband Charles made in 1851 suggested its scope when it specifies that she should have "all the Books, which [Lydia] brought into the family when married, or which came to her from her father, or which she has acquired since marriage from other sources."[1] Since she was a fervent Congregationalist and social reformer, her library likely featured many of the periodicals, tracts, and books that like-minded Protestants printed in vast numbers during her lifetime. She drew on that literature to write *Traits of the Aborigines of America,* an 1822 epic poem about the history of contact between Indigenous and settler peoples in North America. Seeking to explain the origins of Indigenous peoples, she crystallized views on Indigenous religions then popular in the literature of reform that crowded her shelves:

In various forms arose
Their superstitious homage. Some with blood

Of human sacrifices sought to appease
That anger, which in pestilence, or dearth,
Or famine stalk'd; and their astonish'd vales
Like Carthaginian altars, frequent drank
The horrible libation. Some with fruits,
Sweet flowers, and incense of their choicest herbs,
Sought to propitiate HIM, whose powerful hand
Unseen, sustain'd them. Some with mystic rites,
The ark, the orison the paschal feast,
Through glimmering tradition seemed to bear,
As in some broken vase, the smother'd coals,
Scattr'd from Jewish altars.[2]

In copious footnotes, she explained that the first group of Indigenous people described, whom she compared to Carthaginians because they practiced human sacrifice, were the Nahua peoples of the Aztec Triple Alliance. The second, whom she depicted as gentle worshippers of an unknown god, were the Andean peoples of the Inca Empire. Her description of both these groups fit a common, though not universal, Christian assessment of the peoples they variously called "heathens" or "pagans." According to this view, all humans had vague knowledge of God, "whose powerful hand / Unseen sustained them," but tended to elaborate on that knowledge with increasingly perverse ceremonies that could end in the "blood / Of human sacrifices."[3] The third group, however, was different. These were the Indigenous nations of North America then in closest contact with the United States, such as the Lenape (Delaware), Muscogee (Creek), Cherokee, and Haudenosaunee (Iroquois). These nations, she argued, practiced ceremonies in which the trained eye could see "through glimmering tradition . . . the smother'd coals / Scattr'd from Jewish altars," that is, the religion of ancient Israel.

The idea that Indigenous people were Israelites, while not a majority position in the early United States overall, had more support among those who, like Sigourney, dedicated themselves to what historians have called the "benevolent empire" of Protestant reform organizations. This "empire" of interconnected voluntary societies had an outsized influence on early American literature and news media. From the 1790s through the 1840s, reformers' publications often expressed support for Israelite Indian stories or at least treated them as credible. Although Jedidiah Morse, a Congregationalist geographer and textbook author, was skeptical of the idea, he allowed in his 1789 *American Geography* that "it is the opinion of many learned men, supported by several well established facts, that the Indians of America are remains of the ten tribes of Israel."[4] Similarly, Congregationalist minister and educator Elijah Parish did not commit himself to the idea but spent three pages in his popular 1810 textbook, *A New System of Modern Geography*, listing reasons to believe there was a connection between Israelites and Indigenous people before concluding, "the subject is curious, and deserves further investigation."[5] Missionaries, too, often proclaimed support for the idea in letters and diaries that were subsequently published in missionary journals and literature, as with an 1824 letter in which the missionary Calvin Cushman wrote, "I think there is much reason to believe [the Choctaws] are the descendants of Abraham."[6] With these authorities lending credence to Israelite Indian stories, pro-reform newspapers tended to treat them as plausible at least. Thus *The Philadelphia Recorder*, a missionary newspaper, published a piece in 1826 claiming that a Seminole leader's speech so resembled the story of Jacob and Esau that it must be "a piece of circumstantial testimony in favor of the opinion, that the savages of our country are descendants of the lost tribes of Israel."[7] Although only a minority of these Protestant reformers seem to have supported Israelite Indian narratives, they gave the idea a platform with their unparalleled networks for distributing books, pamphlets, and journals.[8] Through these networks, the idea entered the national conversation. Hence, if

Israelite Indian stories were "in the air" in the early United States, as many historians have observed, reformers' publications were one of the main reasons.[9]

When Protestant reformers turned to Israelite Indian stories, they did so for two key reasons. First, the stories allowed them to construct what they believed to be a unitary "Indian religion" based in the rituals of ancient Israel. They used this fictitious religion both to cultivate attachment to Indigenous people among their supporters, who were trained to think of themselves as the spiritual heirs of Israel, and to imply that Indigenous people needed missionaries to guide them to the supposed fulfillment of Israelite religion in Christianity. Second, by telling these stories reformers sought to evoke in their White readers feelings of hope and anxiety about missions to Indigenous people. If the Indians were Israelites, they argued, then God would judge the nation that treated them harshly. Only by slowing the pace of settlement and funding missions to Indigenous people could the United States retain God's favor.

Understanding the appeal of Israelite Indian stories to these early nineteenth century reformers requires understanding who they were. They were overwhelmingly, though not exclusively, bourgeois White members of Congregationalist, Presbyterian, Dutch and German Reformed, and, to a lesser extent, Episcopal churches in the northeast and northwest of the United States— meaning by the latter term the states of Ohio, Indiana, and Illinois as well as Michigan and Wisconsin Territories. Their benevolent empire grew from a heritage that emphasized the collective responsibility of Christians to make their society "godly," by which they meant orderly, deeply hierarchical, and ruled by church members. Christians were responsible for their society, they argued, because of providence, meaning God's arrangement of events to reward faithful communities and punish unfaithful ones. Through the lens of providence, they saw the rise and fall of nations in the historical record as evidence that God struck covenants with certain nations—most especially Israel and nations ruled by Protestants—to allow them to prosper and endure, but only so long as they retained their orderly and pious character. All others God would eventually destroy, even if he kept them going in the meanwhile for his own purposes. As Ephraim T. Woodruff, an Ohio Presbyterian minister, put it in 1826: "When nations, as nations, are guilty of departing from the service of the true God, then are they punished of God in their national capacity in this world. They are pursued with the judgments of heaven until, deeply sensible of their national guilt, they either abandon those courses of national folly to which they have been long addicted, or their remembrance is cut off from the earth." [10] Correct worship of God and respect for hierarchy were, therefore, the foundations of national security.[11]

Through most of the eighteenth century, the Congregationalist, Presbyterian, Dutch Reformed, and German Reformed churches in the British colonies of North America tended to focus on maintaining God's favor for their local communities. This was especially the case in New England, where the inheritors of the puritan movement regarded themselves as a nation apart. During and after the Revolution, however, members of these churches came to see the entire nation through a providentialist lens. God, they argued, had helped the United States to win the War of Independence so that it could become a free, Christian nation and would only support it so long as it fulfilled that purpose. But the new country was far from their ideal of a pious, orderly village. Many Americans, especially in the rural south and west, belonged to no church at all or, almost as bad, to the Baptist and Methodist movements that leveled social distinctions and stirred up worshippers' emotions to dangerous heights. Even worse, an increasing number were Catholics, whom most Protestants saw as a dire threat to democracy because of their supposed allegiance to the Papacy. Black Americans, enslaved and free, and Indigenous people, meanwhile, presented different kinds of otherness. Although members of these northeastern churches tended to believe that it was possible for non-Whites to become godly, they had little taste for racial equality even when it came to Black and Indigenous members of their own churches. Faced with creating their vision of the good society out of such a diverse population spread out over such a large country, Protestant reformers vacillated between fear lest they should fail and hope for the Christian nation that might come of their efforts.[12]

The ratification of the Bill of Rights in 1791 and the slow disestablishment of state churches in the first decades of the nineteenth century ensured that these Protestant reformers could not rely too much on state power to enforce religious norms. Instead, they sought to bind Americans to their cause with practices that had swept the world of English-speaking Protestants during the last century, transforming and dividing their churches. This cluster of practices, which historians refer to as evangelicalism, included specific methods of prayer designed to awaken an experience of God's grace, widespread Bible reading, continual scrutiny of one's feelings and actions in private prayer, and active work to transform society.[13] Reformers assumed that these practices slowly educated, disciplined, and nurtured people into Christians over time by altering their feelings toward others and toward God. In this, they differed sharply from evangelicals in the Baptist and Methodist traditions who expected the dramatic upheaval of a conversion experience to launch a person into a Christian life. Reformers argued instead that only regular nurture, training, and discipline could allow a person to possess the highest form of human feeling: "disinterested benevolence," or the desire to help others without either an expectation of reward or a pre-existing social connection to motivate them.[14]

Seeking to train Americans to feel such benevolence toward the poor, the enslaved, and those without Christian education, reformers from 1800 to 1830 founded society after society dedicated to causes like temperance, antislavery, Bible distribution, education,

and—most consequentially for Indigenous peoples—the conversion of "the heathen" at home and abroad. Out of the interde-
nominational coalition building required to sustain these reform
societies emerged a new political and doctrinal consensus, one
that downplayed distinctive theologies in favor of emphasis on the
need to ensure the triumph of middle-class morality, orderly hierarchies in the home and the public square, and the public dominance of Protestantism over religious skeptics and Catholics.[15]

Despite this new consensus, these northern reformers remained
distinct from other evangelicals, such as members of the Methodist, Baptist, and Restoration movements then making inroads
throughout the west. For understanding Israelite Indian stories,
one important distinction was the extent to which reformers from
the Congregationalist, Presbyterian, and Reformed churches—
who organized and bankrolled the largest reform societies in the
first half of the century—relied on the idea of Israel to articulate
their vision of themselves and of a future, transformed United
States. They often referred to themselves as "Israel" and to the
United States, or the United States as they imagined it to be, as
"Canaan."[16] Pro-reform publications invited their readers to
imagine themselves as allies of this future, fully Christian nation
by referring to them as "friends of Zion," a term that recalled
both Israel, for which "Zion" was and is a common synecdoche,
and the Protestant idea of Zion or "New Jerusalem," which stood
for God's coming kingdom on earth.[17] When reformers called
Indigenous people Israelites, therefore, they made an assertion
not just about their origins but about their future as members,
though not equal ones, in this coming Christian nation.

Emotion and the Construction of "Indian Religion"

The Israelite Indian stories that reformers told were, in part, a
type of comparative religion. They constructed a unitary "Indian
religion" out of accounts of Indigenous customs and ceremonies,

compared that religion to Protestant understandings of ancient Israel, and used the comparison to arrive at conclusions about Indigenous people. Grounded in the idea that similarity of practice indicated similarity of descent, these comparisons featured weak logic and strange leaps of deduction. Their appeal lay not in their intellectual consistency but in the emotions they helped cultivate. In this respect, comparing Indigenous people to Israelites was not the same as comparing them to any other group. Reformers regarded Israelites as a chosen people who, like themselves, had a covenant with the Christian God. They used these stories to cultivate and express the emotions that tied missionaries and their supporters together into the "Zion" of evangelical reform. Their stories also implied, however, that Indigenous people had degenerated from their former status as God's chosen nation. They could not know what was best for them and their religious life and should accept the guidance of White missionaries to "return" to their earlier practices. Hence, the Israelite Indian stories that these "friends of Zion" told helped cement an unequal relationship between missionaries and missionized.[18]

To construct her vision of "Indian religion," Sigourney drew on the most significant publication on Israelite Indian ideas for evangelical reformers: Elias Boudinot's 1816 *A Star in the West*.[19] Boudinot, a New Jersey lawyer, member of the Continental Congress, and director of the U.S. Mint, gave generously to evangelical reform societies after his 1805 retirement. He quickly rose to prominence in the benevolent empire, becoming a trustee of Princeton, the first president of the American Bible Society, and the first president of the American Society for Meliorating the Condition of the Jews.[20] In *A Star in the West*, he laid out what would become the standard Israelite Indian narrative in the early United States. Indigenous people, he claimed, were the descendants of the lost tribes exiled from the Northern Kingdom of Israel in the eighth century BCE and made "outcasts from the nations of the earth." These tribes found the idolatries of Assyria revolting and left, traveling to the extreme northwest of Asia. There, "God again appeared for them, as he had done for their fathers of old at the Red sea . . . [and] stayed the flood, or perhaps froze it into firm ice," bringing them across the Bering Strait to North America. Once in America, they slowly lost their religious traditions until only faint traces of Israelite ancestry were visible. White Americans could reap God's blessings by converting his lost, chosen people to Christianity. Doing so, they would ensure their national prosperity and advance the reign of Jesus's kingdom on the earth.[21]

Boudinot's was not the only Israelite Indian story in wide circulation among evangelical reformers. However, it was perhaps the most widely reprinted and, because of Boudinot's stature, the most respected. Missionary periodicals excerpted and debated it, and subsequent accounts of Israelite Indians that circulated among Protestant reformers usually drew on it heavily.[22] Ethan Smith, a Congregationalist minister in rural Vermont, reconfigured and restated Boudinot's arguments with some modifications in his 1823 *View of the Hebrews*. The chapbook author Josiah Priest, in turn, excerpted Smith's book in his 1826 *The Wonders of Nature and Providence, Displayed* and, in modified form, in his 1833 *American Antiquities*. The latter ran through three editions in its first year, including one print run of 22,000 copies, at a time when a popular novelist like Sir Walter Scott got a print run roughly half that size.[23] Because versions of Boudinot's arguments reached a wide audience, analyzing them reveals broader trends in the use of Israelite Indian narratives among reformers.

Kinship and Sympathy

Most of Boudinot's argument that Indigenous people were Israelites depended on the idea that any parallels between Indigenous practices and those described in the Bible indicated common descent. He drew not only on earlier authors who proposed versions of the Israelite Indian hypothesis but on a forest of details about Indigenous practices drawn from the reports of travelers, missionaries, and chroniclers. He spent one chapter on specious parallels between words in Indigenous languages and Hebrew, a second on stories that seemed to echo those in the Bible, and a third on the custom in some nations of separating women during their menstrual periods in a seeming parallel to Israelite practices. Each supposed piece of evidence was, individually, inconsequential. For example, it is hardly convincing that a Dutch minister in New York met a Mohawk woman in 1644 who told him "that her forefathers had told her that the great spirit once went out walking with his brother, and that a dispute arose between them, and the great spirit killed his brother," no matter how much Boudinot insisted that "this is plainly a confusion of the story of Cain and Abel."[24] For those who wished to be convinced, however, Boudinot supplied arresting details.

From his leaps of logic and questionable evidence emerged a theory: that underlying all Indigenous ceremonies, cultural practices, and stories were Israelite beliefs and practices. "Their religious ceremonies," as Boudinot put it, were "more after the Mosaic institution, than of pagan imitation." Contemporary Protestant theories of religion admitted of only two types of religion: revealed and invented. The former came from God's revelations, first through the Hebrew prophets and then, in fuller form, through Jesus. The latter came from humans and included the use of images or "idolatry," all practices of non-Christian "heathen" or "pagan" religions, the "superstitions" of the ignorant, and the ceremonies of the Roman Catholic Church. All these were similar, they argued, because in each case humans became confused and substituted a created thing for the divine creator.[25] Hence, to prove that Indigenous people had a revealed religion, Boudinot had to insist that they perceived God correctly, if dimly, and did not worship created things. They were, he argued, "never known . . . to pay the least perceivable adoration to images or dead person, or to celestial luminaries, or evil spirits, or to any created being whatever."[26] Any reports to the contrary were the result of malice or misunderstanding.

For Boudinot's readers in the evangelical community, the most convincing and most often-cited piece of evidence in this argument was his belief that Indigenous people used the four-letter personal name of God, YHVH, that appears in the Hebrew text of the Bible but which observant Jews traditionally do not pronounce. In one of the few sections of *A Star in the West* based on his personal experience, Boudinot claimed that, at an unspecified time, he had heard "Indians," use this name in "a religious dance" to commemorate a meeting between the governor of New Jersey and what was probably a Haudenosaunee or Lenape delegation. As Boudinot and "a very large company of gentlemen and ladies" watched, "between twenty and thirty Indians came in, wrapped in their blankets" and began a circular dance, quickening on each rotation around the center and singing, until at the end of the fourth round "they cast off their blankets entirely" and danced vigorously "in a mere frenzy, twisting their bodies, and wreathing like so many snakes, and making as many antic gestures as a parcel of monkies." To Boudinot's ears, the song they sang sounded like "y-he-ho-wah."[27] This was exactly what he hoped to hear.

Boudinot came prepared to hear the name of God in this song because of his reading of James Adair's 1775 book, *The History of the American Indians*.[28] Adair, a British Indian trader, argued from his firsthand observations of the Chickasaw and Muscogee that their religion was Israelite. Reformers read and excerpted his book fairly widely—including Boudinot, who cited it frequently in *A Star in the West*—but rejected Adair's skepticism about the value of sending missionaries to Indigenous people.[29] Adair believed that the Chickasaw used the name "Yo-he-wa" for God, either because he latched on to a few syllables that sounded familiar in sacred songs or because he misheard a ritual phrase, "yahola," used when serving the Black Drink, an important ceremonial medicine.[30] Boudinot added his own hearing or mishearing of "y-he-ho-wah" to Adair's.

The suggestion that Indigenous people remembered the name of the God of Israel seized sympathetic readers' imaginations. The Congregationalist missionary Daniel S. Butrick, for example, interrogated his Cherokee congregants about what he called the "hymn to Yowah" in the hope of learning more about the ancient religious practices of "Israelite" Indians.[31] Authors who made only brief references to Israelite Indian stories, likewise, often made sure to mention the idea that Indigenous people used this name of God.[32] The idea had broad appeal because knowledge of the four-letter name of God would be a sure sign of a revealed religion. After all, according to the text of the Bible, God first used this name when speaking to Moses, whom Protestants thought of as the main recipient of the true religion revealed to the Israelites.[33]

Signs of Israelite revelations in Indigenous practices, reformers believed, would indicate that their supposed "Indian religion" was like Christianity. For them, Israelite religious practices were less a distinct religion than "rites of the ancient church," that is, an older part of Christianity.[34] Some of them even insisted that the prophets of Israel had believed in the Christian doctrine of the Trinity, increasing the imagined resemblance between evangelical Protestants and Israelites.[35] Building on these tight religious links between Israel and themselves, reformers told Israelite Indian stories to help feel that Indigenous people were like them as well, at least insofar as they too practiced a revealed religion derived from that of Israel. Even as Boudinot made racist comparisons of the Indigenous people he saw to "snakes" and "monkies," he saw their invocation of the Israelite name of God as "contrary to the usage of all the heathen world" and a sign that they were his spiritual kin.[36]

The emotional stakes of discovering a hidden kinship with Indigenous people were high. Again and again, reform publications emphasized that what was truly needed to transform the nation, and the world, were sorrow and love. The true Christian, a pseudonymous author wrote in the missionary magazine *Panoplist*, "feels, tenderly feels, for the honour of his heavenly Father, and for the immortal souls of men. When therefore he looks around him, and sees iniquity prevailing, vice triumphing, and multitudes travelling the downward road in peace, he is pained and grieved." Only by allowing oneself to perceive and be wounded by "iniquity" and "vice," the article continued, could a person be motivated to work toward reform. A feeling of zeal, then, and not greater depression, should follow this initial grief. But zeal alone, the author warned, was not sufficient and could easily lead to the "false fire of the hypocrite" seeking to demonstrate their own moral superiority. Instead, the ideal Christian reformer should be driven "by love to God and his cause, by love to mankind and their best interests, by love to the persons, the souls of his enemies, and the enemies of religion."[37] This emotional progress, reformers believed, eventually led to the noblest form of emotion: disinterested benevolence. Such benevolence was, for them, "an inclination to seek the happiness or welfare of others—Or a good will toward mankind in general" without seeking reciprocal benefits for oneself. Crucially, benevolence did not occur naturally but had to be learned through Christian training and practice. Such benevolence was more than a personal feeling. According to reformers' providentialist understanding of American politics, maintaining benevolence toward colonized people would ensure God's continued favor for the nation.[38]

That reformers saw disinterested benevolence as difficult to achieve indicates that they expected that even most of the "friends of Zion" who supported reform causes would need help to bridge the gap between themselves and the subjects of their charity. Help, that is, to see them as familiar enough to feel the love for them that drove reform onward. The excitement with which evangelical reformers treated the idea, however improbable, that

Indigenous people might have an Israelite religion hints that they believed that telling and retelling Israelite Indian stories could help awaken such a sense of familiarity and affection for Indigenous people in their supporters. After all, if Indigenous religion was a form of Israelite religion, "contrary to the usage of all the heathen world," then loving them would be easy: more like loving other Christians than it was like loving "heathens." The same affection that united church congregations with each other into a spiritual "Israel" could then be extended outward to the "Israelites" of America, leading to ever greater heights of benevolence.

At times, the association seems to have worked in the other direction, as feeling love for individual Indigenous people led evangelicals to imagine them as Israelites. Sophia Sawyer, a Congregationalist teacher in a mission in the Cherokee Nation, invoked Israelite Indian stories in 1822 to express her affection for the Cherokee girls, most under ten, with whom she lived in the mission school's dormitory. In a letter back home to New Hampshire, she wrote, "I must have a cold heart indeed not to love them. . . . I have a sweet little Sarah who I thought would never speak a word of our language. I passed her bed the other day [and she] called 'Miss Sawyer I want a kiss.' Never was a sound sweeter to a Mother's ear than this to mine." Reveling in her warm feelings for the girls in her charge, Sawyer remarked, "I am from day to day led to believe them the real descendants of Abraham. Yes, I believe these wandering children of the forest will ere long be seen and gathered as the ancient covenant people. O may the time soon come when they & the fullness of the gentile nations shall be brought into the fold of Christ."[39] For Boudinot, identifying Indigenous people with Israelites was a way to cultivate benevolence toward them, but for Sawyer the association worked in the opposite direction. Seeking to communicate the love that drew her to her students, she turned to Israelite Indian stories that allowed her to imagine the day when the Cherokees would "be seen . . . as the ancient covenant people" and "brought into the fold of Christ." Israelite Indian stories, then, allowed Sawyer to follow the love she felt for these particular children into a vision of the grand mission of redemption that would have legitimacy to friends and relatives who saw her charges as just more "heathens," no more deserving of love than any others.

Stories about Israelite Indians, therefore, helped evangelical reformers cultivate feelings of kinship, familiarity, and love toward Indigenous people. Imagining "Indian religion" as Israelite religion allowed evangelicals to think of it as fundamentally like their own religion and of Indigenous people as worthy of their benevolent care. Details such as the supposed preservation of the name of God were, to them, convincing arguments that Indigenous people were secretly akin to evangelicals and, thus, natural objects for the love and benevolence that they believed drove support for reform organizations. This affective connection was not entirely a matter of political calculus, however. Evangelicals like Sawyer, trained from an early age to feel a thrill of kinship with Israelites and Israel, at times identified Indigenous people as Israelites to express and make sense of their attachment to them.

Hierarchy and Authority

The love and benevolence that these reformers cultivated for Indigenous people, however, did not presume equality. They saw Israelites as like themselves, yes, but in an earlier, lower stage of religious development. As Jedidiah Morse put it in his *American Universal Geography*, Israelites "offered sacrifices . . . as types merely; and were required, together with them, to offer the sacrifice of the heart. This religion ceased in effect at the death of the Redeemer; for then the Spirit from on high was withdrawn, and God refused to accept the offering of the worshipper." The sacrifices described in the Bible, in other words, symbolized an inner "sacrifice of the heart," or the self-surrender that Protestants believed necessary to receive grace. After the arrival of Jesus, these sacrifices became useless. Most Israelites, however, had not understood the inner meaning of the sacrifices they offered, and "considerable numbers . . . have in every subsequent age, observed the rites of the synagogue," or rabbinic Judaism.[40] Not only were Protestants the heirs of Israelite religion in this reading, but, from their position in time after the coming of Jesus, they were able to understand it correctly as most Israelites had not.

Equating Indigenous practices with Israelite religion implied that they, too, were outdated. Israelite Indian stories claimed that Indigenous ceremonies, like those of ancient Israel, anticipated Christian truths and had been meant to prepare Indigenous people for conversion to Christianity. Although these rituals had become degenerate, so that their true nature was apparent to only a careful observer, they still laid a firm groundwork on which missionaries could build. By associating "Indian religion" with their own religious past, moreover, evangelical reformers foreclosed all options for Indigenous peoples' futures other than conversion to Christianity. If their traditions were Israelite, and Israelite religion was essentially incomplete Christianity, then their traditions could have no resources for them that Christianity did not. Although this vision of Indian religion encouraged evangelicals to feel for and value Indigenous people as potentially like them, therefore, it also justified stark differences in power between missionaries and the missionized.

According to Boudinot, Protestant readers of *A Star in the West* and other Israelite Indian stories already understood what Indigenous ceremonies really or originally meant. He argued, for example, that the Green Corn Ceremony—a large communal festival of purification common among Indigenous nations with traditional territories in the southeast—was a version of the Day of Atonement described in the Bible.[41] Although this ceremony purifies and rectifies the community through fasting and the renewal of a ceremonial fire, it did not and does not necessarily draw on Christian, Jewish, or Israelite ideas about sin and expiation.[42] Boudinot's description, however, told a different story. Using the word "beloved" with which English speakers often translated the Muscogee and Cherokee words for that which is sacred or revered, Boudinot described the renewal of fire in the Green Corn Ceremony in terms meant to echo the Day of Atonement. For example, his description of the renewal of the sacred fire echoes the description in Leviticus of the high priest entering the Holy of Holies on the Day of Atonement.[43] "Now every thing is hushed. Nothing but silence all around. The great beloved man, and his beloved waiter, rising up with a reverend carriage, steady countenance, and composed behavior, go into the beloved place, or holiest, to bring them out the beloved fire."[44] In his reverential imagining of a ceremony he likely never witnessed, Boudinot juxtaposes "the beloved place" with the term "holiest," he invites readers to identify that which is "beloved" with that which is "holy," complete with the heavy theological load that term carried in Christianity and Judaism. This act of translation from Indigenous to Israelite religious concepts was meant to occur to readers as if they had thought of it themselves.

These analogies were far-fetched, but neither Boudinot nor any other author of Israelite Indian stories expected them to be otherwise. Indigenous people, they claimed, had degenerated from their Israelite past, helped along by contact with the wrong sort of White settlers. As Ethan Smith put it in *View of the Hebrews*, "a great change has been produced among the Indians. They have . . . much degenerated as to their traditional religion. Their connexions with the most degenerate part of the white people . . . have produced the most deleterious effects. They have felt less zeal to maintain their own religion . . . and to transmit their own traditions."[45] Hence, Boudinot argued that Indians "are not to be wondered at, if they have forgotten the meaning and end of the sacrifices," that is, the Christian truths to which Israelite religion supposedly gestured. "They are rather to be pitied . . . for having forgotten the blessing was not in the outward sign, but in the thing signified or typified by that sign."[46] The "pity" that Boudinot encouraged as the proper response to Indigenous religions had political consequences. Pity is not an emotion between equals but a hierarchical one, in which the one who pities possesses something the pitied person does not.[47] In this case, White, Protestant readers possessed the knowledge of the "thing typified or signified" by Indigenous ceremonies, namely Christianity. Only by funding missions could they extend that knowledge to the Indigenous peoples Boudinot called on them to pity.

By constructing a unitary Indian religion modeled on Israelite religion, therefore, reformers argued that the inner or true meaning of Indigenous practices was Christian. Not only did this make Indigenous people fundamentally like evangelicals, since their religion was simply an older version of Christianity, it also meant that evangelicals had the final authority to interpret Indigenous ceremonies and traditions. Only by recognizing the truth of the interpretations Boudinot proposed could evangelicals feel the pity that was the proper affective orientation toward Indigenous people. This theory of Indigenous religion cast White evangelicals as the authors of the coming triumph of Christianity in America. After all, if Indigenous people were Israelites, then their religions already pointed toward Christianity. Evangelicals' plans to convert them and integrate them into a national order based on a shared idea of Christian covenant, therefore, were not only possible but necessary.

Israelites and the Political Order

For evangelical reformers in the early nineteenth century, the dominant political mood was anxiety about a nation that seemed balanced on the edge of a knife. As the Presbyterian missionary T. Charlton Henry put it in 1824, "Whether it be an honour to live in such an age [as ours], or whether it be a curse, is a choice left to ourselves. Whether we are active instruments of good, in a season of such singular opportunity—or whether we are will-fully blind to all that is passing, is a subject of individual delib-eration. One thing is certain: a signal blessedness, or a signal woe . . . will be the fate of every one of us." Charlton spoke dur-ing a time of intensifying debate about expansion. How rapidly should the United States acquire new territory? As it did so, should it incorporate Indigenous nations through missions or force them to move away from White settlements? He, like most evangelical reformers, read this debate in religious terms. God would not hold blameless those who "could cooly devise on paper a project for [the] Government to hasten" Indigenous peoples' demise.[48] Only swift action to prevent this sin by funding mis-sionary work could avert God's judgment.

Evangelicals' versions of Israelite Indian stories dramatized and intensified these anxieties about imperial expansion. After all, if Indigenous people were God's chosen nation, would he not pun-ish those who afflicted them even more? Surely these American Israelites would play a key role in God's plans for the millennium, or the thousand-year reign of peace on earth that would herald the return of Jesus. If Americans worked to convert Indigenous people, they would simultaneously fulfill two parts of God's mil-lennial plan: the restoration of the Jews to Israel and the conquest of America by a thoroughly Christian and righteous United States.[49] After all, if Indigenous people were truly Israelites, then they surely would not want to stay in the land of their exile. White Americans could then claim the land of North America as a reward for their good deed, free from the guilt of violent dispos-session.

"Cursed Is He Who Curseth the Indians!!": The Politics of a Chosen People

White evangelicals who embraced Israelite Indian stories often argued that only recognizing Indigenous people as Israelites would prevent genocidal warfare. A traveler named Jacob Lindley put the issue this way over dinner in Detroit one summer night in 1793. Lindley was part of a Philadelphia Quaker delegation whom Indigenous leaders had invited to Detroit to mediate treaty negotiations that, they hoped, would end the Northwest Indian War. The journey fell short of its purpose—the war would continue for two more years—but Lindley's interactions with Indigenous people along the way fired his imagination. He became convinced that they were "the dispersed tribes of Israel" and "they would be restored—not to a Jewish, ceremonious Israel, but to a spiritual Israel," that is, to Protestant Christianity. Hence, it was "our duty to use endeavours to promote, and pray for this [restoration], in preference to effecting their extermination." He had heard, in fact, that some White settlers were already planning to exterminate Indigenous people by using "dark and diabolical machinations," such as supplying them with poisoned liquor.[50] The choice he presented was stark: either Indigenous people were Israelites, with all that implied about their religion, and would soon convert to Christianity, or White settlers would kill them all.[51]

Lindley's way of framing the issue of Israelite descent was not unusual among reformers. Some elaborated on it by claiming that, if Indigenous people were Israelites, then slowing settlement in favor of missions would not only save Indigenous peoples from destruction but would forestall God's judgment on the United States. As Boudinot argued, if White Americans did not work to benefit God's chosen people, then "he will afflict and destroy, without mercy. . . . He will be found no respecter of persons; but will . . . inflict all his threatened curses on obstinate offenders."[52] The millennialist preacher Harriet Livermore expressed the same idea when she exclaimed that, because Indigenous people were Israelites, "blessed are they that bless the Indians; and cursed is he who curseth the Indians!!"[53] Whether to recognize Indigenous people as Israelites, therefore, was a life-or-death choice for White settlers as well as for Indigenous peoples. Fear of God's punishment of disobedient nations—a fear familiar from countless sermons in northeastern Protestant churches—would, they hoped, drive their audience onward if benevolence would not.

This perception of urgency was not entirely misplaced. Democratic-Republicans, later called Democrats, rose to power after 1800 on a platform of free markets, rapid expansion, and White supremacy. Crucially, for Democrats the body politic that constituted the republic consisted of White citizens and only White citizens. Because they excluded Black Americans and Indigenous people from political personhood, Democrats saw them largely in terms of the labor and land they could provide to White people.[54] Acquiring more Indigenous territories, they argued, was the only way to advance the economic prosperity, political stability, and republican virtue of the nation, as well as to avoid the revolutions rocking Europe. More land would allow poor White people to become farmers, thereby guaranteeing their prosperity and their republican virtue. But farms could and did fail, and the frequent economic crises of the early United States demolished many poor White people's attempts to achieve the financial independence they saw as their right. To prevent this tension between ideals and reality from stirring up dangerous levels of discontent, Democrats clamoured throughout the first half of the nineteenth century for the United States to provide a constant supply of land for settlement by killing or forcibly removing Indigenous people. After the passage of the Indian Removal Act of 1830, this ideology would lead to waves of genocidal forced migrations.[55]

Reformers attributed the rise of this aggressive expansionism in the Democratic party to a lack of Christian feeling. In an 1814 article by Washington Irving that Boudinot reprinted in *A Star in the West*, Irving lamented that,

> even now, we perceive a disposition breaking out to renew the persecutions of these hapless beings [Indians]. Sober-thoughted men, far from the scenes of danger, in the security of cities and populous regions, can coolly talk of

"exterminating measures," and discuss the *policy* of extirpating thousands. If such is the talk in the cities, what is the temper displayed on the borders? The sentence of desolation has gone forth—"the roar is up admist the woods;" implacable wrath, goaded on by interest and prejudice, is ready to confound all rights, to trample on all claims of justice and humanity, and to act over those scenes of sanguinary vengeance which have too often stained the pages of colonial history.[56]

The problem here was that not enough White Americans had experienced the Christian nurture that would properly cultivate their feelings. While expansionists in the cities were too detached to feel the full moral weight of their "exterminating measures," rural White people displayed unrestrained passion, an "implacable wrath, goaded on by interest and prejudice." Neither group, in this account, was motivated by the sorrow for sin and love for those in need of help that reformers cultivated so carefully.[57]

Israelite Indian stories sought to display these cultivated sympathies for Indigenous people while, like Irving, excoriating expansionists and opponents of missions as heartless or enraged. White enemies of God's chosen people surfaced frequently in these stories, as with the unnamed persons whom Lindley accused of planning to poison Indigenous people or the White settlers whom Smith blamed for Indigenous "degeneration." By reviling often unnamed White opponents, they framed the political conflict between reformers and their Democratic opponents in favorable terms. A performed disgust for other White people highlighted reformers' benevolence and Christian concern while aligning them with God's chosen people, the "Israelites" of America, against emotionally stunted and unchristian settlers and land speculators.

Israelite Indian stories also make clear, however, that the warm feelings and sense of kinship that reformers rehearsed in their accounts of Indigenous people were not racial egalitarianism or expressions of a desire for equal partnership. When they identified Indigenous people as "Israelites" arrested in an earlier stage of revealed religion, they positioned White evangelicals as the superior parties in the relationship, who both understood the supposed inner truths of Indigenous traditions and knew what was best for Indigenous people going forward. Indeed, these stories insisted that reformers were Indigenous peoples' only allies against other White people's rapacity and violence.[58]

Christian Nationalism and Dispossession

Even when reformers saw Indigenous people as the chosen people of God, they were unwilling to give up on expansion entirely. Because Indigenous people were native to Israel, not North America, they would surely want to leave for their "true" home once converted. Imagining Indigenous people as Israelites, although entangled with the love reformers cultivated toward Indigenous people, therefore had a cruel side in that these narratives often authorized the dispossession of Indigenous lands. The reformers who told these stories distinguished themselves from expansionist Democrats by insisting that converting Indigenous people before taking their land, as they proposed, would save the United States from God's looming punishment.

Reformers feared that, with the last judgment and millennial reign of Christ over the world rapidly approaching, the United States' unjust treatment of Indigenous people might draw God's wrath down on the nation.[59] "Have not the Europeans been the cause of [Indians'] sufferings?" Boudinot asked. "Are we not in possession of their lands? Have we not been enriched by their labours? Have they not fought our battles, and spilt their blood for us, as well as against us?"[60] The personal and collective shame that he expected this history to make his audience feel seemed to require a miraculous expiation if the nation were to escape judgment. Happily, Boudinot found a promise of just this kind of expiation in an idiosyncratic translation of Isaiah 18: 1–2, 7 by the Anglican divine George Stanley Faber:

> Ho! land spreading wide the shadow of thy wing, which art beyond the rivers of Cush, accustomed to send messengers by sea, even in bulrush vessels, upon the surface of the waters. Go! swift messengers unto a nation dragged away and plucked; unto a people wonderful from the beginning hitherto. . . .
>
> At that season a present shall be led to the Lord of Hosts, a people dragged away and plucked, even of a people wonderful from the beginning hitherto; a nation expecting, expecting, and trampled under foot, whose land rivers have spoiled, unto the place of the name of the Lord of Hosts, Mount Zion.[61]

To read this passage, Boudinot relied on the idea that the Bible was, in the words of a passage he copied into his commonplace book, "constructed on the symbolic principles of the Hieroglyphics, which were not vague, uncertain things, but fixed & constant analogies."[62] If one took the images in this passage as "hieroglyphics," the United States was obviously the "land spreading wide the shadow of thy wings," since its heraldic symbol was the eagle. He associated the "nation dragged away and plucked" with the tribes of Israel who had suffered exile and come, at last, to America. Finally, the "place of the name of the Lord of Hosts, Mount Zion," was the land of Israel. Decoding these symbols, he concluded that the United States must build ships to transport Native people to Israel. "Who knows," he asked, "but God has raised up these United States in these later days, for the very purpose of accomplishing his will in bringing his beloved people to their own land." After all, "we are a maritime people—a nation of seafaring men" able to accomplish such a feat.[63]

Boudinot did not explicitly say what would happen to the North American continent once Indigenous people were gone, but other authors of Israelite Indian stories were clearer on this point. In 1799, the evangelical poet Charles Crawford argued that "all the descendants of the house of Israel, among which are many Indians, will be restored to the land of their forefathers . . . Many of the Indians will then relinquish their land to the white people."[64] Ethan Smith was somewhat more modest, imagining that only "a portion of that nation [Israel] will in due time be offered, to return to the land of their fathers, where they may form a kind of centre or capital to the cause of Christ on earth." Yet, eventually, "the wilderness and solitary place of *our vast continent,* containing the lost tribes of the house of Israel, will, on a most enlarged scale, rejoice and blossom as the rose, when the long lost tribes shall be found there, and shall be gathered to Zion."[65] Once "the long lost tribes" were returned to Israel—"Zion"—the "wilderness . . . will . . . rejoice and blossom" under White missions and settler cultivation. Missions to Indigenous people, therefore, would end by winning for the United States the same land that expansionists sought to take by force. Although reformers proposed that White settlers earn that land through missionary effort, they still insisted that God intended it for them.

The idea that the discovery of "Jewish" or "Israelite" Indians portended radical transformations had been part of such stories since before Aaron Levi landed in Amsterdam. The expectation that Israelite Indians would gladly gift their land to settlers was new, however. This redemptive scenario implied both that God intended the United States to possess Indigenous territories and that even converted Indigenous people descended from God's chosen nation could not share North America with White people. Like the growing calls for Indian removal, Israelite Indian stories assumed that settlers and Native people could not coexist. Indigenous people, then, would have to move.[66]

Israelite Indian stories emerged from a tangle of thought about the role of evangelical reform in guaranteeing the safety and prosperity of the United States. "Israel" was a charged concept for the "friends of Zion," one they referred to when they sought to imagine their communities, themselves, and their nation. By including Indigenous people in their imagined Israel, they envisioned how a Christian nation could expand across North America. The rapid growth of the United States in extent and imperial reach, however, seemed to threaten that future. Spreading narratives about Israelite Indians allowed evangelical reformers to associate missions with these hopes and fears. If Indigenous people were Israelites, then reformers really were as central to the fate of the nation as they wished to be. They were the only ones who had cultivated their emotions so as to feel the correct benevolence toward them. More, if the Indians were Israelites, then the anxiety they felt for the fate of a rapidly expanding and changing empire was justified. Their action or inaction would determine whether Indians were redeemed and returned to Israel, opening the way for the United States to claim the continent with a clear conscience, or whether God would destroy the United States as he had Assyria, Babylon, and Rome.

Evangelical reformers helped bring Israelite Indian stories to national attention. Once there, however, they slipped out of their control. "Israel" was a powerful, emotion-laden metaphor for more people than just White reformers. Its association with a "chosen people" and a "promised land" made it especially appealing to those trying to create new ways of binding peoples into nations. As I will show, although the spread of Israelite Indian stories in the early republic followed the paths of missionary networks, they were used to reconceive the nation in ways that veered off reformers' mental maps.

2

The Remnant of Joseph

In the late summer of 1840, excitement and fear ran through the Mormon community in Kirtland, Ohio.[1] Kirtland had once been the center of Mormon life, the place where Joseph Smith, the prophet of the new Christian movement, had hoped to make a model of God's kingdom on earth. But after the collapse of a church-owned bank and rumors that the prophet had relationships with multiple women divided the Kirtland Mormons, Smith abandoned those hopes. He left for Far West, Missouri, in July 1837, with no plans to return. Meanwhile, the church high council in Kirtland tried for three difficult years to calm internal dissent and keep peace with their neighbors.[2] But that August, a visiting missionary named Jonathan Dunham brought new disquiet to the bruised community.

According to a complaint that Thomas Burdick, a member of the Kirtland high council, sent to Smith, Dunham had torn through Kirtland while traveling from the Indian Territory to take up a mission to Haudenosaunee communities in New York. Dunham paused in Kirtland only long enough to publicly preach that "the nation," that is, the United States, "was about to be destroyed," with only Mormons surviving to build a new world. Indigenous people, he claimed, would be God's instruments of destruction. Some of the sense of Dunham's preaching comes through in his own words about this mission: "I am not sent to the Gentiles, neither to the Cities of the Sameritans [sic], but to the promised people of the house of Jacob, who if they go through &c."[3] By the "house of Jacob," he meant Indigenous peoples, whom Mormons then identified as "Lamanites." This term, drawn from the Book of Mormon, referred to some of the descendants of a band of Israelites who had settled in North America around 600 BCE.[4] Dunham's phrase "if they go through &c." referred to a prophecy in the Book of Mormon that Lamanites would destroy the unrepentant "Gentiles"—a term that usually referred to non-Mormons—to make way for the kingdom of God: "And my people who are a remnant of Jacob shall be among the Gentiles, yea, in the midst of them as a lion among the beasts of the forest, as a young lion among the flocks of sheep, who, if he go through both treadeth down and teareth in pieces, and none can deliver."[5] Only then, according to Dunham, could God establish his rule on earth.

Non-Mormons in Kirtland heard Dunham's implicit threat. One, in response, growled to a crowd in the post office that "the Mormons ought to be seen to." Burdick begged Smith to rein in the missionary, saying that "such teachings are not understood in this place, they are calculated to make excitement & what the consequences may be I am not able to say."[6] The anti-Mormon violence of the coming years would, in fact, be worse than Burdick could say. By the time of his letter, the Missouri militia had already driven Mormons from that state by force of arms. Before the decade was out, a mob would murder Joseph Smith and his brother Hyrum. In response, an enraged church would embrace prophecies of a Lamanite army destroying the nation that had failed to protect them.

Dunham's story was divisive, but that was the point. Early Mormons used Israelite Indian stories to cultivate, communicate, and model emotional responses to Smith's new revelations. In the process, they formed a new group identity and, over time, a new religious nationalism invested in Zion, a term that meant both any community where Mormons gathered together and the physical city of God that they believed would be built in North America. Imagined intimacy with Lamanites allowed Mormons to feel themselves to be citizens of Zion, distinct from their White Protestant neighbors and families. By telling stories about Lamanites, they sought to evoke feelings about their new church and its relationship to the United States. In Lamanites stories, Mormons performed their love for their supposed Lamanite kin, their hope and sorrow about the cataclysmic destruction their prophecies anticipated, their wonder at living in what they believed to be a new age of miracles, and their anger at non-Mormons.

Stories about Lamanites also influenced Mormons' approaches toward Indigenous people. They interpreted Indigenous earthworks as Lamanite monuments, Indigenous people's remains as Lamanite bones, and living Indigenous people as Lamanites in the flesh. In this process, Indigenous people became part of Mormons' emotional lives but not allies in their political projects. This was not for lack of opportunities. Despite the failure of an early mission to the Delaware nation in 1830–31, Mormons continued to make some overtures to Indigenous nations and attempted, with some limited success, to convert individual Indigenous people.[7] During the period between the 1830 publication of the Book of Mormon and the 1847 migration of the largest faction of the church to Utah, however, Mormons did not make their attachment to Lamanites the basis of sustained relationships with Indigenous nations.

"Indian History" in Early Mormon Thought

Stories about Lamanites accompanied the rise of the Mormon movement. Smith, who before his prophetic career was a farmer and treasure hunter living in upstate New York, gave several accounts throughout his life of the events leading up to the founding of his church. All these agree, however, that he became convinced as a young man that the true church had vanished from the world and, after several visionary experiences during the 1820s, that God had given him new revelations to help restore it. In 1828 and 1829, he began work on the longest of these revelations: the Book of Mormon, a scripture that Smith claimed to have translated from a series of shining metal plates found a few miles from his home in New York. The printed version of the Book of Mormon came out just before Smith founded what he called the Church of Christ in April 1830. Its narratives about Israelite Indians swiftly became key symbols for the new movement.[8]

The Book of Mormon recounts a history of the Americas from the arrival of a band of Israelites led by a man called Lehi in 600 BCE up until the destruction of Lehi's last righteous descendants in 384 CE. In the intervening years, Lehi's descendants split into two main groups: a smaller, largely faithful group called the Nephites and a larger, largely unfaithful group called the Lamanites.[9] The Nephites, who are the protagonists of most of the narratives, prospered when they were faithful to God and suffered when they were not. The Lamanites eventually overcame and destroyed the Nephites, but not before the Nephite prophet Moroni buried the metal plates containing their histories to preserve them for a future age.[10]

Because early Mormons understood the Lamanites to be the ancestors of the Indigenous people of North America, they saw the Book of Mormon as a miraculous revelation of an otherwise lost "Indian history."[11] They invited prospective converts to read it in the context of other Israelite Indian stories, calling it "a history of the origin of the Indians," "a record of the aborigines of this continent," and "a full account of the aborigines of our country, [which] agreed with many of their traditions."[12] Both historical and contemporary critics have made similar comparisons, speculating that texts by James Adair, Ethan Smith, or Josiah Priest were direct sources for some portions of the Book of Mormon.[13] But the Book of Mormon's relationship to other Israelite

Indian stories was always more complicated than any of these comparisons implied. The text differed from these other stories both in its narrative complexity—like the Bible, it has multiple narrators and voices—and in that it presented itself as scripture, not historical speculation.[14] Of course, any, all, or none of these specific sources could have inspired Smith in a more general way to think that Israelites had once lived in North America. The evangelical reformers discussed in the previous chapter spent considerable effort sending missionaries, periodicals, and tracts to lower-class, rural White people such as Smith's family, so it is not impossible that they helped bring Israelite Indian stories to the Smith household.

As they told and retold "Indian histories" from the Book of Mormon, early Mormons came, like evangelical reformers, to read the political future of the United States in terms of those histories. They arrived at radically different conclusions, however. Where evangelical versions of Israelite Indian stories argued that the United States would prosper and acquire Indigenous lands if it behaved benevolently, early Mormons prophesied the destruction of the United States. In the first twenty years of the movement, Mormons emphasized that they and Indigenous peoples would soon gather in God's kingdom: Zion. Although "Zion" could mean any refuge for Mormons, it referred most specifically to a future holy city in Jackson County, Missouri.[15] This was not an arbitrary location. Western Missouri lay "on the borders of the Lamanites," that is, at the edge of the Indian Territory that the federal government had reserved for Indigenous people.[16] God's city, therefore, would emerge at a rupture in the U.S. political order: where states ruled according to the collective will of their White male citizens ran up against a colonial territory administered by the Department of War.[17] In Mormon thought, both these legal dispensations would disappear when Zion's rule extended over the continent. Only the Lamanite descendants of Israel and the White Americans who joined them through baptism into the Church of Christ would have a share in that new nation.

Understanding this sacred history, Mormons believed, should lead one to imitate God's love for Lamanites. As a Mormon preacher argued in 1842, Protestants' ideas of God "made him an unjust God, a partial God, a cruel God, a God worthy only of hatred; in fact, 'the greatest devil in the universe.'" Because they believed that the Bible was God's sole revelation, Protestants implied that "this vast continent of America had been destitute of all revelation for five thousand years" even as God judged, and presumably condemned to Hell, generations of Indigenous people. If so, the preacher continued, then "God was most horribly unjust," and he "would never love such a God; he could only hate him."[18] For this Mormon, accepting the truth of Smith's revelations was not only about the reasoned consideration of their content but also about having the right feelings. Accepting that God intended the Book of Mormon, in part, as a testimony to the Lamanites meant rejecting "an unjust God, a partial God, a cruel God, a God worthy only of hatred" in favor of a God worthy of love. Loving that God, in turn, meant cultivating love for Lamanites in anticipation of future union with them in Zion.

This idea of Zion promised that God would reward his faithful with territory in North America. As the Book of Mormon had it: "[Thus] saith our God: I will afflict thy seed [the Lamanites] by the hand of the Gentiles; nevertheless, I will soften the hearts of the Gentiles, that they shall be like unto a father to them; wherefore the Gentiles shall be blessed and numbered among the house of Israel. Wherefore, I will consecrate this land unto thy seed [the Lamanites], and them who shall be numbered among thy seed, forever."[19] Here, as in some other early texts, "Gentiles" does not refer to non-Mormons, but to all peoples, Mormon or not, who were neither Jewish nor Lamanite. As early Mormons read this passage, those "Gentiles" who afflicted the Lamanites were the non-Mormon Whites who oppressed Indigenous people.

When God ended that oppression and gave the land to the Lamanites, however, not all gentiles would suffer. Some of them would be "numbered" with the Lamanites, meaning that they would become their spiritual kindred and a part of the new nation of Zion. Early Mormons, who believed that their baptism inducted them into the family of Israel, identified themselves as those so numbered.[20]

Early Mormons mapped this understanding of the "Lamanite" past and the future of Zion onto Indigenous people and lands. Smith, for example, did so in a vision he had on June 3, 1834, while traveling to Clay County, Missouri, at the head of a Mormon militia intent on defending Mormon settlers from Missouri troops.[21] Seeing an earthwork mound, Smith took a small group to inspect what they believed to be a site of one of the conflicts described in the Book of Mormon. On its top, they found that "human bones were strewn over the surface of the ground" and uncovered "the skeleton of a man" with the "stone point of a Lamanitish arrow" between his ribs. Surveying the surrounding prairie, Smith experienced a rush of feeling that led to a new connection with what he saw as the sacred past. He wrote later that "the contemplation of the scenery around us produced peculiar sensations in our bosoms; and . . . the visions of the past . . . [were] opend to my understanding." He proclaimed that these remains were those of "a man of God" named Zelph, who had been killed in battle with the unrighteous Lamanites.[22] His presence there testified that the Mormons' coming conflict with Missouri troops put them in a long lineage of righteous warriors fighting for the "land of Promise" given by God to his faithful.[23]

Smith's prophecy hinted as well at the future relationship of White Mormons and Lamanites. Although Zelph had fought alongside the Nephites, he was a "white Lamanite" from whom "the curse was taken . . . or, at least, in part."[24] By this, Smith meant that God removed from Zelph what the Book of Mormon refers to as the "skin of blackness" with which he cursed the

Lamanites for being "a lazy and an idolatrous people . . . a wild, and ferocious, and a blood-thirsty people," in other words, a people who conformed to the worst nineteenth-century stereotypes about "savage" Indians.[25] Smith understood dark skin as a curse in the context of his belief that flesh and spirit were one substance, allowing the sins or righteousness of ancestors to appear on their descendants' bodies. But Smith also embraced the idea that religious ceremonies and righteous living could exalt the spirit. Zelph's lighter skin hinted that perhaps the bodies, as well as the souls, of Indigenous people who embraced Smith's new revelations would become like those of White Mormons. On the strength of this promise about the future transformation of Lamanites, the Mormon leader Wilford Woodruff carried one of the body's femurs with him to Missouri, intending to bury it at the site of the grand temple that would be built in Zion.[26]

Both the miraculous lightening of Zelph's skin and Woodruff's desire to anchor Zion with a part of an Indigenous man's body point to the ways that Lamanite stories refracted racial hierarchies. Some parts of these stories correspond with the larger culture of White supremacism in nineteenth-century America. White evangelicals, for example, also associated light skin with righteousness and hoped that Christian education could lighten the skin of Black and Indigenous people.[27] Woodruff's and Smith's treatment of this unknown Indigenous man's remains, similarly, reflected White Americans' cavalier attitude toward opening Indigenous graves and using their contents to imagine a past that flattered their beliefs.[28] However, Mormon thinking did not fit with the then-dominant belief that White Americans were the only ones fit to rule the continent. They argued instead that God would grant the land of North America to the heirs of Israel: both Lamanites who came from the lineage of Israel and Mormons who became kin to Israel through baptism. Therefore, although Mormons resembled other White Americans in making sovereignty over the land a matter of descent and in believing in the superiority of White skin, the kinship they imagined between themselves and Lamanites such as Zelph opened a space to imagine a future that included both themselves and Indigenous people. Perhaps it was this feeling of closeness to the Lamanites of the past, and the hoped-for converted Lamanites of the future, that filled Smith's bosom with "peculiar sensations."[29]

As early Mormons mapped the histories of the Book of Mormon onto the world around them, they called the expansionist projects of the United States into question more than had evangelical reformers who told Israelite Indian stories. However, although Lamanites were the victors, and occasionally the protagonists, in the histories of the Book of Mormon, early Mormons' deployment of that sacred history neither entirely undermined American racism nor uncomplicatedly embraced Indigenous people.[30] Smith's vision of Zelph clarified that although Mormons believed that Indigenous peoples would inherit North America, they also expected that conversion would transform their bodies to make them as suited for the coming Zion as White Mormons already were. As much or more than it was an "Indian history," then, the Book of Mormon was a sacred history for White Mormons that mapped out their place in this future dispensation.

Lamanites and the Feeling of Empire

Early Mormons rehearsed their belief in the Book of Mormon's narratives in worship, writing, and prophecy. By envisioning and discussing Lamanites, they performed confidence in Smith's revelations and rehearsed the joy, sorrow, and anger that would accompany the coming transformation of the world. Sharing these feelings did more than simply affirm their faith, however. It also positioned White Mormons as a part of the coming kingdom of Zion and as a nation apart from "gentile" settlers. More than any reasoned theological argument could have, the feelings that Mormons cultivated toward Lamanites through worship and through recounting prophecies cemented them to each other and to their imagined Israelite Indian kin.

Some early Mormons went so far as to blur the lines between themselves and Lamanites during worship. At the end of 1830, newly converted Mormons near Kirtland worshipped by entering ecstatic states in which they spoke in Lamanite languages and acted out scenes they associated with Lamanites. According to observers, they mimed preaching to Lamanites, baptizing Lamanites, and traveling to the Lamanites in imaginary canoes. At times, they playacted the millennial destruction of White gentiles at the hands of the Lamanite hosts, "going through all the Indian maneuvers of knocking down, scalping, ripping open, and taking out the bowels" of unseen victims.[31] Those who performed these "maneuvers" had all been members of the Family, a revivalist Protestant group whose worship incorporated dramatic performances such as fainting, laughing, crying, barking, and shouting.[32] For the Family, as for other revivalists, salvation was a matter of authentic feeling. If God were truly present in a person's life, they would feel guilt and alienation as they became aware of their sin, and joy and relief when they were forgiven. Physically and emotionally demonstrative worship helped revival participants produce these emotions in themselves and communicate them to others.[33] For the former members of the Family, their "Indian maneuvers" demonstrated the truth of Smith's revelations and of the spirit of God that inspired them. The presence of that spirit, for them, came with invisible Lamanite audiences, Lamanite languages, and Lamanite movements.[34]

Joseph Smith put an end to these Lamanite "maneuvers" in February 1831, but Mormons continued to associate themselves with Lamanites during worship. Worshipping Mormons spoke and sang in what they understood to be Lamanites languages as late as 1838. "Spiritual gifts" such as speaking in tongues confirmed for early Mormons that theirs was the true church of Jesus, so this practice emphasized that to belong to that true church was to be intimate with imagined Lamanites. Just as Smith had felt "peculiar sensations" during close contact with the imagined Lamanite "Zelph," so too did other Mormons at times perform intimacy with Lamanites during worship to demonstrate their confidence in their new church.[35]

Most commonly, however, early Mormons brought Lamanites into their worship and their daily lives by recounting and elaborating on key prophecies about them. These prophecies expressed both their connections to their new communities and their opposition to the "gentile" world. They dwelt on the millennial destruction of the unrighteous at the hands of Lamanites and on the creation of Zion that would follow. Using these prophecies to cultivate sympathy for Lamanites and excitement about the future vindication of Smith's new revelations confirmed Mormons' sense of themselves as a people apart from the White, Protestant majority. Their hopes for the future, however, went together with a quietist approach to expansion and Indian removal. White Mormons expected Lamanites to acquiesce patiently to removal and to turn on White gentiles with wrath when the day came. White Mormons, however, would take a different emotional tone. They would look on with sorrow and pity, first as the United States forced Indigenous people west and, later, as vengeful Lamanites destroyed the unrepentant.

Early Mormon discussions of these prophecies frequently drew on Parley Pratt's 1837 *Voice of Warning and Instruction to All Peoples*. Pratt depicted Lamanites as the agents of the building of Zion. "[A] New Jerusalem," he wrote, "is to be built in America, to the remnant of Joseph (the Indians) like unto or after a similar pattern, to the old Jerusalem in the land of Canaan."[36] Indian removal would be the instrument for the gathering in Zion because the Indian Territory was "the very place, where they [the Indians] will finally build a New Jerusalem."[37] Hence, Pratt urged Indigenous people to see removal as "a blessing from the hand of God" because "the Gentiles shall not again have power over you;

but you shall be gathered by them, and built up, and again become a delightsome people. . . . [T]herefore lay down your weapons of war, cease to oppose the Gentiles . . . suffer them peaceably to fulfill this last act of kindness, as a kind of reward, for the injuries you have received from them."[38] By framing Indigenous peoples' dispossession within Mormon sacred histories, Pratt could understand it as an "act of kindness." Though violent, removal would convey "a blessing from the hand of God." Therefore, he argued, the proper emotional response to removal was not distress or anger but forbearance and hope.

In Pratt's account, settler Mormons felt along with Indigenous people as removal went on because they, too, experienced both the tribulations and the triumph of being God's chosen people. Speaking from this position, Pratt described how "it is with mingled feelings of Joy and sorrow that I reflect upon these things, sorrow, when I think how you have been smitten; joy when I reflect upon the happy change that now awaits you; and sorrow again, when I turn my thoughts to the awful destruction that awaits the Gentiles, except they repent."[39] Pratt's "mingled feelings of Joy and sorrow" modeled for White Mormon readers how they should temper sympathy for Indigenous people with submission to God's plans. Removal caused immense suffering to which sorrow was a natural response, but faithful Mormons should school themselves to feel "Joy" as well as sorrow. Paradoxically, then, his optimism about and sympathy for Indigenous people discouraged any opposition to Indian removal.[40]

Similarly, although Pratt depicted White Mormons as feeling the sorrow of their Israelite Indian kin, he also models a distinction between the two groups. Where Lamanites could simply look forward to a "reward, for the injuries you have received," Pratt felt sorrow again "when I turn my thoughts to the awful destruction that awaits the Gentiles, except they repent." By modeling this sorrow, Pratt set White Mormons apart from both the "Gentiles," whose "awful destruction" they would witness, and the

Lamanites, whose violence would accomplish that destruction. Unlike those Whites who did not join with Israel, Mormons would remain safe. Equally, unlike Lamanites, they would retain the fine sense of sympathy necessary to sorrow over the destruction of non-Mormon settlers.

Early Mormons incorporated Pratt's interpretations into their visionary culture following the trauma of the 1838 Missouri Mormon War.[41] In 1839, while fleeing the Missouri militia, the Mormon schoolteacher Elizabeth Haven expressed her anger by attributing it to Lamanites. She wrote in a letter that "several hundred Indian Chiefs," probably from the Mandan, Hidatsa, Nakota (Assiniboine), and Arikara peoples, "have had meetings this winter, what it is for, none can learn but it is fear[e]d by the people in the upper Missouri that [it] is a preparation for War. . . . The prophecies must all be fulfilled, and when the remnant of Jacob pass through there will be none to deliver. . . . How soon they will pass through we know not. They are very wrathy toward the whites and we hear many things which they threaten."[42] Haven positions "we," presumably settler Mormons, as separate from "the people in the upper Missouri" who have something to fear from "wrathy" Indians. Mormons could look forward to the prophesied division of the saved and unsaved "when the remnant of Jacob pass through there will be none to deliver." Despite her light skin, Haven was part of a people apart from "the whites" precisely because of the millennial violence of the Lamanites. While "the whites" suffered and Lamanites were "wrathy" in their vengeance, settler Mormons would be able to look on calmly.

Mormons similarly turned to Lamanite prophecies to express their outrage at the murder of Joseph and Hyrum Smith. In January 1845, a Mormon woman named Sally Randall wrote to her parents and family back east about the mood in Nauvoo following the Smiths' death at the hands of a mob the previous June. Although there were rumblings that anti-Mormon violence would recur in the spring, Randall claimed that "we don't fear them much for we never shall be drove from here . . . there is already ten hundred thousand of the Lamanites baptized into the Church and they are waiting very impatient to avenge the blood of Joseph and Hyrum. We have to keep men among them to keep them back or they would [have] been here before this time." Although only a handful of Indigenous people had become Mormons when she wrote, in Randall's mind her anger at the death of the prophet became an army burning for vengeance. As in Haven's letter, White Mormons in Randall's account are both allies of the Lamanites and able to restrain Lamanites' emotions, even to the point of "keep[ing] . . . back" an angry army.

Mormons did not confine the angry rehearsal of Lamanite prophecies to letters. Eliza R. Snow, a plural wife of Joseph Smith, recorded an 1847 prayer meeting in her diary that suggests how ordinary Mormons used these prophecies in their worship. The meeting happened in the home of Lyman Leonard at Winter Quarters, a camp in Nebraska where Mormons leaving Nauvoo for the Great Basin waited in tents and sod shelters for their travels to begin. That winter evening, Snow wrote, "Great instruction was brought forth—br. L[eonard] spoke of the American government—its fall &c. after which the Lord manifested the contrast of the happiness of the saints and the suff'ring of the gentiles when the Lamanites go forth. Language cannot describe the scene."[43] The phrase "the Lord manifested" likely means that those who attended the prayer meeting followed Leonard's sermon on the destruction of the United States with a period of spontaneous, ecstatic worship in which they imagined and performed "the contrast of the happiness of the saints and the suff'ring of the gentiles when the Lamanites go forth." These dramatic performances, like Pratt's *Voice of Warning*, evoked joy as a response to the destructive anger of the Lamanite armies who would destroy the American government. But, during the turbulent decade since the publication of Pratt's text, the proper emotional response to imagining this event had shifted. Where Pratt had anticipated that White Mormons feel both joy and sorrow as Lamanites destroyed White non-Mormons, Snow, Leonard, and the others performed the "happiness of the saints" as the only correct emotional response to the "suff'ring of the gentiles." Displaying these feelings of joy, then, marked their separation from the United States.

The stories that early Mormons told about Lamanites helped to bind them into a coherent religious movement. By sharing prophecies about Lamanites, expressing their confidence in the truth of Smith's revelations, and manifesting in worship the day "when the Lamanites go forth," Mormons sought to feel an intimacy with their "Lamanite" allies that would separate them from other White Americans. This helped cultivate the sense members of the Mormon movement already belonged to a new nation. They presented themselves to each other and to non-Mormon audiences as patiently awaiting the overthrow of the United States. For now, they performed restraint by imagining themselves holding back Lamanites' anger and by enjoining Indigenous people to accept Indian removal. But this restraint depended on its own forms of release: the expression in texts and worship of the unrestrained joy and anger with which White Mormons and Lamanites, respectively, would greet the nation's fall.[44]

The Politics of Prophecy: Lamanites in Mormon Governance

When Dunham, speaking in 1840, identified the Haudenosaunee with "the promised people of the house of Jacob," he drew on Book of Mormon histories and stories about Lamanites discussed so far in this chapter. His dire warning that "the nation was about to be destroyed," however, gestured to another part of early Mormon storytelling about Lamanites: prophecies arguing that these Israelite Indians would soon overturn the United States in favor of a new, perfected nation. Between the murder of Joseph Smith in 1844 and the migration of Brigham Young's faction of the church to Utah in 1847, these prophecies helped form a new, distinctively Mormon, religious nationalism focused on the idea of Zion, the future kingdom of God in North America. This nationalism shaped how Mormons perceived and related to Indigenous people. They expected, after all, that building Zion would require joining with Lamanites. Behind closed doors, their leaders took some steps toward political alliances with Indigenous people against the United States. After Young's faction moved the headquarters of the church to Utah, however, their enthusiasm for alliances with Indigenous people waned even as their investment in the idea of themselves as a nation apart grew stronger.

The development and transformation of Mormon nationalism in this period is particularly obvious in the minutes of a council called "the Kingdom of God," or, more commonly, the Council of Fifty. Smith established the Council of Fifty in 1844 as the basis of a civil government that, he hoped, would rule both Mormons and non-Mormons in Nauvoo. He organized it as a "theocracy" or "theodemocracy," meaning that it based its decisions not only on the will of its members but also on prophetic revelations. This arrangement reflected Smith's increasing awareness that Mormons' new revelations, new rituals, clandestine practice of plural marriage, and apocalyptic expectations of alliance with Indigenous people all placed them beyond the pale of what the United States considered respectable or tolerable in a religion. Smith saw the federal government's refusal to protect Mormons during the Missouri Mormon War of 1838 and during outbreaks of anti-Mormon violence thereafter as the result of a system that harkened to the voice of the popular majority but not to the voice of God. After Smith's murder, the Council of Fifty's suspicion that American democracy was rotten only intensified. Under the leadership of Brigham Young, it expelled its few non-Mormon members, and the remaining councilmen took to describing Mormons as a "nation" set apart from the United States.[45] They planned political and spiritual union with Indigenous people both as a practical defense against federal interference and as a step toward the formation of a new, perfected nation: Zion.

The minutes of the Council of Fifty are an unusually candid record of its members' thinking about this nationalist project. Although summaries rather than word-for-word transcriptions, they contain enough detail about individual member's speeches to make it clear that the council members dealt in the emotional as well as the practical side of creating a new nation. They declared their anger at the United States, their trust in God, and their faith in Smith's revelations. Doing so, they attempted to make their nascent nation feel real and to sever the emotional ties binding them to the United States. As council member Orson Spencer put it, "The kingdom of God is set up and we are in a different attitude to what we ever were before, so that what was once unpatriotic now becomes patriotic . . . we are no longer obligated to [the United States]. We have been organized into a kingdom and it would be beneath our dignity to crouch to any nation."[46] Another, Reynolds Cahoon, proclaimed: "These United States has set us off as a nation to ourselves and what does it prove to us. I just feel that we are a nation to ourselves and we have no concern with them."[47] The members of the Council of Fifty rehearsed these rejections of federal power because nations, just as much as religions, rely on the emotional lives and ritual practices of their members. Only by performing for themselves and others their feelings about a collective identity, whether national or religious, can individuals make an abstract label like "Christian," "Mormon," or "American" feel real and specific to them.[48] In this way, by rehearsing their anger toward the United States and insisting that Mormons were "a nation to ourselves," Spencer and Cahoon made their image of Zion feel solid.

Before the 1847 migration to Utah, the Council of Fifty assumed that they would need Lamanites to establish God's kingdom on earth. Soon, they expected, Lamanites and White Mormons would gather in Zion, where they would be strong enough to declare independence from the United States. The appointment of Lewis Dana, an Oneida Mormon, to the council in March of 1845 symbolized this expected gathering. Sadly, the minutes record very few of Dana's thoughts on the council's debates. His actions, however, expressed hope for the coming gathering of the Lamanites. He helped to organize the Council of Fifty's most substantial attempt to form an alliance with Indigenous nations: the "Western Mission." This mission saw Dana and three other council members—Jonathan Dunham, Phineas Young, and Charles Shumway—travel to the Indian Territory in April 1845 to attend what he believed would be a large gathering of the leaders of all the nations in that region.[49] There, they planned to convert Indigenous leaders and convince them to form their own church to help prepare for the coming of Zion.[50]

The Council of Fifty reached the high-water mark of its enthusiasm for allying with Indigenous nations during the spring of 1845 as members planned the Western Mission. Believing strongly in Indigenous peoples' Lamanite identity and their prophesied role in the destruction of the United States, council members believed that they would swiftly embrace the offer to help throw off federal rule and build God's kingdom. George Miller, for example, charged the missionaries that "when you get into an Indian tribe assemble the chiefs . . . and then tell them your mission and that God has set up his kingdom. This is the only Israel on the earth, the fullness of the gentiles has come in and we have nothing to fear."[51] By "the fullness of the gentiles has come in," Miller meant that all Whites who were going to become Mormons—and hence part of Israel—had already done so. All that remained was for the Lamanites to convert so that they could overturn the government of the United States and help replace it with the kingdom of God, "the only Israel on the earth," of which the Council of Fifty was the first foundation stone.

The council hoped, as well, that Indigenous people would see Mormons as their allies because the new movement had suffered at the hands of the United States. Orson Spencer exhorted Dana to "call upon the red men to come speedily to the help of the Lord against the mighty. They have been driven from their homes and the graves of their fathers and massacred like unto us . . . carry the fire amongst to them and tell them that God has set up his kingdom and that the day of deliverance is at hand."[52] For Spencer, Indian removal had put Indigenous nations in a similar position to Mormons. They had also "been driven from their homes and the graves of their fathers" when they fled Missouri and "massacred" in incidents of anti-Mormon violence. Because of this shared history, he assumed, the creation of a new, Christian nation separate from the United States would thrill a Lamanite audience just as it did him.

Spencer was not entirely wrong to think that Indigenous nations might recognize Mormons as potential allies. Four years earlier, in August 1841, a delegation of around fifty Sauk and Meskwakie (Fox) people had arrived in Nauvoo to meet with Smith. The Sauk leader, Keokuk, who headed the delegation, brought with him a copy of the Book of Mormon that Smith had given him, which he likely saw as a sign of a diplomatic relationship with the Mormons specifically. He came seeking allies in resisting removal from his nation's remaining land in what is now Iowa, not far from Nauvoo. Smith, however, saw this as an opportunity to convert the Sauks and Meskwakies rather than ally with them. Through an interpreter, he "instructed them in many things which the Lord had revealed unto me concerning their Fathers, and the promises that were made concerning them in the Book of Mormon" and exhorted them to behave peacefully. Keokuk responded politely but generally, saying that "I also am a Son of the Great Spirit. I've heard your advice—we intend to quit fighting and follow the good talk you have given us."[53] Mormons have tended to interpret Keokuk's reply as an acceptance of Smith's sermon, but this is a misreading. It was standard diplomatic protocol among Indigenous leaders to affirm an ally's speech, as well as to build alliances based on kinship, in this case, through the "Great Spirit."[54] Keokuk was most likely interested in political, and possibly military, aid, not in Smith's vision of future happiness that would arrive only after his nation "behaved peaceably" and suffered further removal.

Some other Indigenous nations made similar attempts right up to the 1847 migration of Young's faction of the church to Utah. The Potawatomi of the Council Bluffs reservation, for example, repeatedly hosted Mormon missionaries and maintained diplomatic relations with the movement for years, even after Smith declined their 1843 invitation to join a mutual defense alliance of ten nations in the Indian Territory.[55] The few Indigenous nations who opened diplomatic relations with Mormons all had in common that they were facing or had endured removal. In need of settler allies, they seem to have regarded Mormons as a nation apart from the United States, or at least as an organization that, like Protestant missionaries, could intercede with the federal government on their behalf. Sparse evidence makes it difficult to know what they thought of Mormon prophecies about Lamanites, although Keokuk's polite evasions on the subject seem to have been typical. Building "the only Israel on the earth" did not excite them as the Council of Fifty hoped.

The Council of Fifty reversed Smith's coolness toward allying with Indigenous nations because of the practical appeal, as well as the millennial consequences, of such alliances. Some members of the Council of Fifty believed that Mormons would be free from the United States if they were able to get permission to settle on a reservation in the Indian Territory. They interpreted the Nonintercourse Acts—laws that regulated trade with Indigenous people and claims on Indigenous land—to mean that reservations in Indian Territory were outside the reach of the law. Hence, if the Western Mission could obtain permission to settle on a reservation, they would finally be safe to build their ideal community without interference from the states or the federal government. Others appealed to a higher authority than the Nonintercourse Acts to justify the sole legal sovereignty of Indigenous nations over their territories. Miller argued soon before the Western Mission departed that "this is all the Land of the Lamanites and the White people are nothing but intruders; the devil gave it to them. If we can form an alliance with the Lamanites we don't care about the Whites nor any thing else."[56] Such an alliance, he argued, was the only way to make secure claims on "the Land of the Lamanites" and get protection from "the White people" by sheltering under the legal sovereignty of Indigenous nations.

The Western Mission was a serious attempt at forming the kind of alliance Miller envisioned. Dana and Dunham, who led the mission, had deep experience as missionaries to Indigenous nations and prepared well. On Dana's advice, they brought along Solomon Tindall, a Mohegan Mormon and an adopted member of the Lenape nation who probably had connections in the Indian Territory. Hoping to speak at a multitribal council to be held near Fort Gibson, they wisely sought a letter of introduction from the Stockbridge leader Thomas Hendrick. Hendrick, who knew Dunham and was likely one of Dana's relatives, had contacts in the Cherokee Nation who, the missionaries hoped, would secure them the right to speak at the council. When the missionaries arrived in the Cherokee Nation with Hendrick's letter, however, they met with disappointment. The anticipated pan-tribal council was, in fact, a more limited discussion between Muscogee, Cherokee, Pawnee, and Comanche leaders. Worse, it had already taken place. Shumway and Young returned to Nauvoo to deliver their report while Dunham and Dana remained. Dunham would never return. He died, likely from illness, in July 1845, a little less than five years after he arrived in Kirtland proclaiming the imminent rising of a Lamanite army.[57]

Initially, some on the Council of Fifty hoped to try again the next year, but that hope soon faded. Brigham Young argued that it would be better to approach and attempt to convert Indigenous nations one by one than to attempt to form a political union with several nations in order to secure the right to live in the Indian Territory. "It is impossible at present to affect a union amongst the tribes . . . so that we can live in their midst, all that we can do is to go and sow a little seed, and reap and sow, until we can come back and sweep Jackson County [Missouri] and build the Temple" in the place that Smith had first designated for it.[58] From this point on, Mormons under Young's leadership would not seek to settle with Indigenous people but would concentrate on building their own Zion that, they hoped, would attract Lamanites to their cause. As Young put it, "Let us get by ourselves and in a little while the Indians will join in with us, and as soon as we get cousin Lemuel [i.e., the Lamanites] converted I don't fear."[59] To do this, he insisted, they should seek a refuge not in the Indian Territory but in Upper California, a region comprising much of what is now the Southwest of the United States.

By seeking to "get by ourselves" over the Rocky Mountains, the faction of the church under Young put themselves in conflict with the nations they encountered on their migration. On their journey westward, for example, Mormons clashed with the Omaha and Otoe when members of those nations took cattle in response to what they saw as the Mormons' overuse of local resources.[60] These and other conflicts made many Mormons, including Young, leerier of alliances with Indigenous people by the time they arrived in the Great Basin region of what is now Utah. There, they stumbled into complex political relationships and enmities among the Utes, Goshutes, Paiutes, and other nations. Although they made sporadic efforts to convert members of these nations, Mormons' arrogation of local resources and mismanagement of diplomatic relations ignited clashes with Great Basin peoples that would continue through the 1850s.[61]

Practices anticipating the day when the Lamanites would join with the saints in Zion were just one casualty of these conflicts. By 1848, the Council of Fifty was already warning against the heresy of "Lamanism," or "Lumanism," meaning the belief in the imminent arrival of a Lamanite army to help Mormons recapture Zion by force.[62] From 1855 to 1857, the church leadership used the same term again to condemn an outbreak of millenarianism focused on Lamanite prophecies during a period of heightened tensions with the United States.[63] Ultimately, Young's faction of the movement chose to assert their sovereignty over what became Utah by emphasizing not their closeness to Indigenous people but their status as White settlers who, like other settlers pushing into Indigenous territories, could constitute their own polities under U.S. law.[64]

It is unclear from surviving records what Dana, who remained the Council of Fifty's sole Indigenous member throughout his life, thought about this pivot away from alliance with Lamanites to build Zion. Certainly, he continued to concentrate on converting Indigenous people after Young disinvested from the idea. He and George Herring, a Mormon of either Shawnee or Mohawk descent, tried to form diplomatic alliances with nations in the Indian Territory throughout 1845 and may have secured permission for White Mormons to settle near the Cherokee in the Indian Territory. Since Young's plan to move westward prevailed, that offer, if it was indeed made, was never tested.[65] By July of that year, Dana hoped to lead a coalition of Oneidas, Senecas, and Cherokees westward to settle near Young's faction. This plan, too, never gained momentum.[66] Instead, in the winter of 1847, Dana joined with his fellow member of the Council of Fifty, Alpheus Cutler, to create a mission station for Lenape in the Indian Territory.[67] With the main body of the church moving west, Cutler believed it his duty to continue missions in the Indian Territory in the hope of building Zion and, perhaps, nucleating the Lamanite army that would overthrow the United States.

During the three years when Dana oversaw the Lenape mission, the church leadership became more and more concerned that Cutler would stir up trouble with non-Mormon neighbors. Orson Hyde, whom Young had left in charge of the Mormon congregations in Iowa, warned in 1850 that "everything is precarious here. Indian Cutlerism in 500 forms would rage like wild fire through the country if the strong arm of power were not upon it all the time."[68] In a stunning shift from Randall's vision of White Mormons holding back "ten hundred thousand of the Lamanites" from attacking non-Mormons, now the ascendant faction of the church leadership under Young saw itself as holding off the rage of those Mormons who had been infected with Lamanism or "Indian Cutlerism" and their Indigenous allies. That rage, Hyde feared, would consume the churches in Iowa. Again, Dana's feelings on the matter seem to have gone unrecorded. However, when Cutler's continuing Lamanism—including a commitment to send missionaries only to Indigenous people, not to settlers— led to a final break with Young, Dana went with him. He was present at the founding of Cutler's breakaway church in 1851, and after Cutler's death in 1861 went with most of its remaining members to Minnesota.[69]

Whether or not Dana and others continued to hold on to prophecies that Lamanite armies would help build Zion, the Council of Fifty's debates from 1844–47 suggest that early Mormons cultivated the feeling that they were a political community by telling stories about Lamanites. They saw their suffering mirrored in the displacement of Indigenous communities by Indian removal, anticipated an imminent political union with Lamanites, and reinforced their confidence in the triumph of God's kingdom by anticipating Lamanites' violence. Sharing their feelings about imagined Lamanite allies, even to the point of looking for a refuge in the Indian Territory, reaffirmed the sense that Mormons were, as Cahoon put it, already "set . . . off as a nation to ourselves." Once that nation was "set off" in Utah, however, expressing hope for the arrival of a Lamanite army became suspect in, rather than a mainstay of, Mormon political culture.[70]

Lamanites, unlike the imagined "Israelite Indians" of evangelical discourse, did not stay in texts and conversations. Inspired by early readings of the Book of Mormon as an "Indian history," they appeared in the bodies of worshippers and were projected onto the bodies of Indigenous people, living and dead. The emotions early Mormons cultivated for Lamanites shaped their political attitudes toward imperial expansion. They reframed the racial hierarchy of the United States by connecting all the descendants of "Israel" to each other and opposing them to "White" settlers, even as their own narratives continued to associate White skin with religious purity. They made Indian removal a millennial event, charged with hope, sadness, and the certain expectation that it would give way to Zion. Finally, these feelings led Mormon leaders to seek alliances with Indigenous people as part of envisioning themselves as an independent nation. Lamanites were, in this way, vital to the coalescence of the Mormon movement into a people who saw themselves, by the time of the migration to Utah, as a nation apart.

For all this, however, the feelings that White Mormons invested in Lamanites also clouded their perceptions of Indigenous people. As the Zelph episode demonstrates, Indigenous people were at times simply props in the articulation of Mormon sacred dramas. Yet there was another strain to the movement, which Dana exemplifies, which followed Mormons' feelings for Lamanites into diplomatic overtures toward Indigenous nations. Smith and Young, both for their own reasons, passed up opportunities to make alliances with Indigenous peoples. Under Young, trusting in them too much became a heresy. Dana's actions suggest, however, that for at least some early Mormons, and perhaps especially for the handful of Indigenous Mormons, such alliances continued to point the way to a millennial future.

3

Our Common Father

In the spring of 1837, New York City's Clinton Hall resounded with public debates about who Indigenous people were and where they had come from.[1] Like other lecture halls or "lyceums" built in the first half of the nineteenth century, Clinton Hall hosted speeches on transcendentalism, utopianism, abolitionism, temperance, and other topics meeting the intellectual interests of middle-class Americans. That spring, Mordecai Manuel Noah, one of the most prominent American Jews of his generation, appeared several times to explain why he believed Indigenous people were Israelites. His interest in the topic was not new. Just over a decade earlier, the idea that American Jews and Indigenous people were related had figured into Noah's attempts to found a Jewish colony in western New York. That plan fizzled, but Noah's address did not. By late March, he was turning down invitations to repeat his performance in Albany and planning to publish his remarks.[2]

So popular were his lectures that a second speaker appeared that spring to combat "the notions of Major Noah on the ten tribes [of Israel]." This speaker, referred to in the newspapers as "Metacomet" and "Gos-kuk-wa-na-kon-ne-di-yu," was probably William Apess, a Pequot preacher who advocated for the rights of the Indigenous peoples of southern New England. Apess lived in New York City at the time and was one of the few Indigenous people to appear on the lyceum circuit. The pseudonyms also made sense for him. "Metacomet" was a variation on Metacom, the name of the seventeenth-century Wampanoag leader whom Apess memorialized in his 1836 "Eulogy on King Philip," while "Gos-kuk-wa-na-kon-ne-di-yu" was a variant spelling of Sganyodaiyo, or Handsome Lake, a famous Seneca religious leader and reformer whom Apess may have seen as a predecessor.[3] If "Metacomet" was indeed Apess, then he was disavowing an idea he once found compelling. Stories linking Indigenous people to Israelites informed many of his early writings, including his 1829 autobiography, *A Son of the Forest*, and his 1831 sermon, *The Increase of the Kingdom of Christ*.

Both men turned to Israelite Indian stories to navigate the populist White nationalism that came to dominate American culture during their lifetimes. The ascent of the Democratic Party after 1800 strengthened a new American nationalism arguing that the source of sovereignty was "the people," who were able to participate as free agents in a democratic government and a free market. Although their rhetoric hailed universal liberty, in practice "the people" meant White people alone. This populist language soon became general but was particularly important to Democrats, whose electoral success relied on holding together a coalition of working-class people of European descent, wealthy expansionists, and slaveholders by using rhetoric portraying them all as members of a unified racial caste with common interests.[4]

Apess and Noah both drew on this ascendant political rhetoric, even as it excluded them to varying degrees. Although Apess appealed to the rhetoric of freedom that Democrats favored, their notions of "the people" firmly excluded Indigenous people like him. Noah, meanwhile, embraced Democratic political positions even as his Jewish ancestry put his claim on whiteness into question. Although anti-Semitism in America was not as intense as in many parts of Europe, members of the Protestant majority still tended to consider Jews to be less rational in their religion and, therefore, less trustworthy members of the republic. Although Noah enjoyed political rights that Apess did not, therefore, he might well have felt that he was part of "the people" only by sufferance.[5]

Noah and Apess used Israelite Indian stories to navigate the tangled ground between the rhetoric and reality of this populist American nationalism. They addressed them largely to the evangelical reformers for whom talk about "Israel" evoked wonder, sympathy, and excitement. Both tried to mobilize these feelings to the political advantage of their communities. However, Israelite Indians stories also served their communities' internal needs. They used them to describe Jews and Indigenous people as nations with autonomous claims to land and political power. Drawing on the potent symbols associated with Israel, each tried to evoke excitement and sympathy in his audience to induce them to support Jewish or Indigenous nationhood. These alternate religious nationalisms did not attract followers, but challenged the then-dominant assumption that Protestant Christianity, whiteness, and the American state were all consonant. They now stand as unfulfilled dreams and as other visions of what America could have meant.

The claims Noah and Apess made on nationhood reflected the chaotic state of early American expansion. Although the federal government had the sole right to strike treaties with Indigenous nations, it allowed state governments, land speculators, and both legal and illegal settlers to intrude on their territories before negotiations began. This tactic allowed the federal government to disavow responsibility for violence against Indigenous people but usually created a complex tangle of competing land claims and political jurisdictions.[6] Both Apess and Noah tried to take advantage of this chaos to imagine alternate ways of organizing territory and political allegiances. Using rhetoric about Israel, they sought to evoke the pride and hope needed to nucleate new Indigenous and Jewish nationalisms. For Noah, a connection between

Indigenous people and Israelites would give American Jews a claim to belonging and political autonomy in America. Apess, meanwhile, reimagined Indigenous Christians in New England as a new Israel united by kinship and religion. Although neither was typical of his community in his engagement with Israelite Indian stories, the feelings their narratives expressed were not unusual in those communities.

Mordecai M. Noah

Mordecai Noah's turn to Israelite Indian stories reflected his position as a prominent member of a transitional generation in American Jewish history. Born in Philadelphia in July 1785, Noah grew up in a Jewish world radically different from the one he saw in his old age. By the late eighteenth century, most American Jews were Ashkenazim, or descendants of communities from central and eastern Europe, but most synagogues followed the customs of the more established Sephardim, or descendants of communities from the Mediterranean. Noah was part of a post-Revolutionary generation of English-speaking American Jews who tended, more than their parents had, to identify themselves both as citizens and as members of a distinct religious and ethnic community. He came of age as Ashkenazic immigrants arrived in substantial numbers, enlarging American Jewish communities and transforming their culture. These immigrants brought professional religious leaders with them—among them Abraham Rice, the first ordained rabbi in North America—who introduced new ritual approaches and, by mid-century, denominational distinctions to American congregations.[7]

Noah, whose extended family included both Sephardim and Ashkenazim, saw himself as an American by birthright. That perception, however, came under assault throughout his career. Both in his early years as a diplomat and in his long tenure as a newspaper editor in New York, he faced attacks from political and business opponents implying that Jews could not truly belong in the United States.[8] He responded, in part, with allegiance to the Democratic Party. Because Democrats relied on White nationalism, rather than Protestant morality or class interests, to unite their constituencies, they allowed Jews and Catholics of European descent a greater voice in their political organizations than did their Federalist rivals. Noah, who spent most of his career at newspapers that leaned heavily toward Democratic positions, embraced party lines on race. He hailed chattel slavery as a beneficial system and was unwaveringly opposed to suffrage for free Black Americans. This commitment, seemingly, helped him shore up his sense that Jews were White and therefore part of the American body politic.[9]

To be White in early America was not only to have light skin but to be "rational" and "civilized." Rationality and civilization, in part, meant a due reverence to Protestant Christianity because it was based on what White Protestants portrayed as a common-sense reading of the only valid source of religious knowledge: the Bible. Jews, Catholics, Mormons, and religious skeptics who, to this way of thinking, rejected the obvious authority and meaning of the Bible put their rationality, their fitness for civilization, and, ultimately, their whiteness into question. Protestant critics of these groups often implied that they were akin to or allied with Black Americans, Indigenous people, or Chinese immigrants. The implication was that these religious outsiders, no matter their skin color, had as little right as racialized groups to the membership in the nation that came along with whiteness. By contrast, a Protestant confession tightly bound the legal and political category of "White" to a person of European descent and demonstrated that not only their skins but their souls were fit for citizenship.[10]

In different ways, Catholics, Jews, and Mormons all struggled during the nineteenth century to maintain their "irrational" distinctiveness in religion while also asserting that they were White and, therefore, deserved political power. Paradoxically, asserting kinship to Indigenous people allowed Noah to strike this balance. Like most American Protestants, he argued that ancient Israel was the birthplace of American governance and true religion. Jews, therefore, could be full members of a nation founded on Israelite principles by reason of their descent from Israel. Many other American Jews argued this much, but Noah went further.[11] He argued that if Jews were relatives of Indigenous people, then they also had a claim by birthright to the land itself, not just to citizenship. Of course, claiming that Jews were related to Indigenous people ran the risk of implying that they were not White. To avoid that conclusion, Noah argued that Indigenous people were not, in fact, a distinct race from White people. Their physical differences from Europeans, he argued, were due to climate and upbringing, not inherent to their bodies. They could therefore attain all the political and economic privileges of whiteness, just as he hoped Jews would.

"The Government of the Jewish Nation": Land and Nationhood in Noah's Thought

At dawn on September 15, 1824, a salute boomed out from the steps of the courthouse in Buffalo, New York, echoing over the still surface of Lake Erie. At eleven that morning, a procession of civil officials, Freemasons, and militia marched through the streets to St. Paul's Episcopal Church. Noah came in the rear, dressed as a "Judge of Israel [in] black, wearing the judicial robes of crimson silk, trimmed with ermine and a richly embossed golden medal suspended from the neck." The procession entered the church to a march from Handel's "Judas Maccabeus." On the church altar, Freemasons used grain, wine, and oil to consecrate the cornerstone of Ararat, a colony for European Jewish immigrants that Noah planned to build on Grand Island, a flat, heavily wooded island in the Niagara River.[12] This "laudable and prosperous project," as Noah called it, was many things. It was a Zionist dream, fitting in with Noah's lifelong belief that American

Jews could help unify Jewish communities worldwide and inaugurate a return to Palestine. It was a plan to recover Noah's finances, which had collapsed into insolvency when he lost his position as editor of the Democratic *National Advocate* earlier that year. It was, however, also a plan that depended on Noah's conviction that Indigenous people were his long-lost kin, whose descent from ancient Israel conferred on their Jewish relatives unique claims to belonging in America.[13]

Speaking from the pulpit, Noah proclaimed "the approach of that period, when . . . [Jews] are to be gathered from the four corners of the Globe, and to resume their rank and character among the governments of the Earth." They would soon reestablish the government of Israel in Palestine, but in the meantime the United States, with its comparatively broad scope of Jewish civil rights, was the ideal place to incubate the civic institutions they would need to do so.[14] He therefore proposed to "revive, renew and reestablish the Government of the Jewish Nation under the auspices and protection of the constitution and laws of the United States of America, confirming and perpetuating all our rights and privileges, our name, our rank, and our power among the nations of the earth as they existed and were recognized under the government of the JUDGES," that is, the pre-monarchical government of ancient Israel.[15] Under this suitably republican government, Ararat would be an "asylum in a free and powerful country, where ample protection is secured to [Jews'] persons, their property, and religious rights," allowing Jewish immigrants from Europe to prosper and prepare themselves for the return to Palestine. Noah intended for Ararat to have some form of political sovereignty and republican governance. He never precisely worked out its extent, however, aside from casting himself as one of its ruling "judges" and proposing that all Jews contribute to its finances with a capitation tax of "three shekels in silver . . . or one Spanish dollar."[16] He may have delayed deciding for tactical reasons. Amid the ambiguities and competing claims of this early period of expan-

sion, he could have hoped for anything, from municipal autonomy, to statehood, to semi-independence as a nation within the
United States.[17]

Noah meant the dedication ceremony to perform and evoke
feelings about the "Jewish Nation." Nations, under most circumstances, are invisible, theoretical entities. They become real and
tangible both through obvious exercises of power, such as the
enforcement of laws, and, crucially, through emotionally laden
practices of allegiance and affiliation, such as parades, commemorations, and speeches. In these, citizens both evoke attachment
to the nation in themselves and perform this attachment for others
and in their practice of these emotions make palpable the often
airy concept of national identity. In the early republic, all political parties used processions like Noah's to cultivate both the amity
believed necessary to unite citizens in a republic and the strong
party loyalty required to win elections.[18] For Noah's proclamation to function, he had similarly to create in his audience the feeling that the "Government of the Jewish Nation" existed and, as
he wrote to his friend and business partner Peter B. Porter, "produce abroad the conviction that the project is sanctioned by the
people."[19]

European Jews did not respond with the enthusiasm Noah
hoped for. One reason was that Noah appealed specifically to the
special place of Israel in American self-understanding. His
"judge" costume, his speech, and the Freemasonic dedication
ceremonies—which explicitly recalled Solomon's temple—all
sought to constitute a new government by evoking an Israelite
past.[20] For an American audience, this was a natural strategy.
Americans of all political and religious stripes mined the histories
of Israel for both metaphors and practical models to understand
their nation.[21] Potential immigrants in Europe, however, heard
denunciations of Ararat from leading European rabbis, who read
the colony only as an overweening attempt to preempt the divine
plan for Israel. "God alone knows the epoch of the Israelitish

restoration," thundered Abraham de Cologna, a prominent French rabbi; "every attempt on our part to re-assemble with any politico-national design is forbidden." When God did restore Israel as a nation, he added, it would be to its original site, not to "a marsh in North America."[22] For Americans, imagining a "marsh in North America" as a place of refuge for Jews cohered with decades of discourse about the United States as a "new Israel" where human effort could create a perfected society. For critics like de Cologna, who did not share that context, the idea was blasphemous.

Nations are not solely composed of feelings, however. They also include territories. Although it is possible that Noah never actually owned any part of Grand Island, he intended Ararat to demonstrate that Jews could claim land in North America.[23] Land ownership, after all, underpinned both economic and political independence in Democratic thought. The denial of land to European Jews, he argued that day in Buffalo, had kept them in intolerable dependence, but in Ararat they could "till the land, reap the harvest, and raise the flocks which are unquestionably their own."[24] Like other Democrats, Noah associated national and personal autonomy with land ownership. As other historians studying Noah have pointed out, he was preoccupied with the question of how to ensure that Jews could remain Jews while becoming fully American.[25] But to be fully American in Noah's Democratic worldview was, more specifically, to be White. Whiteness, in turn, meant reaping the benefits of enslaved labor and appropriated land. The "land . . . unquestionably their own" that he promised Jewish immigrants was, to him, not only an economic resource but also the guarantor of their full membership in a White supremacist nation.

Jews, Noah implied, had strong claims to territory in North America because the original holders of the land were their kin. He invited the "Indians of the American Continent" who were "in all probability the descendants of the lost tribes of Israel," to join Ararat for this reason. Reunited, Jews and Indigenous people would become a "nation—the first of people in the old world, and the rightful inheritors of the new." Kinship with Indigenous people, in Noah's view, secured rather than undermined American Jews' status because it gave them a connection to the land that predated even the first Protestant settlers. At the same time, that kinship was not total. Indigenous people could become full citizens of Ararat only if they submitted to "measures . . . to make them sensible of their origin, to cultivate their minds, soften their condition and finally re-unite them with their brethren the chosen people."[26] These "measures" likely resembled the tactics used by the dominant missionary groups in Noah's day, who insisted that Indigenous people embrace Christianity as a total way of life, including European agriculture, patriarchal families, and ordered towns divided among private landowners.[27] Noah's "measures" likely would also have sought to make Indigenous people assume what he saw as rational, republican manners befitting White citizens.[28]

Noah's Ararat project was far-fetched, but he was not the only American Jewish writer to find the idea of a connection with Indigenous people useful. Isaac Leeser, a prominent Jewish religious leader and opponent of Reform Judaism, wrote articles praising the idea that Indigenous people might be the lost tribes of Israel throughout the 1850s and 1860s. Like Noah, he saw Israelite Indian stories as reasons to think that American Jews might have a better claim to land in North America than did White Protestants. However, the Reform rabbi Isaac Meyer Wise probably spoke for the majority of American Jews when he argued, against Leeser, that there was no literal, genealogical connection between Jews and Indigenous people.[29] Through the rest of the nineteenth century, other American Jews compared themselves with Indigenous people in order to lay claim to western lands, to navigate tensions between ethnic and political belonging in America, and to understand the place of Jews in America's racial hierarchies. These comparisons did not usually rest on assertions that Indigenous people and Jews were ethnically related, however. Both the precarious place of Jews in the American racial caste system and strong community proscriptions again forming blood ties with non-Jewish peoples militated against the idea.[30]

Like many planned colonies in the early United States, Ararat failed. American Jews showed little interest in relocating to Grand Island. Although Noah had originally planned to gather enough adult Jewish men for his ceremony "to form on that Spot a *Sanhedrin*," or judicial council, to govern Ararat, the only other Jew known to have been in attendance was Abraham Benjamin Seixas, the nephew of one of Noah's most admired childhood teachers.[31] When the anticipated flood of Jewish immigrants did not arrive in Ararat, Noah abandoned it within a year.[32] By 1833, according to one version of events, he was embarrassed enough to ask a friend to abscond with the Ararat cornerstone, then lying behind St. Paul's Episcopal Church, and to "place it in some secure spot . . . where it would not excite comment."[33] Noah did not again try his hand at land speculation, but he continued to turn to Israelite Indians to understand his community's place in an expansive empire.

"The Lineaments of His Race": Israelite Ancestry and Race in Noah's America

Shortly after his Ararat proclamation, Noah paid several young Seneca men to advertise the project by boarding a five-ton ship—unsubtly named the *Noah's Ark*—that would join Governor DeWitt Clinton's ceremonial cruise down the length of the newly completed Erie Canal from Buffalo to New York Harbor. A contemporary newspaper described the boat as "laden with animals and birds of various descriptions, and two young Indian hunters of the Seneca tribe, dressed in their costume." Any plans for using *Noah's Ark* as an advertisement were spoiled, however, when it became stuck in a lock on the canal and arrived days too late to join the governor's triumphant ceremonies in New York Harbor.[34]

This failed stunt points to how Noah's use of Israelite Indian stories invited White American onlookers to associate Jewish and Indigenous bodies. Noah meant for the Seneca men he hired, "young Indian hunters . . . dressed in their costume," to symbolize the Israelite past, and the claims on North America, that Indigenous people and American Jews putatively shared. Given that Noah wanted Ararat to grant Jews political autonomy in America, however, suggesting that their bodies were like Indigenous bodies was risky. Democrats like Noah, after all, insisted that the capacity for political sovereignty was a racial characteristic that only White people possessed. As discussed above, the "irrational" practice of Judaism could make White Protestants question Jews' racial status. Noah experienced this to some extent. His friend Lewis F. Allen, for example, described his physical appearance this way: "Although a native of the United States, the lineaments of his race were impressed upon his features with unmistakable character; and if the blood of the elder Patriarchs or David or Solomon flowed not in his veins, then both chronology and genealogy must be at fault."[35] The features in Noah's face that Allen saw as Jewish seemed to him unexpected for a "native of the United States," meaning a White man. His evocations of biblical patriarchs, moreover, expressed both the respect Allen had for Noah and his condescension toward Jews, whom most American Protestants regarded as an outdated people belonging to the past.[36] Noah suggested a new way of reacting to the physiognomy that Allen found so un-American by connecting Indigenous people to the same Biblical history in both his 1824 Ararat dedication speech and in the 1837 publication of his Clinton Hall address, *Discourse on the Evidences of the American Indians Being the Descendants of the Lost Tribes of Israel*.

"The Indians are not Savages," Noah proclaimed in his Ararat speech, "they are wild and savage in their habits, but possess great vigour of intellect and native talent, they are a brave and eloquent people, with an Asiatic complexion, and Jewish features."[37] In other words, their culture, not their bodies, prevented them from membership in the United States. This idea was a mainstay of assimilationist approaches to Indigenous nations such as those that missionaries favored. Noah varied this common argument by claiming not only that Indigenous people were fit for citizenship but also that they had "Jewish features." These suggested that the same "lineaments" in Noah's own face that Allen saw as foreign to America were, in fact, the signs of kinship with America's original inhabitants and suitability for U.S. citizenship. Noah's exhibition of Seneca men's bodies on *Noah's Ark*, read in this context, was a performance that insisted that those "Jewish features" were plain for anyone to see. Rather than appealing first to prophecy and biblical history as had evangelical reformers, Noah appealed to the American habit of sorting people into racial categories based on quick readings of their physical appearance and the emotional reactions that accompanied them.

In his *Discourse on the Evidences*, first delivered more than thirteen years later, Noah returned to this theme. He approvingly quoted a letter from the painter George Caitlin claiming that "the first thing that strikes the traveller in an Indian country as evidence of their being of a Jewish origin . . . is the striking resemblance which they generally bear in contour, and expression of head, to those people."[38] This kind of immediate recognition that "strikes the traveler" was what Noah was most interested in. It was a snap judgement of appearance based on immediate, "commonsense" sensory impressions and feelings. Based on just such judgments, Democrats argued that a hierarchy between the races affirmed the natural order.[39]

Noah's invitation to onlookers to identify his body with Indigenous bodies had similar functions to contemporary White Americans' use of "Indian costume" and redface makeup on the stage, in protests, and in fraternal organizations. These costumes asserted that their wearers were "Native Americans," a term that anti-immigrant groups then used to denote White, American-born Protestants. By performing their status as "Native Americans," these men—and they were almost always men—asserted that their ties to the land and capacities for violence in defense of it matched those they attributed to Indigenous people. At the same time, the fact that they could remove their costumes and makeup and return easily to their everyday appearance established that they remained White people capable of rational citizenship in a republic.[40] Similarly, by claiming that Jews were relatives of Indigenous people while also insisting that they were "civilized" already, and indeed capable of civilizing Indigenous people, Noah could have it both ways. Jews, in this rendering, were original Americans with both ancestral claims on the land and the rational capacities needed to constitute a republican government.

The shared Israelite ancestors of Jews and Indigenous people, Noah continued in *Discourse on the Evidences,* were "a singular race of men, with enlarged views of life, courage, constancy, humanity, policy, eloquence, love of their families; with a proud and gallant bearing, fierce in war, and, like the ancients, relentless in victory."[41] They embodied, in other words, the ideal that northeastern Americans held for men's regulation of their emotions during the first half of the nineteenth century: physical courage and capacity for violence tempered with self-control and affection for one's family.[42] For Noah, a lineal connection to such a group of people would have helped combat the terms in which he, as a Jewish man, was degraded. As suggested by Noah's concern that Jewish immigrants to Ararat learn to farm, he was stung by anti-Jewish tropes that depicted Jewish men as defective of body and, especially, incapable of the farm work that was the cornerstone of independent citizenship in Democratic ideals.[43]

For Noah, then, Israelite Indian stories presented a way of reimagining the place of American Jews in an expansive empire. They suggested that American Jews were distinct as a nation descended from Israel, and should remain so, but that that distinction did not negate their whiteness. Rather, as it did for countless White Americans who dressed in "Indian" costume on the stage or in political protest, it reaffirmed their ties to the land. The outlandishness of the idea, like the spectacle of Noah's Ararat performance, was likely part of its appeal. It attracted excitement and invited audience to feel the pull of the associations of belonging, of connection to land, and of national identity that the idea of Israel evoked. For him, Israelite Indian stories brought these feelings together and associated them with the glorious future progress of an American empire that fully included Jews. But for Apess, who would argue against Noah's *Discourse on the Evidences* in 1837, the association between Israel and the state was neither so smooth nor so painless.[44]

William Apess

Like Noah, William Apess used Israelite Indian stories to reimagine his community's place in the United States. His context, however, was radically different. A Pequot by birth and a Wampanoag by adoption, he belonged to nations that White Americans regarded as vanished or vanishing. Most Pequots and Wampanoags did not remain on reservations, as White observers expected of "Indians," but lived in, near, and between majority-White settlements, at times migrating to gather seasonal resources and at others engaging with the settler economy in trades like itinerant labor, whaling, and handicraft manufacture. Meanwhile, public commemorations of New England's past emphasized Indigenous peoples' tragic demise and lionized a few individuals as "the last of their nation" while eliding the continuity of Indigenous communities in the region. The local racial system completed this apparent vanishing through a sleight-of-hand. White settlers often classified both Black New Englanders and Indigenous people as "colored," a caste marker that implicitly subsumed "Indian" status.[45]

Apess was one of only a few northeastern Indigenous people in this period who could contest this narrative of vanishing in writing and public addresses. Indigenous people in the region had engaged with settlers' forms of writing for generations, principally through spiritual autobiographies, but often White coauthors or redactors shaped those texts.[46] Apess's writing, by contrast, was his own, as reflected in its combination of revivalist evangelical piety with forthright arguments about the rights of Indigenous people. Evangelical Christianity was not just a source of useful rhetoric for Apess. After a troubled childhood and adolescence, he found a stable Indigenous community in a mixed-race Methodist congregation in which his aunt, Sally George, was a lay preacher. In southern New England, independent Christian congregations like George's were hubs of Indigenous life that provided social connections and gathering places even to nonmembers.[47] Apess saw evangelical Christianity, then, as a way to strengthen rather than attenuate Indigenous communities. He began testifying in camp meetings in 1818 and by 1827 was an exhorter, licensed to expound on others' sermons but not to preach himself. Two years later, he received a preacher's license in the Protestant Methodist Church.[48]

Although he rejected Israelite Indian stories by the time of his 1837 appearance in Clinton Hall, Apess included them in all his writings between 1829 and 1833.[49] By imagining himself as an "Israelite," Apess named his feelings of pride in his ancestry and pushed back on shame he had been made to feel as an "Indian." He also evoked White evangelicals' affection for and familiarity with the idea of Israel to exhort them to feel differently toward Indigenous people, hoping that changed hearts would lead to changed politics. Finally, "Israelite" was a national as well as a racial category for Apess. He argued that Indigenous Christians would belong to "Israel" both by descent from ancient Israel and conversion to the spiritual Israel of evangelical Christianity. Unlike White missionaries, he nurtured the hope that such an

"Israel" would be both fully Indigenous and fully Christian. He seems to have imagined it uniting dispersed, autonomous Indigenous Christian communities as White settlement increasingly encroached on traditional territories.[50]

"The Original Complexion of Our Father Adam": Racialized Israelites in Apess's Thought

Apess emphasized race in his thinking about Israelite Indians in part because, for much of his early life, blood was the main claim he had on his national identity. As he relates in his autobiography, *A Son of the Forest*, he was born near Colrain, Massachusetts, in 1798 to William and Candace Apes, both members of the Pequot nation.[51] When he was very young, his parents moved to Colchester, Connecticut, home to his mother's kin and the only school in the state set aside for "colored" children. This time of comparative comfort came to an end when his parents separated. William Sr. returned to Colrain, while Candace left William and his siblings with her parents to travel in search of work. But Apess's grandparents were physically abusive: his grandfather beat him nearly to death when he was around four. He survived only because of the quick intervention of his uncle, Lemuel Ashbo. Ashbo brought the children's desperate situation to the attention of the town selectmen who, following the customary New England method of providing for orphans, separated the Apess children and bound them out as indentured servants. William remained a servant with a succession of White families in the area until he ran away in 1813. His biography emphasizes that he was cut off from Pequot society during his indenture—although Ashbo may have visited him at least occasionally—and Apess remembered this as a time of isolation and cultural disconnection.[52]

Apess became painfully aware of the political and social meaning of the category "Indian" during childhood. In an otherwise warm portrait of David Furman, who first held his indenture, Apess recorded only one direct quotation from the man: Furman saying, as he prepared to whip Apess after another child accused him of attacking her, "I will learn you, you Indian dog."[53] That Apess remembered this angry outburst decades later indicates, perhaps, that Furman rarely spoke this way but also that the term "Indian dog" was all the more painful for coming from someone he thought of a "good . . . dear man." The young Apess learned well the lesson behind the beating: "I thought it disgraceful to be called an Indian."[54] More, he learned that Indigenous people were frightening and dangerous. As a child, he fled from dark-skinned women he encountered while out berry picking near Colchester because of "the many stories I had heard of [Indians'] cruelty toward the whites—how they were in the habit of killing and scalping men, women, and children."[55] To be an Indian, the young Apess learned, was to be both a source and a target of violent cruelty.

It is not surprising, then, that as an adult Apess found the term "Indian" shameful. "I have often been led to inquire where the whites received this word [Indian]. . . . I could not find it in the Bible and therefore concluded that it was a word imported for the special purpose of degrading us."[56] Like some of his Black contemporaries, Apess sought a history for his people in the Bible as a way of constructing a dignified meaning for the racial category assigned to him.[57] He emphasized that "the proper term which ought to be applied to our nation . . . is that of 'Natives'— and I humbly conceive that the natives of this country are the only people under heaven who have a just title to the name, inasmuch as we are the only people who retain the original complexion of our father Adam."[58] That is, the "tawny," or "olive" complexion that White observers attributed to Indigenous people was, in his argument, the original human color.[59] The same "complexion" that had been a basis for degradation and shame was, to Apess, a reason to link Indigenous people to the Bible.

Here, as elsewhere in *A Son of the Forest*, Apess's use of Israelite Indian stories accorded with the dominant understanding that

"Indian" was a stable racial category that included shared descent, shared appearance, and shared "character." However, he used his evangelical audience's familiarity with stories of Israel to change the meaning of that category. In an appendix to *A Son of the Forest*—one nearly as long as the autobiographical narrative—Apess selected parts of Boudinot's *A Star in the West* that argued for the positive qualities of Indigenous people as a race. He reprinted, for example, an essay on "Traits of Indian Character" by Washington Irving that Boudinot included in his work.[60] "No being," wrote Irving, "acts more rigidly from rule than the Indian. . . . The moral laws which govern him, to be sure, are but few, but then he conforms to them all."[61] This rectitude stemmed from "stern resolution . . . unbending pride, and loftiness of spirit."[62] For Apess, these qualities were reminiscent of Israelites, whom Christians then thought had obeyed God's uncompromising law while remaining ignorant of Christian grace.[63] "[The] great similarity of the manners and customs of the Indian natives and those recorded of the Jews," he wrote, made "many learned men . . . come to the conclusion that the Indian tribes are none other than the descendants of the Ten Lost Tribes of Judah [sic]."[64] Here, Apess conceded the idea that Indigenous people had a unified racial character that allowed the construction of "Indian" as a racial caste. However, by connecting that supposed racial character to the histories of Israel, he recast it in favorable terms.

For Apess, tying an illustrious past to the bodily differences that had been made a source of shame for him allowed him to express pride in his lineage to his audience and, crucially, to himself. Taught that his "complexion" and the "character" it supposedly indicated were signs of savagery and ancestral opposition to the White settlers of New England, Apess reimagined them as signs of descent from the people described in the Bible. More, since many of his readers were evangelical Christians, he could hope that convincing them that "Indian character" was firmly rooted in the biblical past would shift their political attitudes toward Indigenous people.

Christianity and Indigenous Nationhood in Apess's Thought

Apess came into his own as a political thinker after he helped represent the Mashpee Wampanoag nation in the "Mashpee Revolt" of 1833. With Apess as a spokesman, the Mashpee successfully protested the administration of their church and their communal lands by the trustees of Harvard College. In the ensuing years, Apess developed his mature thoughts on Indigenous autonomy in his 1835 *Indian Nullification* and his 1836 *Eulogy on King Philip*. These works express a full sense of Indigenous peoples' rights under both the laws of the United States and Indigenous legal systems. They anticipate the tribal sovereignty movements of the twentieth century by insisting both that Indigenous individuals receive equal treatment under U.S. law and that the federal government honor its treaty relationships to Indigenous nations.[65]

Before his involvement in the Mashpee Revolt, however, a younger Apess used Israelite Indian stories to support more limited forms of Indigenous autonomy. His 1831 sermon, *The Increase of the Kingdom of Christ*, has received less attention than his later works in part because it seems, on the surface, concerned only with the question of saving souls. Read in the context of the Israelite Indian stories that Apess took up and transformed in it, however, *Increase* becomes a far more political document. It emphasized that, because Indigenous people were Israelites, conversion to Christianity would preserve, rather than undermine, their communities.[66]

For Apess, the "kingdom of Christ" included all those he regarded as true Christians, that is, those who had undergone an emotional conversion experience and affiliated themselves with an evangelical church.[67] It would also, however, soon include all people descended from Israel. "[The] ancient people of God, long despised as outcasts and wanderers among the nations," he wrote, would soon "return to the Gospel, which they have rejected for more than eighteen centuries." [68] This would include not only Jews but also the "Israelites" of North America.[69] The prediction that both Jews and Indigenous people would inevitably convert to Christianity was uncontroversial in evangelical circles. Apess disagreed with most White evangelicals, however, in his insistence that Indigenous people should continue to be culturally distinct and politically autonomous from White Christians even after conversion.[70]

Native autonomy was the will of God, Apess argued, precisely because Indigenous people were Israelites. "Although in ruins, grandeur makes its high abode with the house of Judah and the house of Israel. . . . Earth and hell are not able to accomplish their extermination, or to amalgamate these dispersed people with strange nations."[71] The exclusion of Indigenous people from White social institutions was a result of God's will. "America has utterly failed to amalgamate the red man of the woods into the artificial, cultivated ranks of social life. Has not one reason been that it was not the purpose of God that it should be done— for lo, the blood of Israel flowed in the veins of these unshackled, freeborn men?"[72] Far from insisting that Indigenous people assimilate into White society, as did most supporters of missions, Apess argued that when all "Israel"—both Indigenous people and Jews—became Christians, they would reclaim the "grandeur" hidden by their circumstances. They would neither see "extermination," as expansionists desired, nor would they "amalgamate . . . with strange nations" as missionaries and their supporters hoped.

Apess recognized that most missions did not lead to substantial numbers of Indigenous converts. He blamed this on missionaries' tendency to get involved in land speculations that undermined the autonomy of Indigenous communities. The waves of conversions he envisioned would happen only if Indigenous Christians were left to manage their own affairs. If missionaries "sought not their own advancement," he wrote, "the praises of God" would "ascend from the happy wigwams of the natives."[73] Wigwams here are not generic "Indian" dwellings, but a specific kind of building that northeastern Indigenous peoples used when traveling to access different resources. Apess's use of the word, therefore, could indicate that he was thinking of Christian communities following Indigenous practices of seasonal land use rather than the permanent agricultural settlements required by missionaries.[74] This made sense given that Apess wrote in a region where mobility was often the only way for Indigenous people to survive and where a network of majority-Indigenous churches, like Sally George's congregation, helped link dispersed communities. He seems to have envisioned Israelite identity as a way of cultivating those religious ties to more tightly link Indigenous people as they moved through the territories they were forced to share with White settlers.[75] This vision of "happy wigwams" whose inhabitants both maintained their traditional lifeways and embraced Christianity was, for Apess, associated with the idea that Indigenous people were Israelites. Immediately afterward, he made the seemingly non sequitur comment that "it is my opinion that our nation," that is, the "nation" of Indigenous people, "retains the original complexion of our common father, Adam. This is strongly impressed on my mind."[76] That "original complexion," presumably, marked Indigenous people out as a chosen nation whom God wished to preserve.

For Apess, Israelite Indian narratives not only promised that conversion would not undermine Indigenous autonomy but also appealed to White evangelicals. In calling for missions that would ensure Indigenous autonomy, Apess sought to reach the feelings of his largely White audience. "Let us pray for Zion," he exhorted, "and let us remember her scattered and peeled people in their sorrowful season of desertion." If they did so, they would ask with

Apess, "When shall the desert break out into songs of praise, loud and high, like the lion cry of Judah's warriors in the day of triumph! When shall the proud, strong, and fleet warriors of the western wilds, the remnants of powerful tribes, come up to the help of the Lord against the man of sin, as strong and bold for Christ as they are in council, and in deeds of arms!"[77] A new Israel would be born, connected by faith to the "Israel" of evangelical Christianity.

But not yet. White Christians ought to yearn "for the greater increase of the kingdom of Christ, which takes hold of our heart and causes our bowels to yearn in sympathizing sorrow."[78] This call for evangelicals to feel deep sorrow at the plight of the unconverted echoed missionary reformers' insistence that true Christians should be wounded by the ills of society and respond with an outpouring of pity and benevolence.[79] Unlike the reformers who built a theory of "degenerate" Israelite religion in need of missionary aid, however, Apess dwelt on imagery of strength. He imagined Israelites who would praise the Christian God in voices "like the lion cry of Judah's warriors in the day of triumph," and "warriors of the western wilds . . . strong and bold for Christ." Here, he called on his audience to sorrow for the wrongs done to Indigenous people, and to work on behalf of missions, but pushed back on the pity that was the dominant emotional tone of missionary thought about Indigenous people. Instead, he asked his audience to feel wonder at a vision of Christian, Israelite Indians whose strength and boldness refused White observers' pity.

Apess's appeals to feeling suited both his church and the ascendant Democratic politics of his time. More conservative evangelical reformers thought about emotions using a model developed in the eighteenth century, which valued most those emotions, like disinterested benevolence, that Christian education cultivated. Methodists like Apess, however, valued what they saw as authentic, uncultivated emotions. This is not to say their emotions were truly more natural. When Methodists worshipped with tears, shouting, clapping, and singing, they were both using techniques that engaged their emotions and performing the reactions their community expected of beings transformed by God. Instead, the difference between them and the evangelical reformers discussed in the first chapter is that Methodists regulated their emotions differently, valuing "natural" outbursts in worship.[80] Apess's Israelite Indians raising "the lion cry of Judah's warriors" and his "happy wigwams" ringing with praise recalled such spectacles. Affirming that Indigenous people would respond appropriately to conversion, Apess depicted them, as well, as capable of the kind of affections that animated American politics. Particularly after the War of 1812, the ascendant Democratic political culture relied not on a cultivated sense of duty but on heartfelt love for the country to unite the nation. Hence, by the time of Apess's writing, Americans expected a warmer emotional tone from their citizens. Although these same Americans often judged the emotions of non-White people more harshly—seeing them as uncontrolled or animalistic—Apess may have hoped that his audience would see in these properly Christian outbursts signs of the humanity and dignity often denied to "Indians."[81]

Apess's revivalist Methodism, furthermore, posited that all believers were made equal through surrender to the overwhelming feelings of conversion. Methodist churches only rarely lived up to this rhetoric of equality, but Apess insisted on it. Not just Indigenous people but also White people, Apess argued, would need to transform their emotional lives to welcome the kingdom of Christ. "The white man, who has most cruelly oppressed his red brother, under the influence of that Gospel, which he long professed to believe, and just now begins to feel, pours out unavailing tears over the wasted generations of the mighty forest hunters and, now they are almost all dead and buried, begins to pity and lament them." The critique Apess made here reflects larger Methodist critiques of social problems. In Methodist thought, those who truly felt their sins and the grace of God's forgiveness would behave morally. Conversely, immoral conduct was a sign of false or hypocritical feeling.[82] Drawing on this schema, Apess argued that the oppression of Indigenous people was a sign that White Americans did not yet fully feel the Gospel.

Apess's address to his White audience largely traded on their wonder at the idea of encountering Israelites in America and on their sorrow for their own sins. However, like Boudinot and other evangelical reformers, he also sought to awaken anxiety by suggesting that God would punish the United States should it oppress the chosen people. "If," he wrote, "as many eminent men with apparently high presumption, if not unquestionable evidence, believe, the Indians of the American continent are a part of the long lost tribes of Israel, have not the great American nation reason to fear the swift judgments of heaven on them for nameless cruelties, extortions, and exterminations inflicted upon the poor Indians?"[83] That Indigenous people belonged to a chosen race not only meant that they were destined to join the "kingdom of Christ," but also that White Christians would be culpable if they did not repent of colonialism and territorial expansion.

Despite its usefulness for imagining a future "kingdom of Christ," the idea that Indigenous people were Israelites did not sit entirely easily with Apess. He struggled to make sense of the implication in Boudinot's arguments that "Israelite" Indians would vanish from North America. Although Apess looked forward "to the day . . . not far distant when ample justice shall be done to the red man by his white brother," he also seemed to endorse the idea that Indigenous people would disappear regardless of whether that justice was done. He closed the appendix by remarking that living Indians are a "remnant . . . on their march to eternity."[84] On its face, this passage seems to accept the trope of the "vanishing Indian," or the idea that Indigenous people were destined to disappear as White settlement expanded.[85] In the context of Apess's yearning for Indigenous peoples' resurgence after their conversion, however, this passage is perhaps a warning rather than a prediction. If his audience did not work to see that the "Israelite" Indians received the justice Apess hoped for, they would not be "on their march to eternity" but would already be there.

Apess's use of Israelite Indian stories was unusual among northeastern Indigenous people but not unique. Joseph Wolff, a Jewish convert to evangelical Christianity, reported that in 1836 he asked Mohicans he met in New York, "'Whose descendants are you?' They replied, 'We are of Israel.'" It seems they had learned this story from Barbara Simon, a Scottish supporter of the Israelite Indian theory, who had recently traveled through the area.[86] Wolff's description is too terse to clearly determine why these Mohicans repeated Simon's story. Since they also told him a more traditional origin story, they may not have placed much stock in the Israelite idea.[87] Alternately, they may have found the idea useful in concert with ideas borrowed from the Stockbridge community, a group of Christian Mohicans. The Stockbridges, who by the time of Wolff's visit had left New York for Menominee territory near Green Bay, developed a providentialist theology that associated their communities with Israel. According to this theology, the suffering of Indigenous people in the northeast was an affliction from God chastising them for their ancestors' idolatry, much as God had punished Israel for departing from correct worship.[88] If Wolff's interlocutors had already heard a reading of their history that depended on a strong analogy with Israel, Simon's theory might have seemed likely enough to be worth repeating.

Whether Wolff's interlocutors took the idea of their Israelite ancestry seriously or not, that they used it at all was unusual. Even Apess's contemporaries in Christian Indigenous communities tended to ignore or dismiss Israelite Indian stories. The Ojibwe leader and Methodist minister Kahkewaquonaby, or Peter Jones, judged them baseless. Although he had found Boudinot's and Ethan Smith's books compelling, neither he nor Ojibwe elders he spoke to had seen evidence that Indigenous people observed the sabbath, practiced circumcision, built altars, or distinguished between clean and unclean animals.[89] As the results of Jones's investigation hinted, Indigenous people in the northeast seem to have preferred other ways of understanding their history. They connected old and new traditions to significant locations in the region, maintained oral histories, and, in some communities, used Christian theologies and sacred histories in more metaphorical ways than did Apess.[90]

Apess himself abandoned Israelite Indian stories after 1833.[91] The reasons are unclear, but it seems likely that he had grown disenchanted with the White evangelicals he had hoped to reach with tales of Israelite Indians. By the time he appeared in Clinton Hall, he had already faced off with ill-intentioned missionaries in Mashpee. More, the major Protestant missionary organizations had failed to prevent the forced migration of thousands of Indigenous people to the Indian Territory. As for his investment in an "Israel" of Indigenous churches, Apess abandoned the idea in favor of using more recent histories of dispossession and racialization to discuss Indigenous peoples' common cause.[92]

"Israelite" identity was useful to both Apess and Noah, first, because of the hold it had on the emotional lives of White reformers. Both belonged to groups that reformers saw as allies and possible targets of conversion. While they each welcomed alliances with evangelicals to some extent, they shared the dilemma of how to accept help without giving ground on their communities' autonomy. Second, for them stories about Israel not only suggested that specific people were "chosen" as God's favored nation but could also be used to evoke the feelings necessary for political unity among those designated "Israelites." Beyond the strict utility of Israelite Indian stories for swaying evangelical audiences, therefore, they held out new ways of constructing the group identities of Indigenous people and Jewish Americans.

When Apess and Noah spoke in Clinton Hall, the hopes of the friends of Zion had already curdled. The Indian Removal Act of 1830 began waves of forced migration that would continue for the following three decades. Democratic expansionism, it seemed, had prevailed. Although Noah could still hope to benefit from that expansion by cementing his rights to land as a White citizen, Apess could not. Hence, while Noah could continue to use a supposed connection between Israelites and Indigenous people to assert that Jews belonged in an expansive empire, Apess turned away from the idea. Even as he did so, however, a different group of Indigenous intellectuals took up to Israelite Indian stories to argue for the specific land claims of the Cherokee Nation amidst the crises and violence of removal.

4

The Original Customs of Our Nation

On June 7, 1838, the missionary Daniel S. Butrick visited an internment camp at Ross's Landing along the southern shore of the Tennessee River. For the past two decades, Butrick had worked for the American Board of Commissioners for Foreign Missions (American Board) as a missionary in the Cherokee Nation, a constitutional republic ruling part of the traditional Cherokee homeland in what is now Georgia, Tennessee, and North Carolina.[1] Now, however, he was witnessing a man-made disaster as state militias and U.S. Army troops rounded up Cherokees at bayonet point and forced them into internment camps to be prepared for deportation to the Indian Territory. The companies that had already gone westward on what would become known as the Trail of Tears had seen devastating losses, but the camps were little better. Overfilled and lacking adequate sanitation, they were hotbeds for epidemic disease. Until recently, Butrick's main concern had been the care of a small congregation at the Carmel mission station in the central region of the Cherokee Nation near what is now Talking Rock, Georgia. But by the beginning of July, he was conducting so many funerals that he was sometimes confused about which of the day's victims he was to bury.[2]

Writing later that day about the internees, Butrick remarked, "On seeing their habitations, I was insensibly led to exclaim to

myself 'How beautiful are thy tents, O Jacob, and thy taberna-
cles, O Israel.'"[3] Butrick, who believed Indigenous people to be
the descendants of ancient Israelites, knew the original context
of those words. In the Book of Numbers, the non-Israelite prophet
Balaam speaks them when he comes to the camp of the Israelites
to curse them on behalf of the king of Moab. Overcome by the
power of God, Balaam delivers a blessing instead.[4] But Butrick
was not Balaam. He had come intending to bless, but, as the
deaths from removal mounted while the American Board stood
by and sent its missionaries westward, he could have been forgiven for wondering if he had brought a curse instead.[5]

Butrick is now best known for the work that occupied him
between September 1835 and the summer of 1838, when he and
his wife, Elizabeth, left on the Trail of Tears.[6] During those last
years in the east, he worked with the permission of John Ross,
Principal Chief of the Cherokee Nation, to collect reports of what
Ross called "the *Original Customs & Manners* of our nation," and
compile them into a record "for the satisfaction of posterity long
after this present generation shall have returned unto dust." Ross
wanted this record to remain under the Nation's control. He
insisted that it not be published until he, the assistant chief George
Lowrey, and a board of elders had inspected it.[7] This review
process never happened. Too many elders, including many who
contributed to Butrick's project, died during removal. Ross continued to try, however. Before removal, he had asked his friend
John Howard Payne, a playwright most famous for the air "Home
Sweet Home," to collaborate with Butrick and the "antiquarians"
the missionary had been interviewing. Later, he hoped that Payne
would finish what Butrick could not. This hope vanished in 1852,
when Payne died with the book still unpublished.[8]

Many of the stories Butrick and Payne recorded showed clear
influences from the Bible, a fact that the missionary took as con-
firmation that the Cherokees were Israelites. In one of Butrick's
manuscripts, for example, he records a story told by a Cherokee

knowledge-holder named Thomas Smith, or Shield Eater, that was one of several that echoed the passage of the Israelites through the sea during the Exodus from Egypt:

When the Indians started to go to that country God had given them, they were fleeing from their enemies. But as soon as they came to a great water, God told their leader to strike the water with a rod, and it should divide, and give them a passage through, and then flow together and stop their enemies. Thus their leader did, and thus they passed through and their enemies were stopped. God loved them, and therefore he assisted them in this way.[9]

This story was not precisely like the Exodus narrative—Shield Eater clarified in another version that the "waters" in question were rivers, not seas—but it shared enough common elements with it to pique Butrick's interest.[10] Similarly, he was intrigued when another Cherokee man named Nettle told him that once "all people spake the same language, but sometime after that, men attempted to build something that would reach to the clouds; but God was displeased and gave them different languages, & thus separated them from each other."[11] To Butrick, this echoed the story of the Tower of Babel in the book of Genesis. Or, again, he recorded another account that the Cherokee had long ago been "commended . . . to rest from all work every seventh day," which seemed to him to be a memory of Sabbath observance.[12]

Most Cherokees at the time probably did not think that these stories were evidence of their Israelite descent. As George Lowrey, one of the Cherokee leaders who was to review Butrick's eventual manuscript, pointed out, it was far more likely that Cherokee storytellers had learned them at some point during their generations of contact with White Christians and incorporated them into their traditions.[13] Butrick ignored Lowrey's suggestion, convinced by the Israelite Indian stories that he heard from other evangelical reformers. On the surface, then, Butrick's presentation of Cherokee religion as "Israelite" seems to be yet another example of a White evangelical attributing Israelite identity to Indigenous people.

A closer reading of Butrick's manuscripts, however, shows that Cherokee members of the American Board churches shaped both the stories Butrick recorded and how he interpreted them. Nearly two-thirds of Butrick's seventeen named interlocutors belonged to American Board churches at a time when those churches included less than one percent of Cherokee Nation citizens overall.[14] Three older members of those churches—Thomas Nutsawi, Nettle, and Shield Eater—told the majority of the stories that reflected on or reinterpreted the Bible. Finally, Butrick's main interpreter, Andrew Sanders, or Snake, was a committed member of the American Board's Carmel mission church and seems himself to have believed that the Cherokees might be Israelites. Butrick's manuscripts, therefore, record the views of a small subgroup within the Cherokee Nation who told their stories in the context of their church communities' specific political and social circumstances.[15]

Like other Cherokees at the time, members of the American Board churches navigated a rapidly changing society. Decades of political reforms culminating in the 1827 creation of a centralized national government had altered the political significance of being Cherokee. This republican government drew on American political thought to argue that the Cherokee people had sole sovereignty to set laws and elect leaders within well-defined national borders. Simultaneously, it redefined Cherokee identity as a matter of citizenship in the Cherokee Nation and, in an adoption and rearticulation of American notions of race, excluded those with Black ancestors from full citizenship. Older ways of determining who was Cherokee—including membership in a matrilineal clan, the ability to speak Cherokee, and knowledge of Cherokee traditions—remained powerful, however. Meanwhile, both the growing minority of Cherokee church members and White Protestant missionaries raised the question of whether and how one could be Christian and still be Cherokee.[16]

The American Board drew the starkest lines. Christianity, to American Board missionaries, meant membership in a body of visible saints—visible for their clean collars and well-kept households as much as for their good works. Their massive missionary enterprise, therefore, encouraged Cherokees to adopt a patriarchal family structure, have men rather than women work the fields, and otherwise comport themselves like middle-class, White northeasterners. This program was destructive to older Cherokee ways of life and particularly so for women, whose status was higher in traditional Cherokee society than the American Board would allow. Judging by the stories told to Butrick, Cherokee members of the American Board churches seem also to have picked up on another, largely unspoken idea in the missionaries' approach: that Christianity was a matter of nurture and rearing and, therefore, Christians were likely to be the descendants of Christians. The idea that Christianity was heritable accorded with Cherokee approaches to the political importance of descent. Not only did the new citizenship laws rely to some extent on race, but older ways of reckoning Cherokee identity traced connections to sacred beings and political belonging through maternal lineages and a somewhat looser language of Cherokee "blood."[17]

Stories claiming that the Cherokees' ancestors had been chosen by the Christian God and led to their current homeland used this cross-cultural importance of heredity to make a series of arguments about the relationship of Christianity to the Cherokee Nation as a state and the Cherokees as a people. The small group of Christian Cherokee intellectuals whom Butrick consulted, likely knowing that these stories would have an outsized influence on the record Ross envisioned and, therefore, on future generations of Cherokees, crafted them to specific purposes.[18]

First, they used the idea that their ancestors were the protagonists of the missionaries' Bible stories to support Cherokees' rights
to their traditional homeland. Second, they implied that Cherokees had a claim to Christianity independent from missionary
control, since their "original customs" were a form of Christianity given to their ancestors. Third, they argued that God had
given Cherokees their ceremonies and methods of healing and
that Christian Cherokees could ethically participate in these
despite missionaries' prohibitions. Contrary to earlier historical
readings of these manuscripts, therefore, they did not use Israelite narratives to argue that Christianity embraced all races, but
adopted, inverted, and rearticulated White evangelicals' claims
to be favored by God.[19] Expecting that their stories would be preserved and published with the imprimatur of the National Council, they sought to reform Cherokee society by marking some ideas
and practices they described to Butrick as "traditional" and others
as degenerations or innovations.[20] Israelite Indian narratives
helped in this project by allowing them to argue that their stories
described an original Cherokee religion revealed by the Christian God.

Oral Tradition and Mediation

Butrick's and Payne's notes present more complicated interpretive challenges than many of the other sources used in this book.
These challenges shape my interpretations and limit how far it is
possible to generalize from the surviving records. The stories they
contain followed a chain of mediators, from the Cherokee intellectuals who told them, through the interpreters who summarized
them in English, and finally through Butrick and Payne to, they
all hoped, an audience consisting of both Cherokees and White
people. Each person in the chain of mediation attempted to bridge
the gap between what they understood tradition to be and what
they believed were the needs, abilities, and understanding of their

audience.[21] Read with an eye toward these specific acts of mediation, the stories Butrick and Payne recorded cannot be taken to reveal a general opinion among Cherokees before removal or even among Christian Cherokees. Most likely, the political use of Israelite Indian ideas they reveal was limited to a small group of American Board church members.

Butrick's role in the surviving manuscripts is the most obvious. In part, he reached for the Bible to understand Cherokees because it was an important intellectual resource for him. He was part of a long line of settlers who made this move: as early as 1698, an English official in Williamsburg, Virginia, compared the Cherokees' ceremonies to Israelite rituals enjoined in "leveticall Law."[22] However, Butrick was also entangled in the projects of reform detailed in the first chapter and likely wanted to find Israelites among the Cherokees for reasons similar to those of other evangelicals. That is, the idea allowed him to understand Cherokee traditions as valuable remnants of an earlier Israelite religion rather than as false idolatry. Also like other reformers, he likely felt that White Americans would feel more tenderly toward Indigenous people they regarded as Israelites and give generously to missionary projects as a result. Because Payne largely worked from Butrick's notes, his sections of the manuscripts follow the missionary's interpretations.

Butrick's translators also had a hand in the manuscripts. Although Butrick could speak some Cherokee, he relied on interpreters when preaching and collecting stories. His most frequent translator, Andrew Sanders, seems to have deliberately shaped the narratives he translated to make them correspond more closely to the Bible. Sanders almost certainly knew about Butrick's belief in the Cherokees' Israelite origins. The missionary, according to Cherokees who knew him, did not hide his "opinion that [Cherokees] were descendants of the old Hebrew stock."[23] Sanders, moreover, was a member of the Carmel church where Butrick was pastor between 1832 and 1838.[24] Some sort of relationship seems to have grown from that acquaintance. Not only did Sanders frequently agree to translate for the missionary, but also, after enduring the Trail of Tears, he joined the Dwight Mission church where Butrick was one of the pastors and served on church committees alongside him.[25]

Sanders's views on Cherokee traditions leaned, at least, toward an Israelite interpretation. In a July 1837 letter to John Ross, he summarized the interviews on "Cherokee Antiquities" he and Butrick conducted in a way that corresponded in several important details with the accounts of Israelite Indians in the evangelical literature. The letter claims that, according to the oldest Cherokee traditions, "there existed from eternity, Three Beings above, who were always one in mind, & in all their works," and that "the most sacred name of God is Yi Ho Wa . . . the hymn called Yo wa, is sung to yi ho wa." To an audience familiar with missionary literature, this would have suggested that Cherokees had originally believed in the Trinity, just as many evangelicals believed the Israelites had, and sang the same hymn invoking the supposed Israelite name of God that frequently appeared in missionaries' Israelite Indian stories. Going on, Sanders related that the first "man was made of red earth, & was red," a reference to the creation of Adam as well as the color most often associated with Indigenous people in discussions of race among settlers and Indigenous peoples in the southeast.[26] He then presents summaries of stories that seemed to mirror the narratives of the flood and the Tower of Babel from Genesis, as well as the crossing of the sea and the giving of the law to the Israelites from Exodus.[27]

All the stories Sanders mentions are in Butrick's manuscript but scattered through many conversations and with several different intellectuals. By editing them together into one narrative that followed the sequence of events in the Bible, Sanders exaggerated their similarity to narratives about Israelites. He, unlike the older intellectuals Butrick interviewed, probably could read English, a key skill because most of the Bible was not available in

Cherokee before removal. Spending years in American Board churches would have made Sanders familiar with the structure of the Bible if he was not already. Therefore, Sanders could arrange these stories to match the sequence of events in the Pentateuch, beginning with the existence of God and the creation of humans from earth before moving through the events of Genesis and Exodus.[28] He insisted, however, that these were Cherokee traditions. They "were not received from the whites" because the intellectuals who related them "universally declare that they were handed down from their fathers" who "generally held the white people & their religion in such contempt that there is no reason to suppose they would learn of them." Besides, Cherokee ceremonial practices, to Sanders's eye, resembled Israelite ones: "Many of [the Cherokees'] customs as nearly resemble the customs of the Jews as their [i.e., Cherokees'] traditions do the accounts of scripture."[29] Not all Cherokees agreed. A heavy ink line runs through this last assertion in the manuscript, and Ross omitted it when he later had Sanders's memorandum recopied.[30]

Sanders would have played a crucial role in creating a concise summary in English of an oral account told to a responsive audience. Butrick does not discuss what their interviews with antiquarians were like, but Payne had an experience that suggests how they might have played out. In 1840, Payne met with the famous Cherokee intellectual Sequoyah to record "some ancient memories of the past." Payne, Sequoyah, Ross, and a translator sat in the loft of Ross's house while Sequoyah told stories in Cherokee, "his voice alternately swelling, and then sinking to a whisper, and his eye firing now and then its wild flashes subsiding into a most benignant smile." Ross and the interpreter listened intently, but Payne remained in suspense as no one translated for him. After an hour of storytelling, the interpreter turned to Payne and summarized Sequoyah's words as, "all about the sending of wampum belts from various tribes." He said no more.[31] If Butrick's interviews went anything like Payne's, then Sanders would have controlled what he set down on the page. If, as seems possible from his letter to Ross, Sanders was interested in portraying Cherokees as Israelites, then he would have had a free hand to pick and choose details to relay to Butrick as he translated from what were probably longer and more elaborate stories.

Finally, the intellectuals that Butrick and Sanders interviewed were also mediators between the traditions they had received and the needs of their community. Less can be known about their intentions in telling these stories than about Butrick's or Sanders's. Butrick's terse notes usually recorded only the source of the story and a bare outline. Without knowing the emotional valence they had in their original telling, any interpretation of these stories must be cautious. An American Board missionary named Cephas Washburn found this out during his extended conversations about religion with two Cherokee intellectuals named Takaetuh and Blanket. These men also claimed that similarities between Christian and Cherokee sacred histories proved that the Bible was about their ancestors, and were, Washburn wrote, "very ready to flatter themselves that they are truly descendants of Abraham." Because both were generally skeptical of Christianity, however, Washburn believed that they made the claim satirically. "If the Scriptures of the Old Testament were read to him, [Blanket] would, if possible, find some point of resemblance to their own traditions, and then he was sure to point out something which would tend to exalt his own people above the white people." Blanket, whom Washburn described as "too much of a wag to ever be serious on any subject," probably did this to deflate the missionary's pretensions to total knowledge of "the great fundamental truths of natural religion" that were the basis of their conversations.[32] It is entirely possible that some or all of Butrick's interlocutors teased him in the same way.

The life of Thomas Nutsawi, Butrick's most frequent interlocutor, suggests that this was not the case with him, however. Nutsawi mediated between Cherokee traditions and Christianity in his own life as well as in his conversations with the missionary, making it less likely that he was trying to tease or deflect when he suggested that the two bodies of stories had much in common. He spent most of his life as a ceremonial leader and traditional knowledge-holder, having learned from an older male relative whom Butrick refers to as his "grandfather," although he was probably his maternal uncle. At around age fifty, Nutsawi moved about twenty miles from his home in Ulunyi (Turnip Town)— near what is now Ellijay, Georgia—to the Carmel mission station to work off debts incurred at the mission store. While working at the mission as a saddler, Nutsawi joined the Carmel church. He ceased to officiate at public ceremonies, which dismayed his "grandfather" so much that the older man left Ulunyi. Although he gave up his place as a ceremonial leader, Nutsawi continued to use traditional healing and to counsel other Cherokees as, seemingly, an unofficial lay preacher. During the final months of his life, as Cherokees were being gathered into internment camps, he went from camp to camp delivering comfort and fasted and prayed to call for the help of the Christian God. In August of that year, at about the age of sixty, he fell ill and died. Both American Board missionaries and unnamed Cherokees, who presumably came from the camps or nearby towns, attended him during his final illness and helped bury him near the Brainerd mission station.[33]

Given modern Cherokees' storytelling practices, it is best to read Nutsawi and the other Cherokee intellectuals consulted as occupying a space between earnestly relating the truth and fabricating stories to please or tease the missionary. According to Christopher Teuton's analysis of Cherokee storytelling practices, the truth of a story is contextual to the relationship between the audience and the storyteller. Stories do not create definitive, incontestable histories but bring the resources of one's teachers to bear on a specific situation in the present. Because storytellers speak not to a silent audience of readers but to a discrete set of people within hearing, they may change specific details, events, and the narrative sequence out of a desire to tell the most useful or appropriate version of the story for that audience.[34] Recognizing this is not to claim that the narratives were inauthentic or fictional but to assert that tradition is dynamic and that Butrick's interlocutors told him stories for specific purposes and with an acute awareness of context.

Since I cannot reconstruct the full depth and complexity of each story from Butrick's notes, my interpretations depend on two broader contexts. First, they depend on what we can know about the lives of those who mediated each story during the recording process: Butrick, his translators, and the Cherokee intellectuals they interviewed. As detailed above, each had a distinct investment in the missionary churches in the Cherokee Nation that would have shaped how they related these stories. Second, my interpretations depend on my reading of the history of the Cherokee Nation just before removal. During the years when Butrick collected these stories, the Cherokee Nation faced serious threats to its political independence and underwent rapid cultural change as the adoption of White American slave-holding, farming practices, and material culture changed Cherokees' ways of living.[35] Butrick's interlocutors almost certainly knew that his charge from Ross called on him to help mitigate this cultural change by preserving the "original customs of our Nation" for their "posterity long after this present generation shall have returned unto dust." Each person involved in mediating these stories shaped them in ways that reflected how they wanted that posterity to think of themselves as a people and a nation.

Israelite Stories and the Cherokee Homeland

When Butrick began his research in 1835, the Cherokee Nation was in a precarious position. In December of that year, a small group of Cherokee leaders signed the Treaty of New Echota, which ceded the Cherokee Nation's remaining land in exchange for land in the Indian Territory. This touched off a desperate three-year legal fight as the Cherokee National Council, which had the sole right under Cherokee law to sell land to White buyers, explored all available ways to keep title to their homeland. The National Council had reason to hope that the American Board missionaries and their supporters would help them. In the past, the American Board had published tracts opposing Cherokee removal, given platforms to Cherokee speakers, and helped open doors in Washington to Cherokee delegations. Some individual missionaries continued to support the Cherokee Nation after the Treaty of New Echota, but the American Board itself refrained from doing so on the grounds that their involvement might provoke a secession crisis by drawing the federal government further into conflict with the state governments attempting to seize Cherokee land. Soon, they officially abandoned their missions in the Cherokee Nation.[36]

This political situation likely informed the telling of several stories Butrick collected that recounted how a deity strongly implied to be the missionaries' God had created the Cherokee people, chosen them from among the nations, and given them their promised land in North America. These stories deployed narratives about Israelite Indians in a way starkly different from how they were used in the missionary press. White Americans who told Israelite Indian stories at times openly advocated for the dispossession of Indigenous territories.[37] Butrick did not argue that Cherokees should "return" to the historical territory of Israel but saw removal through the lens of Bible narratives that interpreted the exile of Israelite leaders to Babylon as a consequence of national sin. Similarly, he argued, God allowed removal to punish Cherokees for continuing traditional ceremonies that he saw as idolatrous.[38] The stories told to him, however, drew on histories of Israel in the Bible to imply that God gave the Cherokees their traditional territories unconditionally and without plans to remove them elsewhere.

Several of the stories Nutsawi told used narratives from Genesis to recount the creation of the Cherokee and claim that they were a chosen people. "The first man and woman were red. The family saved in the ark were red. The Red people therefore are the real people, as their name yv-wi-ya, indicates."[39] Here, like Apess, Nutsawi reimagines the story of Genesis as occurring to Indigenous people and positions them as the original progenitors of all humanity. Unlike Apess, however, Nutsawi was more concerned with the claims his nation could make than with creating a Christian identity that could link Indigenous nations. Certainly, when Nutsawi talked about "Indians" as a whole, he often seemed to be thinking of Cherokees, as when he retold the story of the twelve sons of Jacob, or Israel: "They once had an ancestor who had twelve sons, and from him came the twelve tribes, or great families. . . . At first there were twelve tribes of Indians, but after a while, one tribe violated the law of God by intermarrying in an unlawful manner, and therefore they resolved to reduce the number of the tribes to seven."[40] Although the record reads "tribes of Indians," it is more likely in context that he meant Cherokee clans. By historical times, there were seven such clans, but oral histories record that there were originally more.[41] It is possible, then, that Nutsawi was relating an earlier version of this tradition, rather than claiming that there had once been only twelve "tribes of Indians," a claim that would be unlikely in light of the Cherokees' familiarity with a larger number of Indigenous nations.

Not only were Cherokees, or Indigenous people in general, the first people in Nutsawi's stories, but they had also been favored by the Christian God. In his version of the Tower of Babel narrative, for example, "the red people" did not participate in building the tower, and so they continued to speak the original human language.[42] Not only that, but God chose them to receive revelations and political power. "Long ago God made himself known to the Indians, chose them for his people, and told them they should be the father of all other nations."[43] This was a religious claim, in that it asserts that Cherokee religion was, in the missionary's terms, a true, revealed religion. It was also a political one. Throughout eastern North America, in Indigenous diplomacy it was common to use the language of fatherhood and brotherhood to express political relationships between nations. "Fathers" did not rule over "sons," but they could expect deference and respect for their territories.[44] In a moment when the United States allowed the aggressive encroachment of newcomers on Cherokee land, this theological argument suggested that doing so violated an order set down by the Christian God. To Butrick and to evangelical reformers whom Nutsawi might have expected to hear this story, this would have been a clear signal that they invited divine wrath if they did not shift the course of U.S. expansion.

God's favor came with a gift of land. Nutsawi told how "God told the leader of the Indians that they must go to a country which He had given them, but they would have to pass some great water before they got there."[45] Shield Eater narrated the same story slightly differently: "When the Indians started to go to that country God had given [them], they were fleeing from their enemies. But as they soon came to a great water, God told their leader to strike the water with a rod, and it should divide, and give them as passage through, and then flow together and stop their enemies. Thus their leader did, and thus they passed through and their enemies were stopped. God loved them, and therefore He assisted them in this way."[46] Nutsawi claimed that God had given Cherokees their traditional territories, while Shield Eater emphasized that God had defeated their enemies to bring them to their land because "God loved them, and therefore He assisted them in this way."[47] In this retelling of the sacred histories of Israel, the themes of a promised land and God's assistance to his chosen people, already present in Exodus, came to the fore. By claiming that their ancestors' migration was to "a country which He had given them," Nutsawi and Shield Eater were appealing to the idea that the God whom White Americans worshiped—and whose mandates they claimed to respect—had ordained that Cherokees should have their traditional homeland. For them, as for many others who turned to Israelite Indian stories in this period, the promised land was not a metaphor but a physical territory.[48]

These stories also implied that God might be willing to defend that territory. Shield Eater, in the example above, claimed that God "assisted them" to escape their enemies and come "to that country God had given [them]" simply because "God loved them."[49] Although Shield Eater ostensibly told this story about events in the far past, he chose to tell it during a period when Cherokee land claims were under serious assault. Butrick could not have collected this story earlier than the beginning of his project in 1835, when the Treaty of New Echota began the last crisis leading to Cherokee removal, or later than Shield Eater's death in 1838. This context suggests that the "enemies" in this story could as easily be Georgia militia or land speculators as unnamed pursuers of Cherokee ancestors.

Such a reading of God's hand in the situation would have directly opposed Butrick's understanding of events, since he did not believe, as implied in these stories, that God had granted the Cherokee people their lands unconditionally. Instead, even as his Cherokee congregants were being gathered into camps for the forced march west, he claimed that God allowed them to lose their land to chastise them for their sins, particularly their "almost universal Saturday night frolicks," meaning social or religious dances, that "carried through the Holy Sabbath."[50] This reflected Butrick's providentialist understanding of history. He wrote in 1831 that "whatever our Rules, i.e. the rules of the United States, see fit to do with [Cherokees], or for them is of but little consequence. They are safe unless their *Rock* give them up," that is, unless God decided to abandon them utterly.[51] Although his providentialism gave Butrick hope that conversion might improve Cherokees' material situation by bringing God's blessings, it left him cruelly unable to offer any explanations for the Trail of Tears that did not blame his congregants.

Nutsawi's and Shield Eater's Israelite Indian stories contested Butrick's interpretation of events. Although they may have hoped that God would assist them against their enemies, they did not argue that God allowed their enemies to attack them because of Cherokees' moral failings. Their uses of Israelite Indian stories also contested the assumption among reformers that if Indigenous people were Israelites, then they should cede their land to White settlers and return to Israel. In these stories, the salvation that God offered to Cherokees was not just a spiritual matter but also included a divine warrant to their ancestral homeland. Whether or not Nutsawi and Shield Eater got the idea that Indians were Israelites from Butrick, therefore, they used it for their own purposes.

Israelite Stories and Cherokee Claims to Christianity

The Israelite Indian narratives that Butrick recorded portrayed Cherokee traditional religion as consonant with the American Board missionaries' vision of Christianity. Nutsawi and some of Butrick's other interlocutors used these stories to assert that their "Israelite" ancestors had once practiced the original, pure form of Christianity. Missionaries, in this understanding, were only restoring to the Cherokee a religion to which they had ancestral rights. Their stories insisted both that the Cherokee had known of the Christian God before the missionaries arrived and that their traditions came from "prophets" whom God had sent to them but not to White people. Equipped with this knowledge, it was Cherokees, not missionaries, who could best reconcile new

Christian rituals and beliefs with their existing traditions and knowledge.

According to Nutsawi, the most ancient Cherokee authorities held that the world had been created by "Three Beings above, always together, and of the same mind" whose names were "U-ha-lo-te-qa, Head of all power," "A-ta-nv-ti, or United" and "U-sqo-hu-la," or "the affections of the heart." "These three," Nutsawi said, "will always continue the same. They created all things, were acquainted with all, and present everywhere, and governed all things. When these called any person, that person must die just in the same way They thought best to have him die." They "sit on three white seats above; and all prayers are to be directed to them. They have messengers, or angels who come to this world and attend to the affairs of men."[52] Nutsawi's narrative here reflected contemporary Congregationalist and Presbyterian theology. The conservative Congregationalists who were the staunchest supporters of the American Board were then locked in combat with an insurgent Unitarian movement over whether to understand God as three persons in one, as had been the traditional Congregationalist position, or as a unity. The conservative faction argued that the prophets and patriarchs of Israel had known about the Trinity and encoded this knowledge in the text of the Bible.[53] By contending that the Three Beings were "of the same mind," "always continued the same," and were all-present and all-powerful, Nutsawi therefore claimed that his ancestors understood the attributes of divinity that the fiercely Trinitarian American Board missionaries insisted were indispensable both to Christian identity and to the religion of the ancient Israelites. No wonder, then, that this story struck Andrew Sanders enough that he placed it at the beginning of his summary of Cherokee beliefs. By asserting that their ancestors had understood Protestant orthodoxies long before the arrival of American Board missionaries, Nutsawi and Sanders implied that the missionaries were only helping them to restore their ancestral religion. Cherokee elders, not missionaries, had the prior claim to knowledge of the Christian God.

Along with stories about the "Three Beings above," Sanders's account also highlighted stories that fulfilled reformers' expectation that the descendants of Israelites would remember God's name. To make this connection, however, he had to smooth over discrepancies in those stories. Sanders claimed in his summary that "the most sacred name of God is Yi Ho Wa . . . the hymn called Yo wa, is sung to yi ho wa." This summary made the identification between "Yi Ho Wa" and the Christian God seem transparent. The story he based this assertion on, however, was somewhat different. Nutsawi related that "Ye-howa was a great King. He was a man and yet was a Spirit. The song or hymn called yowa was sung to him. His name must never be mentioned only by persons selected, & by them, only on the sabbath day."[54] Recording this story, Butrick wrote that "~~God~~ ˇthis Yehowaˇ commanded them to rest from all work every seventh day."[55] His crossing-out emphasized the ambivalence around the identity of "Ye-howa" in Nutsawi's account. To him, Ye-howa could be a "king"—by which Butrick meant the title more normally translated as "chief"—who was "a man and yet a Spirit." But Butrick hesitated, lifting his pen and crossing out the word "God" rather than claim as divine a figure that Nutsawi seemed to think of as a human ruler. To Butrick, humans and God were distinct beings, combined only in the unique case of Jesus. To Nutsawi, raised in a traditional Cherokee world populated by multiple kinds of powerful beings, the categories of "man" and "spirit" were likely more fluid.

Sanders glossed over this moment of incomplete translation to create a smooth, unified picture of "Cherokee Antiquities" supporting three ideas: first, that Cherokees were descendants of Israelites, second, that their national traditions were really or originally Israelite and therefore compatible with Christianity, and, third, that they were living on the land the missionaries' God had given to them. Such a picture was useful because it appealed to the Nation's allies among northeastern evangelicals, who believed that God had clear intentions for the United States that did not include the destruction of all Indigenous nations. Evangelical reformers tended to regard those Indigenous nations that met their standards of "civilization," including adherence to Trinitarian Protestantism, as worthy of sympathy, support, and even of political sovereignty. They saw the Cherokee Nation—with its written constitution, its republican government, and its elite minority who adopted Euro-American manners and family organization—as a prime example of a "civilized" Indigenous nation. Accordingly, they had already provided important aid to the Cherokee Nation by publishing pro-Cherokee articles and tracts, by supporting legal challenges to incursions on Cherokee sovereignty, and by sponsoring speaking tours by prominent Cherokees.[56] It would have been reasonable for Sanders to hope that they would continue to do so, especially if he presented a version of Cherokee traditions that appealed to their sympathies.

Nutsawi made an even bolder claim to the compatibility of Cherokee traditions and Christianity. He attributed Cherokee traditional knowledge to "prophets" whom he implied had been sent by the same God as the missionaries' worshipped. One such prophet, at times referred to as "Wâsi," seems to have been modeled on Moses.[57] In one story about him, for example, Nutsawi said that "God . . . gave new commandments to the Indians, while they were in the wilderness, and marked them on a long smooth stone (having descended on to the top of a mountain) and gave them to their leader and enabled him to read them to the people. He also gave them other instructions which were marked on skins. Their leader, to whom God gave these laws was a prophet, and could see God, and was with Him on the mountain." Moses, according to the book of Exodus, stood in the presence of God on Mount Sinai and received a version of the law that God inscribed on stone tablets.[58] In Protestant understandings at the time, the giving of the tablets at Sinai was a crucial stage in the revelation of the Bible and in continuity with the later revelation of the New Testament. Nutsawi's version, by transposing this revelation into Cherokee history, implied that the Cherokees had known the teachings contained in the Bible long before the missionaries arrived. But, in Nutsawi's story, the Cherokees received more than tablets. God gave them "other instructions which were marked on skins." Inserting these "other instructions" into the story suggested that Cherokees received a more extensive revelation than Moses had at Sinai and, perhaps, that their differing religious practices were the result. Some of Butrick's other interlocutors elaborated on this story to emphasize the importance of distinctive Cherokee traditions. Shield Eater, when he told a version of the same story, said that it was the missionaries' Christ who gave their laws to them. "The top of the mountain appeared bright like the sun, on account of the descent of the *son* of God upon it; and their leader went up, and the *son* of God gave them laws marked on a slate stone. He also then commanded them to sing the hymn which they sing at day break, and at even." In this account, at least some Cherokee ceremonial observances—in this case, traditional morning and evening prayers—came directly from the second person of the Trinity before his birth as Jesus.[59]

In Nutsawi's and Shield Eater's accounts, the Christian God also taught Cherokees methods for communicating with the sacred world that the missionaries believed to be incompatible with Christianity. Missionaries condemned as "conjuring" the practice of using quartz crystals to divine sources of illnesses and social discord during Cherokee ceremonies and traditional healing.[60] When Nutsawi described these practices, he referred to the crystals used in divination as the "word of Wâsi," or Moses.[61] Shield Eater, likewise, claimed that such crystals "were also anciently called Wâsi uto nu hi, Moses' word, and Wâsi intisata in, Moses director &c."[62] Read in the context of this idea, Nutsawi's claim in a different story that "[God] . . . talked with some [Indians], and told them things to come and thus made them prophets," seemed to imply a Cherokee lineage of prophecy distinct from the prophets in Christian tradition.[63] Congregationalist theology of the time taught that the age of prophecy was over, but, as Nutsawi told it, God had given the Cherokee ways of foreseeing the future that continued to that day.[64] Cherokee divination was thus a form of special revelation likened to the direct speech between God and the prophets of Israel in Christian traditions.

This attempt to integrate Cherokee traditional knowledge with the stories the missionaries brought reflected a larger tension in the Cherokee Nation. From the 1820s forward, many Cherokees sought to access Christianity in ways that did not preclude participation in traditionalist Cherokee communities. Most did so in the Methodist and Baptist churches because they had more Cherokee-language preachers and allowed a greater degree of individual latitude. Membership in American Board churches brought a higher level of scrutiny, since these missionaries required potential coverts to pass substantial theological tests and to strictly adhere to their community discipline. On the other hand, American Board churches offered access to schools, to resources such as mills at mission stations, and, especially after removal, to Cherokee-language printing presses vital for the work of creating and disseminating a Cherokee national culture.[65]

Cherokee members of American Board churches responded to this situation by seeking to bridge their investment in Cherokee communities with the more exacting Christianity of their missionary pastors. One common strategy was to avoid missionaries' scrutiny by using the Cherokee language, which most American Board missionaries could not speak with facility. Much of the preaching in American Board churches happened through interpreters, who at times soft-pedaled missionaries' sermons when they believed they would cause discord.[66] Outside formal sermons, worship seems to have often included a component in Cherokee, in which Cherokee lay preachers expounded the lessons of the sermon and the congregation sung hymns in their native language.[67] After the Trail of Tears, furthermore, not all the pastors of the Presbyterian churches that succeeded the American Board communities were White. The American Board ordained only two Cherokee ministers—John Huss and Stephen Foreman—but both preached in Cherokee some or most of the time and pushed forward the incorporation of Christian practice into Cherokee life.[68] One final strategy was to maintain relationships with missionaries to access resources they brought without accepting their authority or formally converting. Cherokees who made use of American Board schools and its printing press, for example, would help develop independent Cherokee educational institutions and humanitarian organizations that shaped the practice of Christianity throughout the Nation.[69]

Nutsawi, Shield Eater, and Nettle may have, similarly, seen these stories as ways to chasten missionary authority and assert Cherokee control over the adoption of Christianity and the use of the resources that missionaries brought. If their description of Cherokee traditional religion as fundamentally Christian had become part of future Cherokees' understanding of the "original customs of our Nation," this would have given more political weight to the voices of Christian Cherokees, perhaps even, and more specifically, to those belonging to American Board churches. By telling Butrick specific versions of Israelite Indian stories, therefore, they may have hoped to ensure that Christian Cherokees, rather than missionaries, would direct future changes in Cherokee society.

Israelite Stories and Cherokee Ceremonies

Joining an American Board church came with costs. American Board pastors were more severe even than other White missionaries about what they saw as "idolatry" and "superstition." Butrick, for example, sought to discourage idolatry by routinely destroying or defacing images of Jesus or the Holy Spirit in missionary publications he received.[70] This uncompromising attitude often put Cherokees affiliated with the American Board missions into difficult positions. Aspects of both traditional healing practices and the public ceremonies that had bound Cherokee communities together for centuries were, in the eyes of missionaries, idolatrous because they appealed to beings and forces other than the Christian God. American Board church members who followed the missionaries' line strictly—and it is unclear how many did—had to separate themselves from their kin and neighbors by abstaining from these vital parts of Cherokee life.

Nutsawi's and Sanders's endorsement of the idea that the ancestral Cherokee religion was a form of Israelite religion pushed back against such separation while tacitly accepting missionary concepts of idolatry. In their account, the difference between Christian and non-Christian Cherokees "consisted only in the objects of worship, and not in ˇoutwardˇ forms & ceremonies. These, in general, were the same, as none had images."[71] Where missionaries saw the "outward forms & ceremonies" of Cherokee life as idolatry, Nutsawi and Sanders here insisted that they were licit because they abstained from the use of images. Non-Christian Cherokees were simply mistaken in their "objects of worship," meaning the beings and forces honored in Cherokee ceremonies, not in their practices. Throughout their narratives borrowing from or commenting on Bible stories, they insisted that Cherokee worship had originally been directed to the "Three Beings Above"—which they heavily implied were identical with the Christian Trinity—and could, perhaps, be restored to that state. This use of stories comparing Cherokees to Israelites echoed the ways that evangelicals used Israelite Indian narratives to argue that "Indian religion" was simply Israelite religion and could be returned to its putative earlier state. However, rather than calling for Christianity to sweep Cherokee religion aside, as missionary narratives did, Nutsawi and Sanders called for some ceremonies and traditional healing methods to be reformed and maintained.

Their implication that such a reformation would leave the "outward forms & ceremonies" intact, likewise, drew on the ways evangelical reformers understood religious rituals. Recall that, to reformers, Israelite ceremonies were valid because, when performing them, Israelites underwent the proper emotional state for worship: "the sacrifice of the heart."[72] This belief that religious ceremonies were valid only so far as participants schooled themselves in the correct feelings was a common attitude among nineteenth-century American Protestants and one that members of mission churches were likely to discern. By insisting that the actions performed in Cherokee ceremonies were correct, but that the beliefs and attitudes of those conducting them needed to change, Nutsawi and Sanders implied that Butrick and other missionaries committed the same error reformers attributed to "degenerate" Israelite Indians: forgetting the meaning of ceremonies while attending to their outward forms. Just as evangelical reformers used Israelite Indian stories to argue that they, not Indigenous people, understood the original meaning of their ceremonies, here Nutsawi and Sanders used them to argue that it was Christian Cherokee who best understood those meanings. They alone were able to reform them by offering the correct "sacrifice of the heart."

Nutsawi would have known from his time living at Carmel that he had to tread carefully when discussing traditional healing around Butrick. The missionary caused a major rift in the Carmel church in the fall of 1830 by condemning Cherokee healing as "the black waters of heathenism" and delivering a blistering sermon on "the great evil & wickedness of addressing our prayers to inferior objects," that is, of petitioning beings and forces other than the Christian God. The key problem was that maintaining proper relationships with sacred beings was central to Cherokee healing practices in the early nineteenth century. Traditional healers taught that diseases had their root in an offense given to a sacred being and that healing required appeasing that being or opposing it by invoking another power. Butrick's rigid condemnation, therefore, forbade what for many Cherokees' was their main or only source of healing. It shocked his congregation so badly that "scarcely a Cherokee attended meeting" the next Sunday, and some left the church permanently.[73]

Nutsawi tried to find ways to use traditional healing that would maintain its "outward forms" while shifting the "object of worship" to the Christian God. Late in life he told Butrick that he was prone to "bleeding at the lungs." His relatives, many of whom suffered from the same condition, treated it with medicine "administered by conjurers," that is, traditional healers. Because he was spending much of his time at Carmel, Nutsawi "had learned the sin of conjuring and resolved to have no recourse to it," and so "went to the woods, and obtained the family medicine, and took it, calling on the Name of the Lord for help. He spent . . . some whole days in fasting and prayer, and soon found his health restored."[74] By gathering the medicine he needed but administering it along with a course of Christian prayers, Nutsawi asserted, or hoped, that new ways of healing compatible with Christianity could be found.

Some of the Israelite Indian stories Nutsawi told seem to explain his reasoning behind practicing traditional healing in concert with Christian prayer by giving some elements of Cherokee traditional healing a grounding in Christian theology. He claimed that in the past "mortal diseases were supposed to arise from the displeasure of God, when any such diseases made its appearance in the country, the people resorted to the A-to-hv-na ["Physic dance," in Butrick's translation] for relief. It is said, God had directed them to do this, though this idea is probably of more modern origin."[75] This explanation of traditional healing, which even Butrick suspected to be an adaptation of an earlier tradition, connected the missionaries' understanding of sickness as a trial from God with Cherokees' understanding of it as the result of a ritual impurity or an offense to a sacred being. According to Nutsawi, God was both the being offended and the being to be propitiated by healing ceremonies: not a far cry from the then-common evangelical practice of responding to disasters and sickness with days of fasting and repentance.

Nutsawi and other American Board church members whom Butrick interviewed seem to have been warier of Cherokee ceremonial life than of traditional healing. Nutsawi, after all, had ceased to officiate at public ceremonies after his conversion. He and Johnson Pridget, another American Board congregant who translated for Butrick, furthermore, seemed to condemn Cherokee ceremonial life in Christian terms. They claimed that

> those who deny the worship of the sun, and adore only the Three Beings above, say that the priests who pray only to them, i.e. to God above, and all others not guilty of lying, stealing, fighting, murdering, fornication, adultery, or causing abortion and destroying children &c. when they die will go above to God, where it will always be light and pleasant.
>
> But all such as are guilty of the above crimes, together with all who pray to the Devil, (by praying to the Devil they mean praying directly to him in order to prevent his hurting them, or praying to the sun &c. in obedience to the Devil) will go when they die to Tsv-ski-no-i, i.e. the place of wicked spirits, and be forever tormented.[76]

This interpretation of the afterlife shows clear Christian influences, both in the idea of an eternal reward or punishment after death and in the list of misdeeds that might merit punishment. Cherokees had not previously censured abortion or infanticide, for example, and sex between unmarried people was normal.[77] It is less clear what they meant by condemning both those who "worship the sun," a reference to normative Cherokee ceremonies, alongside those "who pray to the Devil." Elsewhere in Payne's and Butrick's manuscripts, the word "Devil" refers not to the missionaries' image of an enemy of Christianity who causes all false worship but to malignant beings such as two siblings who caused smallpox or the dangerous shape-shifter Untsaiyi the Gambler.[78] Records of Cherokee traditions from the period associate such beings with witchcraft, or the anti-social use of ritual power, not with pro-social acts such as the Green Corn Ceremony or healing ceremonies.[79]

It is possible that Butrick, not his interlocutors, collapsed these two categories in the parenthetical gloss explaining that "praying to the Devil" included "praying to the sun &c. in obedience to the Devil," especially given that it was common for American Board missionaries to characterize non-Christian religions as service to the Devil. It is also possible that the condemnation of both witchcraft and traditional Cherokee ceremonies here was meant to draw a distinction based on the "objects of worship" rather than the "outward forms & ceremonies" of Cherokee practices. Those who practiced these ceremonies in the manner Pridget and Nutsawi thought correct, that is, with the "Three Beings Above" in mind, could look forward to a pleasant afterlife, whereas those who practiced them incorrectly could not. It is possible, then, that they hoped their stories would lead to changes in Cherokee ceremonial life to make it more compatible with Christianity. Their narratives, after all, insisted that Cherokees were originally Trinitarian Christians related to or identical with the Israelites of the Bible and positioned Cherokee members of the American Board churches as authoritative interpreters of this "original" Cherokee religion. Had their narrative been accepted, they would have been in a powerful position, despite their small numbers, to influence the practice of

Cherokee traditions and make them more palatable to their Christian commitments.

Telling stories about Israelite Cherokees, therefore, was a strategy not only for asserting Cherokee control over their religious lives but for asserting what those religious lives should look like. Adopting and repurposing the strong distinctions that missionary Christianity made between inward feeling and outward ritual, they made room for the traditional healing practices that missionaries condemned and, perhaps, plotted a course for the continued practice of public ceremonies in a Cherokee Nation with an increasing number of Christians.

The strategies these stories offered, however, were not those that Cherokees used to maintain their traditions and their national identity after removal. None of the older men Butrick and Payne consulted survived the Trail of Tears for longer than a year, and in the chaotic period after removal the records of their conversations remained unreviewed and unpublished. It is unclear how much of Butrick's and Payne's manuscripts even Ross got to read.

Both the Cherokee Nation and the American Board church communities survived removal and the tumult that followed, however. Some American Board congregations remained together and founded new Presbyterian churches in the west. Congregants at the Carmel church, for example, tended to join the church at Dwight Mission in the new Cherokee Nation, members of the Willstown church joined a new congregation at Honey Creek, and the members of the Brainerd and Haweis churches formed the New Echota Church.[80] In all, five or six majority-Cherokee congregations, with a total number of members fluctuating between about 200 and about 250, endured in the new Cherokee Nation between 1838 and 1860.[81] These numbers were fairly steady through the Civil War, but pro-Confederate Cherokees' hostility to Presbyterian ministers dealt a blow to the organization from which it never fully recovered. Continuing a pattern from before removal, however, Presbyterian schools and presses remained important to the Cherokee Nation's educational programs.[82]

Butrick recorded traces of how a few Cherokee intellectuals used Israelite Indian stories to argue for the territorial integrity and religious autonomy of the Nation. Although White reformers in the northeast such as Elias Boudinot and Ethan Smith used Israelite Indian stories in ways that undermined land claims, these Cherokee intellectuals used these same narratives to argue that Cherokees' land and traditions had been granted to them by God. Given that evangelical reformers had been allies to the Cherokee Nation in the past, drawing on the broader currency of Israelite Indian stories in their print culture may have seemed a worthwhile strategy to these intellectuals as it once had to William Apess. By casting themselves as the holders of an "original" Cherokee tradition that accorded with, but modified, the missionaries' religion, they argued as well for the importance of Christianity, as they saw it, to the Cherokee Nation and anticipated future social reforms. Although their Israelite Indian stories were never distributed as they had hoped, their use of them shows how such narratives offered strategic possibilities for some Indigenous thinkers in the early nineteenth century. Outside the Cherokee Nation, however, changes in how White Americans thought about the interrelationship of religion and expansion were changing the meaning and popularity of Israelite Indian stories.

5

The Indian War Is
Only Begun

In the summer and autumn of 1860, the archaeologist David
Wyrick uncovered two objects in Newark, Ohio, that would have
thrilled Israelite Indian theorists of the previous generation.
Wyrick was digging in the Indigenous ceremonial mounds known
as the Newark Earthworks, hoping to find clues to a vanished civilization of "Mound Builders." Like most settlers who looked for
the Mound Builders, Wyrick believed they were a vanished race,
unrelated to Israelites or Indigenous people, who had built the
impressive earthworks dotting the Mississippi, Missouri, and
Ohio river valleys. He was more puzzled than excited, then, when
he unearthed a piece of carved pipestone, just small enough to fit
comfortably in his hand, inscribed with Hebrew characters. It was
a long pyramid with four faces and a knob on one end, resem-
bling a plumb bob. The Hebrew on its faces, allowing for errors
and poorly formed letters, read "Holy of Holies," "King of the
Earth," "the Law of God," and "the Word of God."[1]

Many contemporaries suspected Wyrick of faking the find. The
Hebrew on the pipestone was far too modern for it to have been
made by lost tribes of Israelites who had fled the Assyrian conquest. Even more suspiciously, another object—a tablet with the
Ten Commandments in appropriately archaic writing—appeared

in Wyrick's excavation site soon after critics pointed out this incon-
sistency. The origin of these objects, later called the "Newark holy
stones," remains unclear. At the time, Freemasons identified the
first as a ceremonial tool belonging to their order, though they
did not say how it ended up buried in a cornfield. The origin of
the second remained more mysterious, though someone likely
made it in response to the media coverage of the first. The puz-
zlement over the objects in Wyrick's reports on the dig, however,
suggests that he probably did not help make or hide either of them.
They confounded rather than confirmed his theories about
Mound Builders, whom he believed were related to Europeans,
not Israelites.[2] Interest in the "holy stones" faded quickly, as what
thirty years earlier might have caused an explosion of new interest in the Israelite past of North America was, by 1860, just a
curiosity.

The lack of excitement around Wyrick's find does not mark the
end of Israelite Indian stories, but it symbolizes their fall from
respectability among most White Americans. Related stories continue to be told to this day in Mormon culture, affecting both
settler and Indigenous Mormons' conceptions of themselves.[3]
American Jews continued in the nineteenth and twentieth centuries to compare themselves to Indigenous people, usually more
subtly than did Israelite Indian stories, to make claims on American belonging and territory.[4] Among the White Protestant majority, however, Israelite Indian stories had already begun to decline
in popularity by 1830. The meaning of those Israelite Indian stories that still appeared in print shifted at the same time, losing
the providential charge they had in earlier decades. From the
beginning of European speculation about the Americas, there
had been those who claimed that Israelites were the ancestors of
Indigenous people but did not invoke ideas of prophecy or providence as had American evangelical reformers.[5] Through the
1830s and 1840s, publications about Israelite Indians in the

United States increasingly fit this non-providentialist mold. By 1860, not even Wyrick's "holy stones" could reignite interest in the religious meaning of Israelite Indians.

These changes in Israelite Indian stories were not a case of science triumphing over error. Although a scientific guild of professional anthropologists began to offer their own accounts of the American past during this same period, their theories that "Indians" were living fossils of the earliest human societies or that a separate race like the Mound Builders had been active in North America were no more accurate than Boudinot's millennialist prophecies had been.[6] Instead, Israelite Indian stories fell from popularity because of a shift in how White Americans interrelated religion and imperial expansion. Their transformation and decline reveal the growing entanglement of expansionist politics and secular approaches to the regulation of religion.

In this chapter, I trace the rise of secularism as the dominant framework for American thinking about land and settlement in the mid-nineteenth century. This shift both caused the decline of Israelite Indian stories and reconfigured the place of religion in American nationalisms. Expansionists relied on a developing secularism to counter reformers' critiques, to endorse American empire as natural and even to invoke the spirit of the land as an animating force for the push westward. This account complicates earlier depictions of American religious nationalism by suggesting that secular ways of interrelating the state, the land, and religion, not an excess of belief in White Americans' status as manifestly "chosen" by God, accompanied expansion. Where belief in God's special care for America, and particularly for White Americans, may now seem easier to set aside as irrational and mistaken, this secular order of expansion is still with us and, therefore, harder to dispel.

Secularism and Israelite Indians

At the time of the Revolution, one dominant way of relating religious and national feelings was a form of providentialism that argued that the nation's prosperity depended on God's favor. Providential discourses shaped multiple nationalisms in the early United States, not necessarily to the benefit of the imperial state.[7] As the preceding chapters have shown, to invoke the idea of providence was to bring the powerful feelings produced in religious practice into political discussion, often with the effect of making America's empire seem fleeting or helping to nucleate oppositional nationalisms. Even Israelite Indian stories that ultimately endorsed White settlement—such as those of Elias Boudinot, Mordecai Noah, and Parley Pratt—evoked fear of God's judgment and hope for millennial redemption to encourage scrutiny of that empire in terms other than its own political interests. They raised the question of whether God might not, in fact, bless America.

In the first half of the nineteenth century, however, White Protestants developed a new method for relating religion to the state that muted, but did not eliminate, providentialism. I understand this method, which historians of religion in America call "secularism," as a set of interrelated practices for experiencing, describing, and regulating religion. In aggregate, the practices of secularism reinforced the sense that the only religions compatible with American democracy were those cast in the image of White, mainstream Protestantism. Constituent practices of secularism included the enforced reading of the King James Bible in schools, support for Protestant missionary organizations abroad, and the delegation of control over Indian reservations to churches.[8] In each case, White Protestants argued that government support for "true religion" strengthened the nation against the assaults of such forms of "superstition" and "fanaticism" as Catholicism, Mormonism, Indigenous traditional ceremonies, and Black American religious groups. Hence, it opposed not religion in general, as the everyday use of the word might suggest, but those religions that White Protestants considered dangerous.[9]

Evangelical reformers helped create American secularism. They put the Bible in Americans' schools and households, worked for political cooperation between Protestant churches, and inveighed against the influence of the Roman Catholic Church.[10] But, because the culture of secularism sought to embrace all Americans, it was never entirely under the control of any one group. Adopting it demanded that evangelicals, too, make changes. Having accepted the idea that the American state supported true religion, they became less able to imagine that God might destroy that state for disobedience or to envision a different kind of nation. The major exception to this was their continuing critique of slavery, which returned frequently to the idea that the slave system invited God's wrath. They tended, however, to avoid critiquing the United States itself by blaming slavery on hard-hearted plantation owners and southern state governments. Both expansion at the expense of Indigenous nations and U.S. intervention abroad, however, became harder for them to critique because they had so completely accepted the compatibility that secularism implied between Christian morality, liberal ideals of freedom, and the American state. As a result, they became less able to see that the interests of the United States and the interests of Christian benevolence were not one and the same.[11] The Presbyterian missionary T. Charlton Henry had warned in 1824 that, depending on whether evangelicals could save Indigenous people from those who would "cooly devise on paper a project for [the] Government" to eliminate them, they would face "a signal blessedness, or a signal woe."[12] By the middle of the century, however, his successors had accepted that they lived in a blessed nation and, consequently, became less able to imagine how its coolly devised projects could bring about "a signal woe."

Many of the practices making up secularism took hold during the first half of the nineteenth century, with the effect that the mental and religious landscape of the United States in 1840 was very different from how it was in 1800. One index of this change was the shift in how White Americans told Israelite Indian stories. After 1830, White Americans who told such stories increasingly drew on a tradition of using Israelite lineage not to explain the place of a people in God's plans but to locate them within Europeans' mental maps of human diversity. In English, this tradition went back at least as far as Edward Brerewood's 1614 *Enquiries Touching the Diversity of Languages and Religions*. Brerewood argued that any traces of Israelite customs among Indigenous people were evidence that some of the lost tribes of Israel had intermixed with "Tartars"—meaning nomadic peoples of the Eurasian steppe—who later migrated to the Americas.[13] That Indigenous peoples were Israelites, for Brerewood, placed them in the taxonomy of humanity but did not imply that God intended any special destiny for them. After Indian removal began, more and more White Americans writing about Israelite Indian stories followed Brerewood, not Boudinot, in their conclusions.

The transformations that Israelite Indian stories underwent point to key differences between the secularism of the mid-nineteenth century and the providentialism of an earlier generation. These later stories located the truth about the American past in artifacts that supposedly testified to an Israelite past and in bodies: both the remains of dead Indigenous people in burial mounds and the bodies of living people that were scrutinized for signs of racial identity. By turning from biblical prophecy to artifacts and bones, they did more than shift epistemic footing from religion to the emerging discipline of archaeology. This shift made the past, not the millennial future, the focus of their study and changed the emotional tenor of Israelite Indian stories from one of hope and attachment to one of detached, cool speculation. In the process they eliminated the visions, however chauvinist, of a future for Indigenous people that Israelite Indian stories had offered.

These stories focused on reading Indigenous peoples' bodies to classify them according to contemporary American racial categories. They used the supposed Israelite ancestry of Indigenous people to classify them as "Semites," a racial group then taken to include all speakers of Semitic languages such as Arabic and Hebrew. The supposed racial characteristics of Semites varied widely in nineteenth-century accounts. Some classified them as irreducibly distinct from Europeans while others, such as the prolific skull-measurer Samuel George Morton, classified them as nearly "Caucasian," that is, White. American authors who used the term to describe Indigenous people, however, generally claimed that Semites were essentially nomads unfit for settled life or, by extension, for making the legal claims to land that helped undergird White Americans' political status.[14] Hence, these stories dovetailed with the racial hierarchy that American secularism sustained. It asserted that the racial order of the United States rested on a foundation of immutable natural facts about human diversity rather than on God's contingent decisions to punish some nations and exalt others.

This emphasis on reading bodies and artifacts came along with a new emphasis on material evidence. Increasingly, nineteenth-century Americans believed in the power of reasonable people—always implicitly meaning White men—to arrive at truth from interpreting the world around them according to their inborn rationality, or common sense, rather than through education in more complex interpretive frameworks. This set of interpretive practices, which historians call Scottish commonsense realism, was one powerful constituent structure of secularism. It provided a unitary justification for Protestant Christianity as based in "commonsense" readings of the Bible, of democratic governance as based in "commonsense" political decisions, and racial and gender hierarchies as the "commonsense" result of

observing human bodies without the need for intervening interpretation.[15] In practice, this epistemic approach exalted White
men's emotions by making what they thought of as their "natural" feelings and uncultivated impressions into common sense.
Reactions such as disgust for members of other races, violent
anger against Indigenous peoples, and desire for land all became,
in this understanding, obvious readings of the world as it was.

Earlier Israelite Indian stories had used such commonsense
readings of material evidence at times but subordinated them to
Biblical interpretations. It was only in an appendix to the 1825
second edition of *View of the Hebrews* that Ethan Smith described
his research into a Jewish prayer phylactery—a *tefillin*—supposedly
unearthed in 1815 from an Indian burial mound near Pittsfield,
Massachusetts. Smith engaged in materialist interpretation by
lingering over descriptions of the object, searching for traces of
its Israelite origin in the way it had been "sewn up with the sin-
ews of some animal; a thing which," he claimed, "no Jew in Chris-
tendom would have done" and in the apparent age of its leather
case.[16] However, he treated whatever conclusions he drew from
the *tefillin*'s material details as corroborating evidence only. The
bulk of his work relied on parsing Biblical prophecy and European and White American reports of Indigenous customs to
identify the origins of Indigenous people and to warn of the consequences of mistreating them.

After 1830, however, White authors who invoked Israelite Indians increasingly relied on material evidence rather than either
Christian or Indigenous narratives to understand the past. An
early example of this kind of writing was *Antiquities of America
Explained*, an 1831 book by the Baltimore schoolteacher Ira Hill.
Hill argued that the mounds of North America were evidence
that Indigenous people had once been great builders. He hypoth-
esized that their ancestors were Israelites who had come to
America with Phoenician colonists and quickly lost their religious
distinctiveness, though not the mastery of building they acquired

while enslaved in Egypt, through intermarriage. The united Israelites and Phoenicians landed in Nova Scotia and moved south
and west, leaving behind the "least enterprising" and lowest
classes of their society with each move. Hence, the Nahua, Maya,
and Inca cultures that built stone cities were remnants of the most
advanced Israelite–Phoenicians, who had moved the farthest from
Nova Scotia, while the Native peoples of North America were the
descendants of those who had been left behind and had fallen into
disorder without the elite classes of their societies.[17] Although the
impressive mounds and earthworks in North America proved that
Indigenous people had Semitic ancestry, then, they did not show
they were Israelites in any way that had religious significance.
More, since the "least enterprising" Semites remained in North
America, nothing in Hill's narrative questioned prevailing negative stereotypes of Indigenous people as shiftless wanderers.

   Far from wanting to warn against the dangers of mistreating
God's chosen people, Hill argued for the Israelite ancestry of
Indigenous people only to call for further White settlement in the
west. He feared that potential settlers hesitated because of theories, long considered respectable in Europe, that differing cli-
mates created racial differences. If such theories were correct,
White Americans who settled in the west would slowly become
less White, losing the capacity for civilization that, supposedly,
came along with that racial identity.[18] But, Hill argued, since
Indigenous people still looked like Semites, White Americans
were safe from such degeneration. North America had been
"designed by the God of Nature but for one people" who could
live anywhere in the continent without suffering a change to their
bodies.[19] White Americans, therefore, need not fear adverse
effects from westward settlement. They might even find their
bodies improved, since Hill believed that the climate had blessed
Indigenous peoples with robust health and easy child-bearing.[20]
In the context of European debates about White American bodies, the implication was clear: White Americans would inherit the

physical virtues of Indigenous people just as they came to inherit the physical territory in which their "Israelite" ancestors' bodies and artifacts lay.[21]

The pamphleteer Josiah Priest similarly turned to an examination of earthen mounds in his *American Antiquities and Discoveries in the West*. Like Hill, Priest believed Indigenous people to be descendants of groups from the ancient Near East. Like many other European and American ethnographers, Priest divided humanity into three lineages, each stemming from one of Noah's three sons—Shem, Ham, and Japheth—and argued that each son's progeny shared certain racial traits. The descendants of Japheth built cities, the descendants of Ham served, and the descendants of Shem, or Semites, were wandering nomads.[22] Based on their supposed cultural similarities to Israelites, Priest argued that Indigenous people were Semites—perhaps specifically Israelite or perhaps not—who had interbred with and become like the nomadic Scythians and Tartars of central Asia.

For Priest, all Semites were constitutionally incapable of building or settlement and had an inborn propensity to wander. Indigenous people, therefore, must be "usurpers" who, through "bloody warfare," had "exterminated the original inhabitants of America," that is, the same Mound Builders whose secrets Wyrick sought to uncover. Obviously, since they had built earthworks, those original inhabitants had been descended from Japheth, although Priest could not quite decide if they were Celtic or Chinese.[23] Hence, although Israelite Indian narratives influenced Priest's account, his ideas lacked any implication that Indigenous people ought to be redeemed, that there might be redeemable elements of their religion, or that how White Americans treated them would be significant. Rather, they were Semitic simply because Semites, in Priest's thought, were archetypical wanderers and barbarians. Not only did they not have a claim to God's favor, therefore, but, as nomadic usurpers, they had no real claim to the land of North America.

Such accounts stressing the Semitic more than the Israelite identity of Indigenous people continued to crop up in American literature over the next thirty years. As late as 1860, Henry Rowe Schoolcraft, a founding figure in American anthropology, could write that, "the mere conjecture that these tribes are the off-shoots of the Shemitic race of Asia, is important, and becomes deeply interesting when it appears probable, as many men of learning and genius have asserted, that their history, fate, and fortunes, can be connected with that of the Hebrew race."[24] He bases this idea on his observation that Indigenous languages and physiology—by which he largely meant cranial measurements—classed them as belonging to "Hebrew, or at least Shemitic stock—though the questions of *when* or *how* [the Indian] came to this continent, are quite as difficult to answer as the others."[25] Far from turning to the millennial interpretations of Israelite presence, Schoolcraft argued that if Indigenous people were Semites, the histories of the Bible would be called into question. Based on his reading of Apache stories of a global flood that superficially resembled the story of Noah's ark, he supposed that both stories must be fragmentary memories of world-spanning empires connected by great ships that were destroyed in a great deluge. "[Who] knows but the ark of Noah was nothing more than one of those large ships that used to connect the two continents, belonging to some distant colony of the Jews, bound home at the time of the flood."[26] For Schoolcraft, then, the point of identifying Indigenous people with Israelites was simply to explain what he saw as analogies in language, sacred history, and physiology. Their presence in America signified no providential design and even threatened the Bible's assumed place at the center of world history.

It is small wonder that Wyrick's stones, which seemed to hint at specifically Israelite religious practice in ancient America, attracted so little notice when they emerged in the same year Schoolcraft wrote. By that point, most Israelite Indian narratives had for years followed the line of thinking Schoolcraft pursued: that "Semitic" ancestry placed Indigenous people in American racial hierarchies and explained their presence in the United States in ways that did not need to reference the will of the Christian God or Indigenous peoples' own traditions. It was far easier than it would have been decades earlier, when evangelical reformers warned that God "will afflict and destroy, without mercy" those who harmed his chosen people, to dismiss Wyrick's stones as a hoax.[27] By using Israelite identity primarily to give racial classifications to Indigenous people and to justify expansion into their lands without limit, these newer Israelite Indian theories harmonized with the practices of secularism. But, as I will show, secularism was not just a matter of political interest. Its practices evoked feelings, just as telling and reflecting on Israelite Indian stories had.

The Protestant Secular and the Enchantment of Land

In the aftermath of the War of 1812, Democratic politicians came to see the acquisition and distribution of western lands at low cost as the only way to ensure that the United States would survive. Their platform grew from anxiety about what they saw as insidious threats to republican government: foreign influence from European powers, insurrection among enslaved people, the accumulation of wealth in the hands of financiers and industrialists, and financial panics that made a mockery of poorer White Americans' attempts to achieve economic independence or "competency." Only by distributing the land necessary for a republic consisting of White farmers, Democrats argued, could they secure White Americans from serfdom, demagoguery, and revolution. They only dug in more on this position when their program of rapid expansion and land speculation contributed to the disastrous Panic of 1837. Under James K. Polk, they orchestrated the annexation of Texas, seized Oregon in a tense confrontation with the British Empire, and conquered what is now the southwestern United States in the Mexican–American War.[28] Although popular American historical memory still often frames these acts of conquest as economic or demographic necessities, they were in fact ideological choices made out of belief in the power of widespread land ownership to avert national disaster.

This expansionist ideology cohered with secular ways of relating religion and the state. Tracing their connections reveals how spiritual feelings about land abetted American conquest even where openly articulated theologies did not. A lack of obvious theological arguments in favor of Democratic positions has led some historians to conclude that they were less interested in bringing religious ideas into their politics than their Federalist and Whig opponents and, correspondingly, to characterize as politically quietist the revivalist evangelical churches whose congregations tended to vote Democratic.[29] Beginning with the rise of Andrew Jackson, however, Democratic expansionists successfully disseminated the idea that expansion was natural and uncontestable. Although framed in the language of nature, their arguments attributed a salvific, redeeming power to the land and to violence committed in defense of settlers that evoked Christian theologies.[30] Where evangelical reformers invoked their readings of biblical histories and prophecies to argue for political change, Jacksonian Democrats invoked nature. It was natural, they argued, that White men rule supreme, that farming be preferred to industry, that free trade be encouraged, and that the United States continue to expand. Similarly, it was natural that true religion should support all these measures. After all, were they not the result of nature, which was itself the work of God? This, rather than the providentialism of earlier generations, was the context for the famous invocation in the mid-1840s of America's God-given "manifest destiny"—meaning, literally, a destiny that was obvious or "manifest" from the natural order of the world—to possess Oregon and Texas. Democratic expansionists thus neutralized providentialist critiques of expansion by appealing to the idea that God's will was plain in commonsense readings of nature. This common sense, in turn, consisted largely of the feelings and impressions of White men.[31]

Democratic expansionism was secular also in its invocations of spirit. Using the language first of "spirit" and later of "spirituality," Americans adapted to secularism with new practices that located religious truth in human life, and especially in human seeking for the sacred. Interacting with and talking about spirits, feelings, and hauntings became, for many Americans, ways of expressing and relating to the larger forces at work in their society. The movements that embraced this new language—including mesmerism, Spiritualism, and Transcendentalism—tended to keep within the strict terms of acceptable "good religion" by endorsing racial hierarchy, patriarchal families, free trade, and democratic liberalism. Although some strands of these unruly movements bucked this trend by assigning dignified places to Black Americans or approaching gender and sexuality in nonnormative ways, for most White Americans by the midcentury the language of "spirit" was the language of acquiescence to or support for the world as it was.[32] In accounts of American settlement, likewise, the language of spirit tended to become the language of the ascendant politics of the day, that is, expansionism.

Recognizing this widens the boundaries of what might be considered "religious nationalism" beyond churches and politicians' solemn invocations of the Bible to wherever Americans invoked the unseen, or the "spirit," in the muddled emotional territory between religion and nation.[33] Expansionists used spiritual language to evoke and regulate emotions around the extension of U.S. dominion and White settlement. First, they began to discuss expansion in a way that seamlessly blended God's benevolent intentions for White Americans with the processes of nature. This way of talking about land allayed the fears of judgment on which providentialist critiques of expansion relied. Second, they imagined and rehearsed the anger of "martyrs" of the frontier, meaning settlers who had fought with Indigenous people in the past. Inhabiting these stories, even while disavowing the violence they recorded, prepared White Americans to see violence as a natural part of expansion. This, in turn, prepared them to see Indian removal as a "kinder" approach. Even Protestant ministers in the northeast shifted their language in response to the successful coherence of this way of talking about land with the secularism that they had helped shape. They began to gesture toward the territories ruled by the United States as a sign that God's favor was not conditional but was rather revealed in the bounty and texture of the land itself. Where once the idea that God might judge territorial expansion had seemed possible, this new language left no room for the idea that religion might check settlement.

Expansionists preferred to depersonalize White settlement, often comparing it to an unseen fluid moving across the land. "The wave of improvement is still onward to the west, and will not stop its progress till the rich prairies, far in the distance from us, shall have been covered with a mighty flood of population," claimed a column appearing in the *Connecticut Courant* in 1837.[34] An 1839 folk history claimed that "migration to the West . . . may well be compared to the rushing of a fluid into a void . . . a current which, I may safely say . . . cannot be stayed until the great Central and Western voids are filled."[35] And again, in 1848, the New York Democratic senator John Dix dismissed concerns about westward expansion, because "the aboriginal races, which occupy and overrun a portion of California and New Mexico, must . . . give way before the advancing wave of civilization [and] ultimately become extinct by force of an invincible law."[36] Depicting western migration as a fluid acting according to its own physical laws framed as a natural process the massive outlay of military might, political force, and economic risk taking required to accomplish expansionists' aims. These appeals to nature were, in context, religious arguments. Nature revealed the hand of a beneficent God, whose will was apparent not in prophecy and revelation but in the arrangement of the world as it was, including in its racial hierarchies.[37] If expansion occurred because God had designed the world to create White dominion, then attempts to stand against the "wave" of settlement were foolish and doomed.

The very northeastern Protestants who had once thrilled to Israelite Indian stories accepted this reframing of God's role in American history. Over the 1830s and 1840s northeastern Protestants came to emphasize that God had arranged nature to benefit both White settlement and democratic government in North America. The Unitarian pastor George Ellis exemplified this turn when he claimed in an 1854 sermon that the "American system" of government "took its training in part from these once vast wildernesses; from the glorious, solemn old forests, whose living roots were nourished from the mould of ages. The mighty rivers, widening as they flowed, and the fair valleys which they watered, helped to develop this American system."[38] For Ellis, the land of America proceeded from the blessing of God, and the political order of the United States proceeded from the land. Similarly, the Presbyterian minister Horace Eaton argued in 1848 that God had provided White Americans with a "good land" that had rich mineral resources near to waterways, a sign that God had "thought of the myriads that were to swarm this land, and, like a provident father, in the full treasure houses of the earth, made ready for our happiness and elevation."[39] Ellis's and Eaton's audiences could enjoy these lands without hearing the warnings against national sin that were common fifty years earlier in Presbyterian and Congregationalist churches. The God who had made the land to "develop this American system" would pass no judgments on the extension of that system across the continent. Positive feelings about the land—both the pride Eaton evoked in White settlers' use of the land and the aesthetic appreciation Ellis conjured of "glorious, solemn old forests," "mighty rivers," and "fair valleys"—were signs that White Americans' seizure and occupation of territory were right in God's eyes.

Those most invested in expansion, therefore, referred to the power of nature to stir human emotions, not the power of a God who directed history, to justify the aggressive expansionism of the 1840s. Some historians have found the phrase "manifest destiny" a useful label for the belief in the divine imperative that Americans conquer the continent, which developed over the first half of the nineteenth century.[40] This use of the phrase attends to its original context: the 1845 debate in Congress over the United States' rights to the Oregon Territory and Texas. Britain and Mexico, respectively, had sounder claims to those territories than did the United States according to the "doctrine of discovery" that had settled Europeans' disputes over land claims in the Americas since the 1500s. According to this doctrine, the first Christian nation to lay claim to an area obtained title to the entire watershed. But, in 1845, the Democratic newspaper editor John O'Sullivan brushed away "all those cobweb tissues of right of discovery, exploration, settlement, continuity, &c," to claim for the United States "a still better title . . . our manifest destiny to overspread and to possess the whole of the continent which Providence has given us for the development of the great experiment of liberty and federated self-government entrusted to us."[41] "Providence," here, was not the God of earlier evangelical reformers and their colonial ancestors, who struck covenants with communities, judged them according to their piety, and brought weal or woe in response. Instead, this was the God of nature, whose will was "manifest" in the land itself, which, in an undefined, spiritual way, invited, encouraged, and supported White settlement. Despite the more general use of the phrase "manifest destiny" in history textbooks and in some historical studies, then, the idea is most accurately understood as an outgrowth of nineteenth-century secularism, not a perennial theme running from the New England colonies forward through American history.[42] Getting this wrong risks missing its later effects. O'Sullivan and other exponents of manifest destiny did not announce their ideas as "religious" with exegeses about the will of God or the dangers of national sin but blended them with secular ways of talking about the relationship of religion and government that made Protestant beliefs, populist democracy, and imperial expansion all seem the uncontestable works of nature. Rhetoric about the natural order of America, more than ideas of the United States as "chosen," is now the legacy of manifest destiny.

As Americans increasingly gestured to the idea that expansion was natural and necessary for the growth of democratic institutions, they created new justifications for the violence that territorial conquest caused. A new wave of stories appearing in commemorative speeches and sermons, in newspapers, and in collections of folktales encouraged nineteenth-century readers to identify with settlers of the past, feeling their anger, mourning their losses, and forgiving their violence.[43] This spiritual communion with shades of the past evoked and channeled emotions, just as Israelite Indian stories had. These new stories' treatment of emotions differed significantly, however. They participated in a shift in American culture after the War of 1812 away from valuing the carefully cultivated benevolence central to evangelical reform toward valuing emotions thought to reveal a person's authentic, natural self.[44] Those feelings, just as much as talk about the land, encouraged the sense that expansion was simply part of the natural world. Evoking them became one constituent practice of that secularism which insisted on the naturalness of White dominion.

Commemorations of past "Indian wars" during the first half of the nineteenth century rehearsed the feelings of anger, sorrow, and vengeance they attributed to the settlers who had been in these conflicts. These accounts invited listeners and readers to feel the passions that, they claimed, possessed settlers and caused them to act in both un-Christian and uncivilized ways. They both insisted that Christianity forbade vengeance or indiscriminate violence and invited their audiences, presumed to be White Christians, to feel the violent passions that had swept away past settlers' Christian nurture. They made the implicit argument that other, darker spirits were at work along the American frontier. Hatred and vengeance, they argued, would always arise where White and Indigenous people lived together, and, by their very naturalness, these feelings would triumph over the cultivated sentiments of Christianity. Christians, therefore, did not themselves need to feel overwhelming hatred for "Indians" to believe that the lower-class Whites of the rural west inevitably would. Implicitly or explicitly, the literature of the Indian wars argued that, without Indian removal, the same malignant feelings would haunt the frontier and the same horrific violence would result.[45]

One typical work, Alexander S. Withers' *Chronicles of Border Warfare* (1831), cast conflict on the frontier in emotional terms. "There is," he argued, "in the Indian bosom an hereditary sense of injury, which naturally enough, prompts to deeds of revengeful cruelty towards the Whites."[46] Revenge drove White settlers as well, but whereas Indigenous peoples' feelings were the result of a "hereditary sense of injury," Whites' feelings were more understandable. He asked his readers to feel along with them by imagining "parents, in the bloom of life and glow of health, mercilessly mangled to death, in the presence of children, whose sobbing cries served but to heighten the torments of the dying.—Husbands, cruelly lacerated, and by piece-meal deprived of life, in view of the tender partners of their bosoms, whose agonizing shrieks, increasing the anguish of torture, sharpened the sting of death." This suffering created the feelings that caused settlers to act barbarically themselves. "Barbarities such as these had considerable influence on the temper and disposition of the inhabitants of the country. They gave birth to a vindicative feeling in many, which led to the perpetration of similar enormities and sunk civilized man, to the degraded level of the barbarian."[47]

His audience, whom he had asked to imagine tortured settlers, was to sympathize with this "vindicative feeling" to understand, if not justify, the answering "enormities" committed against Indigenous people. Although regrettable, these acts were, in the end, only natural.

Some narratives explicitly opposed these natural emotions to the cultivated sentiments of Christianity and civilization. One popular text of this sort was James Eldridge Quinlan's *Tom Quick, the Indian Slayer*, an 1851 collection of stories about a Pennsylvania woodsman whose decades-long career of murdering Indigenous people had made him a folk hero. Quinlan assumed that Quick's deeds, which included luring Indigenous men into the woods with promises of good hunting before killing them, would horrify midcentury Americans. "[The] murders committed by Tom were unjustifiable," Quinlan allowed, but the emotions that caused them were understandable: "In the struggle for mastery between the aborigines and those who supplanted them, the refined and humane sentiments which are promoted by civilization and Christianity, were obliterated by the dark and unfeeling dogmas which obtain a lodgment in the human mind during perilous and bloody times."[48] In Quinlan's rendering, the "refined and human sentiments" that reformers attempted to inculcate were luxuries. No matter how much "civilization and Christianity" worked to promote them, one act of violence could sweep them away. In Quick's case, because Indigenous men had killed his father when raiding the family's farm during the Seven Years' War, he had embraced "the theology of the unsanctified" and dedicated himself to the "dark and unfeeling dogma" of revenge. Although Quinlan treated Quick as a figure of horror and fascination who belonged to an earlier age, he suggested that the carefully cultivated sympathy for Indigenous people that missionaries and their supporters promoted was but a flimsy veneer. As soon as any violence broke out between settlers and Indigenous people, then "the struggle for mastery" would begin again and more Tom

Quicks would embrace their natural anger. In this understanding of the role of passion in violence, the cultivated emotions of religion, however appropriate to most circumstances, were at best naïve when it came to understanding the frontier. There, natural emotions would win out, and blood would be the result.

This new literature sometimes veered into spiritualizing language by framing less obviously unhinged "Indian killers" than Quick as martyrs to the cause of Christian civilization. The Maine lawyer Charles Daveis sounded this theme at the 1825 centennial commemoration of the Battle of Pequawket, a conflict in what would be Fryeburg, Maine, between Abenaki people and English settlers. Daveis asked his audience to picture Fryeburg, then a town of about one thousand people, as he imagined it to have been in 1725: a "wild region . . . awakened by the war-whoop" where "the green earth sprung up alive with a dark and furious ambush; and the glen was manned at once by its native garrison." In Daveis's telling, Indigenous people and the land blended into a single force of unreasoning opposition against White settlers, who stood against it as a "resolute band of martyrs."[49] Martyrs, of course, die for a purpose: in this case, it seems, the creation of Fryeburg. His audience, gathered to commemorate and celebrate their town, might have easily transferred their pride in and willingness to defend their home to these imagined "martyrs." But the English settlers at the Battle of Pequawket did not die for the town, which would not exist until almost forty years later. On the contrary, they were militia from near Nashua, New Hampshire, who had ventured over a hundred miles to cash in on a British bounty on Abenaki scalps.[50] This detail did not matter to Daveis. In his commemoration, scalp hunters became victims, even "martyrs," whose defeat consecrated the land to future White ownership just as the deaths of martyrs had, in Christian thought, sowed the seeds for the future triumph of the faith.[51]

By retelling these stories in books perused in comfortable parlors, newspapers read out loud at crowded post offices, and in public orations, White Americans in the early and mid-nineteenth century modeled specific emotional responses to expansion. They attributed any sympathy their audiences might feel for Indigenous people to their existence in a more refined and civilized age, when it was possible to mourn the victims of a man like Quick. But as they invited their audiences to vicariously experience the horror of settlers being "mercilessly mangled to death," they prepared them to excuse, and perhaps prepare themselves to feel, "vindicative feelings" that could end only in retaliatory violence. After all, such "vindicative feelings" were natural and only partly restrained by the cultivated feelings of Christianity. Despite the low estimation these stories put on Christian nurture, Christian terminology framed how they discussed violent passions. Following "vindicative feelings" meant embracing a shadow divinity: the "theology of the unsanctified" with its "dark and unfeeling dogmas." At the same time, these narratives also insisted that settlement, by whatever means, promoted civilization and Christianity. Hence, even scalp hunters who died at the hands of Indigenous people could become "martyrs" whose deaths transformed the land from a "a wild region . . . awakened by the war whoop" to a place where the glens and "green earth" nourished American democracy.

Rehearsing these feelings prepared Americans to respond similarly to future conflicts. The Congregational pastor and president of the University of Vermont, Daniel Clarke Sanders, wrote in 1828 that the "worst passions," which had driven settlers to excessive violence during the Pequot War of 1636–38, were not just a thing of the past. Conflicts such as the Creek War of 1813–14, the First Seminole War of 1817–18, and the Winnebago War of 1827 aroused the same passions in settlers. "It is the opinion of many that the Indian war is only begun. The people on the frontiers,

feeling no longer safety, are leaving in great distress" for forti-
fied settlements.[52] For Sanders, forgiving the New England settlers their seventeenth-century "excesses" meant preparing to
recapitulate and excuse them in the new conflicts that he anticipated would come.[53]

These rehearsals of past violence often returned to the idea that
Indian removal was the only alternative to bloody war.[54] At the
end of his commemorative speech, Daveis remarked that "one
[land] cession, after another, must be made to the peace of the
union, and we must compromise again the rights of humanity to
preserve a spirit of harmony" by driving out Indigenous people.
Given this sad necessity "the best expiation we can make, the only
atonement we can offer to the spirit of the Indian . . . [is] to superinduce a more perfect system of social happiness, than he is
providentially qualified to participate; and for that purpose to
unfold all the intrinsic capacities of our situation, and to promote
all its essential principles of virtue, liberty and justice."[55] By mentioning Indigenous peoples' unnamed "providential" deficien-
cies, Daveis alluded to the idea that God had crafted the supposed
character of the races along with the rest of nature. In his estimation, then, the same American system of governance that
expansionists saw as growing from White possession of the soil
of North America could be the only "expiation" that could be
offered to the spirits of the dead. If White settlers did not "compromise again the rights of humanity" by obtaining land cessions
even through illegitimate means, the violence of a century past
would only recur. Better, instead, to "superinduce a more perfect system of social happiness" in which Indigenous people could
not participate.

The narratives about expansion that rose to prominence in the
first half of the nineteenth century, therefore, worked above all
else to make White possession of the land, White victimization
by Indigenous people, and White violence in response all seem
inevitable. In stark contrast to the sense of being chosen for God's

purposes that animated evangelicals, this nationalist literature emphasized that expansionism was simply the result of nature. Any attempts to halt or slow settlement were perversions of nature and, more distantly, of the will of God who had designed it. Writers of the frontier sought to channel their readers' and hearers' feelings along courses that encouraged sympathy with the anger of White settlers, and just enough regret for Indigenous peoples' deaths, to feel that they, as modern and civilized people, were doing better than their ancestors by carrying out the mass violence of removal.

The transformation of Israelite Indian stories from arguments about God's intentions for Indigenous people and the United States to works of racial classification illustrates how White Americans' feelings about Indigenous people changed over the first half of the nineteenth century. Where once it had been possible to imagine that expansion would bring divine judgment, the rise of what I name here as secular ways of relating religion and politics made easier to dismiss the idea that God might not wish for White Americans to expand rapidly across the continent. The God of nature, after all, had created a land that gave rise to the racial hierarchies and expansionism of American empire as easily as soil gave rise to trees. White dominion over the continent, as O'Sullivan and others like him argued, needed no reading of Biblical prophecy to understand when it was "manifest" in the course of history and the land itself to anyone with the common sense to see it.

At the same time, the new literature of the frontier undermined the value of disinterested benevolence toward Indigenous people on which missionaries and their supporters relied. Folk histories, tales, and commemorative speeches argued that contact between White settlers and Indigenous nations only gave rise to violent feelings that could possess even White Christians and drive them to bloody acts. The blood that settlers shed in these conflicts, however they began, made them "martyrs" whose deaths nurtured the "more perfect system of social happiness" that their descendants enjoyed. Only in such a "more perfect system" could reformers' plans for Christian education flourish. In this secular rendering of the relationship between religion and the state, it was not that America's empire needed Christianity to thrive—as past reformers had had it—but that Christianity needed American empire.

Conclusion
The Feeling of Empire

The feelings evoked by Israelite Indian stories and their political meanings are still with us. In January and February 2016, a group of armed protesters occupied Malheur National Wildlife Refuge in Harney County, Oregon. The protesters, led by Ammon and Ryan Bundy—both radical members of the Church of Jesus Christ of Latter-day Saints from Nevada—asserted that their goal was to take federally managed land back from the government and turn it over to "the people." To hear the Bundys describe it, America had gotten off course. Ordinary Americans—by which they largely meant White Americans living in rural areas—were victims of a government that had grown far too large and too powerful to be a guarantor of liberty any longer. The only way to save the people was the same panacea that nineteenth-century expansionists had offered: land.[1]

In December 2015, just weeks before the occupation began, Ammon Bundy justified his presence in Oregon to the people of Harney County. Pacing in front of wreaths crusted with artificial snow on the stage of an assembly hall on the county fairgrounds, he inveighed against federal regulation of western lands and described what he saw as the proper state of the United States government, under the Constitution, in rapturous terms. Holding up a battered pocket Constitution, he insisted, "It's all here, it's all right here." Putting the Constitution down on a card table, he continued, "The growth pattern of this country is that you had states, they were sovereign, independent states, and they united together. The growth pattern is you had territories," he gestured with both hands to enclose the air in front of him in an imaginary border, "that were not states, that territories [were] under the jurisdiction of the federal government . . . but as soon as that territory gets populated enough to become a state . . . the people become sovereign and have their rights within the state. That's the growth pattern." But the federal government had perverted it. "If we didn't have these," he paused, gesturing, looking for a word, "I guess, wicked men if you wanna say, call it what you want, if we didn't have these wicked men, it's a beautiful pattern. Because what can happen is our territories—we can obtain land, whether it's through a war or we purchased it, and we can obtain land that could be a territory. The people can go it and begin to populate that territory, and it can become a state." He gestured hugely above the brim of his black cowboy hat, "We could do that across the whole continent, across the whole world. Right? And make people free across the whole world." Bundy spoke for over an hour about his vision of a freer west, perhaps even a freer world. By the end, tears ran down his face.[2]

Just as surely as had Democratic expansionists, Bundy here assigned a mysterious, even a sacred, power to the settlement of land by "the people." They alone, in his vision, have the power to "populate" land and convert it into a state, that is, a sovereign government. He imagined no end to this process as "the people" extend their settlement across "the whole continent . . . the whole world." Although Bundy and the other occupiers were at pains to distance themselves from the openly racist wings of the American militia movement, it is clear from the way he imagines this expansion that for him, as for his nineteenth-century intellectual forebears, "the people" means White people.[3] Only they could "populate" areas that presumably already have people living there, from whom "we"—the United States, or "the people" themselves?—have already obtained land through war or purchase. Only they could make a territory a state and continue the "beautiful pattern." Only they could "make people free across the whole world." As he spoke, Bundy reached out physically to his audience again and again, trying to convey his love for this vision of the nation, in which political sovereignty arose not from a distant federal government but from the land under the ownership of people like him. White, Christian people like him.

But the Bundys and some of their followers did not give up entirely on the idea that Indigenous people, also, might be part of that "beautiful pattern." The Malheur Wildlife Refuge that they occupied had once been a part of the reservation of the Burns Paiute Tribe, the federally recognized tribal government that represents the Wadatika band of the Northern Paiutes. Opinion in the Burns Paiute Tribe remained against the occupiers, which seemed to trouble the Bundys and some of their followers. Perhaps they thought visible opposition from the Wadatika created a public relations problem for the occupation, or perhaps, as Mormons, they felt some sympathy for people who might, after all, be Lamanites.[4] Late in the occupation, a Mormon occupier named LaVoy Finicum imagined what it could mean for him and his fellow occupiers if the Wadatika allied with them, using terms strikingly like those used in Israelite Indian narratives that cast Indigenous people as allies of White settlers in a millennial scenario. In a video Finicum made, he squats outside and addresses the Wadatika to call for their help:

It is time that we begin a dialogue, Paiute people here of Harney County. It is time for you to throw off the BIA, to become a completely sovereign independent nation without the overlordship, overseership, of the BIA, the Bureau of Indian Affairs. . . . Let us begin this dialogue. I believe in the American people. I believe in the Native Americans. It

is time for them to stand up and throw off the federal government out of their own nations. Having said that, we want
you to know that we desire a good relationship, we desire
respect. . . . Thanks. I hope to see you soon. We'd be on the
same side—we are not enemies.[5]

Finicum would die soon thereafter, the only casualty of the Malheur Wildlife Occupation, with that hope unfulfilled. Like White
Mormons in the early years of the movement, Finicum drew on
his feelings of kinship with Indigenous people to imagine a time
when the United States would be transformed, when the Burns
Paiute Tribe would "stand up and throw off the federal government out of their own nations." In that future conflict with what
Finicum saw as an imperial state, "we'd be on the same side,"
just as White Mormons and converted Lamanites would have
been on the same side in the millennium.

The occupiers of the Malheur Wildlife Refuge echoed many
of the feelings about empire discussed in this book. Not only did
Ammon's adoration of the "beautiful pattern" recall expansionists' beliefs in the sacred power of the land, but Finicum's appeal
to the Wadatika recalled the feelings of kinship to Indigenous
people running through many White Americans' Israelite Indian
stories. To many watching the Malheur Wildlife Refuge occupation, it seemed irrational for a few dozen miscellaneous antigov-
ernment activists and militia members to believe that their actions
could overturn federal control of western land, still less inaugurate a new era of Indigenous and settler cooperation. Seen in the
longer history of expansion, however, the occupiers' hopes under-
line the emotions involved in the creation of America's continental empire. Expansion, to be sure, had economic and political
motives, but that did not make it solely rational. Feelings about
the land, the people, and the nation had their own force, which
found expression in stories about Israelite Indians just as they

more recently did among the occupiers of a wildlife refuge in Oregon.

To the question posed in the introduction—"What did empire feel like?"—I can now answer that, for many Americans, the massive extension of White settlement, the tightening of racial hierarchies, and the state violence of removal felt too overwhelming to understand using anything other than religious terms. Using practices cultivated in religious communities, they evoked, expressed, and disciplined their feelings about transformations in the state, the economy, and the society of America that dwarfed the human scale of their lives. For some of them, Israelite Indian stories were compelling ways of feeling through these changes, useful less because they answered questions about Indigenous peoples' origins than because they suggested possibilities for their future.

Each community studied here helped to shape specific reactions to Israelite Indian narratives. Reading in genteel libraries like Sigourney's, evangelical reformers felt a surge of hope and wonder at the thought that Indigenous people might be God's chosen nation and that missionary work might save the United States. When Mormons fleeing west from Nauvoo gathered in freezing sod cabins in Nebraska, they let loose their anger by envisioning Israelite Indians as incarnations of the wrath of God unleashed against American empire. For American Jews in the lyceum halls of northeastern cities and Christian Cherokees in the log cabins of American Board missions, stories about Israelite Indians became reasons to feel pride in themselves and to hope for political sovereignty. In each case, these stories helped to blur feelings cultivated in religious communities about "Israel" with feelings about American politics. In the process, they seemed capable of creating new national identities or perhaps even of helping to make territorial claims in an empire still defining its boundaries. If they now seem bizarre, it is not because they are less reasonable than myths about the redemptive character of the land or about White Americans' special place in God's plans than because those latter myths took their place as ways of using religious feelings to understand the extension of American empire on a massive scale.

From one perspective, these Israelite Indian narratives failed. None of them, except perhaps for early Mormon stories about Lamanites, had a transformative political effect on American expansion. No new nations, not even the Mormon Zion as early members of the movement envisioned it, resulted, and no territories were redistributed. Attending to them, however, reminds us that expansion was neither inevitable nor uncontested. That it was made to seem so is a function of the triumph of a certain way of feeling about the United States and about the lands and peoples under its control. In the intervening years between the decline of Israelite Indian narratives and now, other nationalisms have been and continue to be constructed that incorporate the feelings cultivated in religious communities. By widening our view of the past to include even failed religious nationalisms, we prepare ourselves to better understand the tumultuous arguments about American empire that continue, as they were at Malheur, to be matters of religion and matters of feeling.

Notes

Introduction

1. Henry Méchoulan and Gérard Nahon, "Introduction," in *The Hope of Israel: The English Translation by Moses Wall*, by Menasseh Ben Israel (New York: Oxford University Press, 1987). The traditional story of these "ten lost tribes" relies largely on 2 Kings 16:9, 15:29; 2 Chronicles 36:21–23, and 2 Esdras. According to the traditional reading of these verses, members of all twelve tribes were deported from Israel, but only the members of two tribes returned. Hence, the traditional number of the lost tribes was ten. Tudor Parfitt, *The Lost Tribes of Israel* (London: Weidenfeld & Nicolson, 2002); Zvi Ben-Dor Benite, *The Ten Lost Tribes: A World History* (New York: Oxford University Press, 2009).

2. Méchoulan and Nahon, "Introduction," 73.

3. "*Converso*" refers to all Jews forced to convert, even if they did not follow Jewish practices. The terms "*marrano*" or, in some modern scholarship, "crypto-Jew" are sometimes used to designate Jews, like Levi, who continued or were suspected of continuing Jewish practices. Irene Silverblatt, *Modern Inquisitions: Peru and the Colonial Origins of the Civilized World* (Durham, NC: Duke University Press, 2004).

4. Menasseh Ben Israel, *The Hope of Israel*, ed. Henry Méchoulan and Gérard Nahon (1650; repr., New York: Oxford University Press, 1987), 106.

5. It was already a well-discussed idea by the time a compendium of theories as to Indigenous origins was published in 1607. See Gregorio García, *Origen de Los Indios de El Nuevo Mundo, e Indias Occidentales* (1607; repr., Madrid: F. Martinez Abad, 1729). The idea was defended as early as 1581 by the Dominican friar Diego Durán, although as the relevant work was not published in his lifetime it is difficult to know exactly how much it circulated. Diego Durán, *Historia de Las Indias de Nueva España e Islas de La Tierra Firme.*, ed. Angel María Garibay K. [Kintana], 2 vols. (1581; repr., México [DF]: Editorial Porrúa, 1967).

6. Méchoulan and Nahon, "Introduction," 74–75.

7. Ben Israel, *The Hope of Israel*, 111.

8. Méchoulan and Nahon, "Introduction," 62–69. Levi's account and Ben Israel's commentary on it contain numerous ambiguities that seem to suggest a genetic relationship between Indigenous peoples and Jews, whatever Ben Israel's intentions. Paul B. Miller, "'Benedito Sea A. Que No Me Hizo Indio Ni Negro': Ethnic Paradigms in Menasseh Ben Israel's Esperança de Israel," *Bulletin of Hispanic Studies* 89, no. 5 (September 2012): 473–82; Méchoulan and Nahon, "Introduction."

9. Richard W. Cogley, "The Ancestry of the American Indians: Thomas Thorowgood's Iewes in America (1650) and Jews in America (1660)," *English Literary Renaissance* 35, no. 2 (March 1, 2005): 304–30; Richard W. Cogley, "'Some Other Kinde of Being and Condition': The Controversy in Mid-Seventeenth-Century England over the Peopling of Ancient America," *Journal of the History of Ideas* 68, no. 1 (January 2007): 35–56; Jenny Pulsipher, *Subjects unto the Same King: Indians, English, and the Contest for Authority in Colonial New England* (Philadelphia: University of Pennsylvania Press, 2005); Jill Lepore, *The Name of War: King Philip's War and the Origins of American Identity* (New York: Random House, 1998).

10. Roy Harvey Pearce, *Savagism and Civilization* (Berkeley: University of California Press, 1988), 61–62; Hilary Wyss, *Writing Indians: Literacy, Christianity, and Native Community in Early America* (Amherst: University of Massachusetts Press, 2000), 12, 161.

11. Albert Weinberg, *Manifest Destiny: A Study of Nationalist Expansionism in American History* (Baltimore: Johns Hopkins University Press, 1935); Ernest Tuveson, *Redeemer Nation: The Idea of America's Millennial Role* (Chicago: University of Chicago Press, 1968); Anders Stephanson, *Manifest Destiny: American Expansionism and the Empire of Right* (New York: Hill and Wang, 1995); Conrad Cherry, *God's New Israel: Religious Interpretations of American Destiny*, rev. and updated ed. (Chapel Hill: University of North Carolina Press, 1998); Steven Woodworth, *Manifest Destinies: America's Westward Expansion and the Road to the Civil War* (New York: Alfred A. Knopf, 2010); Walter Hixson, *American Settler Colonialism: A History* (New York: Palgrave Macmillan, 2013). A useful historiography of the idea that pushes back against such perennialist interpretations is Robert Walter Johannsen, "Introduction," in *Manifest Destiny and Empire: American Antebellum Expansionism*, ed. Christopher Charles Morris and Sam Walter Haynes (College Station: Texas A&M University Press, 1997), 1–7.

12. Jonathan Sassi, *A Republic of Righteousness: The Public Christianity of the Post-Revolutionary New England Clergy* (New York: Oxford University Press, 2001); Robert P. Sweringa, "Ethnoreligious Political Behavior in the Early Nineteenth Century," in *Religion and American Politics: From the Colonial Period to the Present*, ed. Mark Noll and Luke E. Harlow (New York: Oxford University Press, 2007), 145–68; Sam Haselby, *The Origins of American Religious Nationalism* (New York: Oxford University Press, 2015); Peter Onuf, "Imperialism and Nationalism in the Early American Republic," in *Empire's Twin: U.S. Anti-Imperialism from the Founding Era to the Age of Terrorism*, ed. Ian Tyrrell and Jay Sexton (Ithaca, NY: Cornell University Press, 2015); Benjamin E. Park, *American*

Nationalisms: Imagining Union in the Age of Revolutions, 1783–1833 (New York: Cambridge University Press, 2018).

13. Anthony Wallace, *The Death and Rebirth of the Seneca* (New York: Alfred A. Knopf, 1970); Gregory Dowd, *A Spirited Resistance: The North American Indian Struggle for Unity, 1745–1815* (Baltimore: Johns Hopkins University Press, 1992); Alfred Cave, *Prophets of the Great Spirit: Native American Revitalization Movements in Eastern North America* (Lincoln: University of Nebraska Press, 2006); R. David Edmunds, *Tecumseh and the Quest for Indian Leadership*, 2nd ed. (New York: Pearson Longman, 2007); Matthew Dennis, *Seneca Possessed: Indians, Witchcraft, and Power in the Early American Republic* (Philadelphia: University of Pennsylvania Press, 2010).

14. Sylvester Johnson, *The Myth of Ham in Nineteenth-Century American Christianity: Race, Heathens, and the People of God* (New York: Palgrave Macmillan, 2004); Laurie Maffly-Kipp, *Setting down the Sacred Past: African-American Race Histories* (Cambridge, MA: Belknap Press of Harvard University Press, 2010); Sylvester Johnson, *African American Religions, 1500–2000: Colonialism, Democracy, and Freedom* (New York: Cambridge University Press, 2015), 177–208.

15. Johnson, *African American Religions, 1500–2000;* Tisa Wenger, *Religious Freedom: The Contested History of an American Ideal* (Chapel Hill: University of North Carolina Press, 2017); Jennifer Graber, *The Gods of Indian Country: Religion and the Struggle for the American West* (New York: Oxford University Press, 2018); Heather D. Curtis, *Holy Humanitarians: American Evangelicals and Global Aid* (Cambridge, MA: Harvard University Press, 2018); Matthew W. Dougherty, "New Scholarship in Religion and United States Empire," *Religion Compass* 13, no. 5 (May 2019).

16. Walter Hart Blumenthal, *In Old America: Random Chapters on the Early Aborigines* (New York: Walton Book Company, 1931); Lee Huddleston, *Origins of the American Indians; European Concepts, 1492–1729* (Austin: University of Texas Press, 1967); Richard H. Popkin, "The Rise and Fall of the Jewish Indian Theory," in *Menasseh Ben Israel and His World*, ed. Yosef Kaplan, Henry Méchoulan, and Richard H. Popkin (Leiden, Netherlands: E. J. Brill, 1989), 63–82. Accounts emphasizing debates over scriptural inerrancy as an explanatory factor in the existence of Israelite Indian include G. Blair Nelson, "Men before Adam!: American Debates over the Unity and Antiquity of Humanity," in *When Science & Christianity Meet*, ed. David Lindberg and Ronald L. Numbers (Chicago: University of Chicago Press, 2003), 161–182; Steven Conn, *History's Shadow: Native Americans and Historical Consciousness in the Nineteenth Century* (Chicago: University of Chicago Press, 2004), 16–19, 132–33.

17. Garcia, *Origen de Los Indios de El Nuevo Mundo, e Indias Occidentales*.

18. Ben-Dor Benite, *The Ten Lost Tribes*.

19. I translate *gentes* as "lineages" rather than the more usual "peoples" to avoid confusion. Anthony Pagden, *The Fall of Natural Man: The American Indian and the Origins of Comparative Ethnology* (New York: Cambridge University Press, 1982); Robert Bartlett, "Medieval and Modern Concepts of Race and Ethnicity,"

Journal of Medieval and Early Modern Studies 31, no. 1 (2001): 39–56; Kathryn Burns, "Unfixing Race," in *Rereading the Black Legend: The Discourse of Religious and Racial Difference in the Renaissance Empires*, ed. Margaret R. Greer, Walter Mignolo, and Maureen Quilligan (Chicago: University of Chicago Press, 2007); María Elena Martínez, *Genealogical Fictions: Limpieza de Sangre, Religion, and Gender in Colonial Mexico* (Stanford, CA: Stanford University Press, 2008); María Elena Díaz, "Conjuring Identities: Race, Nativeness, Local Citizenship, and Royal Slavery on the Imperial Frontier (Revisiting El Cobre, Cuba)," in *Imperial Subjects: Race and Identity in Colonial Latin America*, ed. Andrew B. Fisher and Matthew D. O'Hara (Durham, NC: Duke University Press, 2009); Joanne Rappaport, "'Asi Lo Paresçe Por Su Aspeto': Physiognomy and the Construction of Difference in Colonial Bogotá," *Hispanic American Historical Review* 91, no. 4 (November 2011): 601–31.

20. Eric Wolf, *Europe and the People without History* (Berkeley: University of California Press, 2010); Johnson, *African American Religions, 1500–2000*.

21. Jonathan Boyarin, *The Unconverted Self: Jews, Indians, and the Identity of Christian Europe* (Chicago: University of Chicago Press, 2009). See also Martínez, *Genealogical Fictions*.

22. Nicholas Guyatt, *Bind Us Apart: How Enlightened Americans Invented Racial Segregation* (New York: Basic Books, 2016).

23. Most literature on this wave of Israelite Indian stories addresses Jewish or Mormon engagements with these narratives specifically. On American Jewish uses of these stories see Rachel Rubinstein, *Members of the Tribe: Native America in the Jewish Imagination* (Detroit, MI: Wayne State University Press, 2010); Sarah Imhoff, "Wild Tribes and Ancient Semites: Israelite-Indian Identification in the American West," *Culture and Religion* 15, no. 2 (2014): 227–49; David S. Koffman, *The Jews' Indian: Colonialism, Pluralism, and Belonging in America* (New Brunswick, NJ: Rutgers University Press, 2019). On Mormon uses, see Lori Elaine Taylor, "Telling Stories about Mormons and Indians" (PhD diss., State University of New York–Buffalo, 2000); Armand Mauss, *All Abraham's Children: Changing Mormon Conceptions of Race and Lineage* (Urbana, IL: University of Illinois Press, 2003); Jared Farmer, *On Zion's Mount: Mormons, Indians, and the American Landscape* (Cambridge, MA: Harvard University Press, 2008); W. Paul Reeve, *Religion of a Different Color: Race and the Mormon Struggle for Whiteness* (New York: Oxford University Press, 2015); Stanley J. Thayne, "The Blood of Father Lehi: Indigenous Americans and the Book of Mormon" (PhD diss., University of North Carolina–Chapel Hill, 2016); Max Perry Mueller, *Race and the Making of the Mormon People* (Chapel Hill: University of North Carolina Press, 2017); Matthew W. Dougherty, "None Can Deliver: Imagining Lamanites and Feeling Mormon, 1837–1847," *Journal of Mormon History* 43, no. 3 (2017): 22–45. I engage with each of these literatures in later chapters.

24. The most extensive bibliography of such theories is Walter Hart Blumenthal, "In Old America—The Ten Lost Tribes of Israel" 1931, MS-229, Jacob Rader Marcus Center of the American Jewish Archives. See also Dan Vogel, *Indian Origins and the Book of Mormon: Religious Solutions from Columbus to Joseph Smith* (Salt Lake City, UT: Signature Books, 1986).

25. The only study to discuss Israelite Indian stories in the context of early American political thought is Eran Shalev, *American Zion: The Old Testament as a Political Text from the Revolution to the Civil War* (New Haven, CT: Yale University Press, 2013). Shalev rightly relates Israelite Indian stories to nationalist rhetoric but does not explicitly engage with colonialism. He discusses Indian removal, for example, only as a natural result of settlement rather than a political policy on which these narratives might have commented.

26. Janet Jakobsen and Ann Pellegrini, "Introduction: Times Like These," in *Secularisms*, ed. Janet Jakobsen and Ann Pellegrini (Durham, NC: Duke University Press, 2008), 1–35.

27. Jane Burbank and Frederick Cooper, *Empires in World History: Power and the Politics of Difference* (Princeton, NJ: Princeton University Press, 2010), 1–22; Paul A. Kramer, "Power and Connection: Imperial Histories of the United States in the World," *American Historical Review* 116, no. 5 (December 2011): 1348–91; Johnson, *African American Religions, 1500–2000*, 2, 107–26, 246–61, 273–376; Wenger, *Religious Freedom*, 26–34.

28. Winthrop Jordan, *White over Black: American Attitudes towards the Negro, 1550–1812* (Baltimore: Penguin Books, 1973); Edmund S. Morgan, *American Slavery, American Freedom: The Ordeal of Colonial Virginia* (New York: Norton, 1975); Mechal Sobel, *The World They Made Together: Black and White Values in Eighteenth-Century Virginia* (Princeton, NJ: Princeton University Press, 1987); Reginald Horsman, *Race and Manifest Destiny: The Origins of American Racial Anglo-Saxonism* (Cambridge, MA: Harvard University Press, 1981); David Roediger, *The Wages of Whiteness: Race and the Making of the American Working Class* (New York: Verso, 1991); Karin Wulf, *Not All Wives: Women of Colonial Philadelphia* (Ithaca, NY: Cornell University Press, 2000); Rebecca Goetz, *The Baptism of Early Virginia: How Christianity Created Race* (Baltimore: Johns Hopkins University Press, 2012); Kathleen DuVal, *Independence Lost: Lives on the Edge of the American Revolution* (New York: Random House, 2015).

29. Thomas Hietala, *Manifest Design: American Exceptionalism and Empire*, rev. ed. (Ithaca, NY: Cornell University Press, 2003); Ned Blackhawk, *Violence over the Land: Indians and Empires in the Early American West* (Cambridge, MA: Harvard University Press, 2006); Patrick Griffin, *American Leviathan: Empire, Nation, and Revolutionary Frontier* (New York: Hill and Wang, 2007); Gordon Wood, *Empire of Liberty: A History of the Early Republic, 1789–1815* (New York: Oxford University Press, 2009); Goetz, *The Baptism of Early Virginia;* Bethel Saler, *The Settlers' Empire: Colonialism and State Formation in America's Old Northwest* (Philadelphia: University of Pennsylvania Press, 2015); Matthew Karp, *This Vast Southern Empire: Slaveholders at the Helm of American Foreign Policy* (Cambridge, MA: Harvard University Press, 2016).

30. The United States was not the only empire in North America. The British Empire, French Empire, and Spanish Empire all had territories in North America and the Caribbean during the years covered in this narrative. Some scholars have argued, furthermore, that Indigenous hegemons in North America should be considered empires alongside European powers. Alan Taylor, *American Colonies* (New York: Viking, 2001); Alan Taylor, *American Revolutions:*

A Continental History, 1750–1804 (New York: W.W. Norton, 2016); Pekka Hämäläinen, *The Comanche Empire* (New Haven, CT: Yale University Press, 2008); Michael McDonnell, *Masters of Empire: Great Lakes Indians and the Making of America,* 1st ed. (New York: Hill and Wang, 2015); Caitlin Fitz, *Our Sister Republics: The United States in an Age of American Revolutions* (New York: W.W. Norton, 2016).

31. Benedict Anderson, *Imagined Communities,* rev. ed. (New York: Verso, 2006); David Waldstreicher, *In the Midst of Perpetual Fetes: The Making of American Nationalism, 1776–1820* (Chapel Hill: University of North Carolina Press, 1997); Onuf, "Imperialism and Nationalism in the Early American Republic"; David Morgan, "Emotion and Imagination in the Ritual Entanglement of Religion, Sport, and Nationalism," in *Feeling Religion,* ed. John Corrigan (Durham, NC: Duke University Press, 2017), 222–41.

32. The term is often used to distinguish settler colonies from colonial systems with other goals, such as extractive colonies created with the goal of maximizing colonial powers' access to local natural resources and labor. Patrick Wolfe, "Settler Colonialism and the Elimination of the Native," *Journal of Genocide Research* 8, no. 4 (December 2006): 387–409; Frederick E. Hoxie, "Retrieving the Red Continent: Settler Colonialism and the History of American Indians in the US," *Ethnic and Racial Studies* 31, no. 6 (September 1, 2008): 1153–67; Hixson, *American Settler Colonialism;* Saler, *The Settlers' Empire.*

33. J.Z. Smith, "Religion, Religions, Religious," in *Relating Religion: Essays in the Study of Religion* (Chicago: University of Chicago, 2004); Tomoko Masuzawa, *The Invention of World Religions, or, How European Universalism Was Preserved in the Language of Pluralism* (Chicago: University of Chicago Press, 2005); David Chidester, *Empire of Religion: Imperialism and Comparative Religion* (Chicago: University of Chicago Press, 2014); Wenger, *Religious Freedom.*

34. Nathan Hatch, *The Democratization of American Christianity* (New Haven, CT: Yale University Press, 1989).

35. Jon Butler, *Awash in a Sea of Faith: Christianizing the American People* (Cambridge, MA: Harvard University Press, 1990); Amanda Porterfield, *Conceived in Doubt: Religion and Politics in the New American Nation* (Chicago: University of Chicago Press, 2012).

36. Tracy Fessenden, *Culture and Redemption: Religion, the Secular, and American Literature* (Princeton, NJ: Princeton University Press, 2007); Jakobsen and Pellegrini, "Introduction: Times Like These"; John Modern, *Secularism in Antebellum America: With Reference to Ghosts, Protestant Subcultures, Machines, and Their Metaphors; Featuring Discussions of Mass Media, Moby-Dick, Spirituality, Phrenology, Anthropology, Sing Sing State Penitentiary, and Sex with the New Motive Power* (Chicago: University of Chicago Press, 2011); Peter Coviello, *Make Yourselves Gods: Mormons and the Unfinished Business of American Secularism* (Chicago: University of Chicago Press, 2019).

37. For this reason, I use the terms "feelings" and "emotions" as experiences that occur within a social setting, rather than the term "affect," which, in some interpretations, denotes a precultural or prelinguistic force. On this approach to affect theory, see Brian Massumi, "The Autonomy of Affect," *Cultural Cri-*

tique, no. 31 (1995): 83–109; Melissa Gregg and Gregory J. Seigworth, "Introduction: An Inventory of Shimmers," in *The Affect Theory Reader*, ed. Melissa Gregg and Gregory J. Seigworth (Durham, NC: Duke University Press, 2010). For a reading of affect that does not take this track, see Donovan O. Schaefer, *Religious Affects: Animality, Evolution, and Power* (Durham, NC: Duke University Press, 2015), 19–35.

38. This discussion of emotions as practices draws especially on Monique Scheer, "Are Emotions a Kind of Practice (and Is That What Makes Them Have a History)? A Bourdieuian Approach to Understanding Emotion," *History and Theory* 51 (May 2012): 193–220; Pierre Bourdieu, *Outline of a Theory of Practice* (Cambridge: Cambridge University Press, 1977). It is also informed by Barbara Rosenwein, *Emotional Communities in the Early Middle Ages* (Ithaca, NY: Cornell University Press, 2006); Pamela E. Klassen, "Ritual," in *The Oxford Handbook of Religion and Emotion*, ed. John Corrigan (New York: Oxford University Press, 2007), 144–58; Nicole Eustace, *Passion Is the Gale: Emotion, Power, and the Coming of the American Revolution* (Chapel Hill: University of North Carolina Press, 2008); Pascal Eitler and Monique Scheer, "Emotionengeschichte Als Körpergeschichte. Eine Heuristische Perspektive Auf Religiose Konversionen Im 19. Und 20. Jarhundert," *Geschichte Und Gesellschaft* 35, no. 2 (June 2009): 282–313; Jan Plamper, *The History of Emotions: An Introduction* (New York: Oxford University Press, 2015); Nicole Eustace et al., "AHR Conversation: The Historical Study of Emotions," *American Historical Review* 117, no. 5 (December 2012): 1486–1531.

39. My readings throughout of how specific communities attach emotions to concepts and link concepts to one another draw on Raymond Williams, *Marxism and Literature*, Marxist Introductions (New York: Oxford University Press, 1977), 130–34; Laura Stevens, *The Poor Indians: British Missionaries, Native Americans, and Colonial Sensibility* (Philadelphia: University of Pennsylvania Press, 2004); Sara Ahmed, "Affective Economies," *Social Text* 22, no. 2 (Summer 2004): 117–39; Sarah Ahmed, *The Cultural Politics of Emotion* (New York: Routledge, 2004) 1–16; Schaefer, *Religious Affects*, 92–146; Morgan, "Emotion and Imagination in the Ritual Entanglement of Religion, Sport, and Nationalism."

40. Méchoulan and Nahon, "Introduction," 69–74.

Chapter 1. Friends of Zion

1. Probate Court (Hartford, Connecticut), "Probate Records," September 5, 1851, 196, Connecticut, Wills and Probate Records, 1609–1999, Ancestry.com; Historic American Buildings Survey, *HABS CONN, 2-HARF, 2- (Sheet 7 of 15)—Lydia Sigourney House, 15 Hurlburt Street, Hartford, Hartford County, CT*, 1933, Photograph, 1933, Prints and Photographs Division, Library of Congress, https://www.loc.gov/pictures/item/ct0169.sheet.00007a/; Jane Donawerth, ed., *Rhetorical Theory by Women before 1900: An Anthology* (Lanham, MD: Rowman & Littlefield, 2002), 141–43; Sandra A. Zagarell, "Lydia Howard Huntley Sigourney (1791–1865)," in *The Heath Anthology of American*

Literature, by Paul Lauter, 5th ed., vol. B (Boston, MA: Houghton Mifflin College, 2005).

2. Lydia Howard Sigourney, *Traits of the Aborigines of America: A Poem.* (Cambridge, MA: University Press, 1822), 7–8.

3. Pagden, *The Fall of Natural Man.* For an American source contemporary to Sigourney, see Jedidiah Morse, *The American Universal Geography; or, A View of the Present State of All the Kingdoms, States and Colonies in the Known World,* 7th ed. (Charlestown: G. Clarke, 1819), 76–77.

4. Jedidah Morse, *The American Geography: Or, a View of the Present Situation of the United States of America* (Elizabethtown, NJ: Shepard Kollock, 1789), 18.

5. Elijah Parish, *A New System of Modern Geography, or, A General Description of All the Considerable Countries in the World* (Newburyport, MA, 1810), 22–25.

6. The letter is reprinted in Robert Benjamin Lewis, *Light and Truth; Collected from the Bible and Ancient and Modern History, Containing the Universal History of the Colored and the Indian Race, from the Creation of the World to the Present Time* (Boston: A Committee of Colored Gentlemen, 1844), 265–66.

7. Philadelphian, "Descendants of Israel," *Philadelphia Recorder,* July 8, 1826, ProQuest: American Periodicals; "The Progress of Knowledge," *Western Recorder,* January 19, 1830, ProQuest: American Periodicals.

8. John Fea, *The Bible Cause: A History of the American Bible Society* (New York: Oxford University Press, 2016); Sonia Hazard, "Evangelical Encounters: The American Tract Society and the Rituals of Print Distribution in Antebellum America," *Journal of the American Academy of Religion* 87, no. 4 (December 2019).

9. Historians have frequently used the idea that Israelite Indian stories were "in the air" to contextualize historical figures who accepted the idea. See, e.g., John Brooke, *The Refiner's Fire: The Making of Mormon Cosmology, 1644–1844* (Cambridge: Cambridge University Press, 1994), 142–43; Richard Bushman, *Joseph Smith: Rough Stone Rolling* (New York: Alfred A. Knopf, 2005), 84–109; Laurie Maffly-Kipp, "Introduction," in *The Book of Mormon* (New York: Penguin Books, 2008), ix–xiii; Philip Gura, *The Life of William Apess, Pequot* (Chapel Hill: University of North Carolina Press, 2015), 127–28.

10. Ephraim T. Woodruff, *A Sermon Delivered Before the Ecclesiastical Society in Williamsfield and Wayne, Ashtabula County, Ohio; On the 4th of July, 1826: In Celebration of the Jubilee of the Independence of the United States of America* (Warren, OH: Hapgood and Quinby, 1826), 5, 7. Nicholas Guyatt, *Providence and the Invention of the United States, 1607–1876* (New York: Cambridge University Press, 2007); Shalev, *American Zion.*

11. Sassi, *A Republic of Righteousness*; Guyatt, *Providence and the Invention of the United States, 1607–1876*; Spencer McBride, *Pulpit and Nation: Clergymen and the Politics of Revolutionary America* (Charlottesville: University of Virginia Press, 2016).

12. Edmund Morgan, *Visible Saints: The History of a Puritan Idea* (New York: New York University Press, 1963); Butler, *Awash in a Sea of Faith*; Christine Heyrman, *Southern Cross: The Beginnings of the Bible Belt* (Chapel Hill: University of North Carolina Press, 1998); Patricia U. Bonomi, *Under the Cope of Heaven: Reli-*

gion, Society and Politics in Colonial America, updated ed. (New York: Oxford University Press, 2003); Sassi, *A Republic of Righteousness*; David Hall, *A Reforming People: Puritanism and the Transformation of Public Life in New England* (New York: Alfred A. Knopf, 2011); Shelby Balik, *Rally the Scattered Believers: Northern New England's Religious Geography* (Bloomington: Indiana University Press, 2014); Kathryn Gin Lum, *Damned Nation: Hell in America from the Revolution to Reconstruction* (New York: Oxford University Press, 2014); McBride, *Pulpit and Nation.*

13. Definitions of evangelicalism vary widely. Perhaps the most commonly used is the "Bebbington quadrilateral," which defines as evangelical any group that embraces the necessity of a conversion experience, a theological emphasis on the atoning work of Jesus, emphasis on the authority of the Bible, and social activism. David Bebbington, *Evangelicalism in Modern Britain: A History from the 1730s to the 1980s* (Winchester, MA: Allen & Unwin, 1989). I have chosen to emphasize a specific lineage of practices over adherence to beliefs because I am more concerned with how different strains of the movement shaped distinct emotional styles than their theological content. Hatch, *The Democratization of American Christianity*; Butler, *Awash in a Sea of Faith*; George Marsden, *Understanding Fundamentalism and Evangelicalism* (Grand Rapids, MI: W.B. Eerdmans, 1991); Mark Noll, *America's God: From Jonathan Edwards to Abraham Lincoln* (New York: Oxford University Press, 2002).

14. Kenneth P. Minkem and Harry Stout, "The Edwardsean Tradition and the Antislavery Debate, 1740–1865," *Journal of American History* 92, no. 1 (June 2005): 47–74.

15. Butler, *Awash in a Sea of Faith*; Robert Abzug, *Cosmos Crumbling: American Reform and the Religious Imagination* (New York: Oxford University Press, 1994); Daniel Walker Howe, "Religion and Politics in the Antebellum North," in *Religion and American Politics: From the Colonial Period to the Present,* by Mark A. Noll and Luke Harlow, 2nd ed. (New York: Oxford University Press, 2007); Sweringa, "Ethnoreligious Political Behavior in the Early Nineteenth Century," 145–68; Porterfield, *Conceived in Doubt*; Emily Conroy-Krutz, *Christian Imperialism: Converting the World in the Early American Republic* (Ithaca, NY: Cornell University Press, 2015).

16. Timothy Dwight, *Conquest of Canäan* (Hartford, CT: Printed by Elisha Babcock, 1785); Abiel Abbot, *Traits of Resemblance in the People of the United States of America to Ancient Israel. In a Sermon, Delivered at Haverhill, on the Twenty-Eighth of November, 1799, the Day of Anniversary Thanksgiving. By Abiel Abbot, Pastor of the First Church in Haverhill.* (MA: From the press of Moore & Stebbins. Published for the subscribers, 1799); Conrad Cherry, *God's New Israel: Religious Interpretations of American Destiny,* rev. and updated ed. (Chapel Hill: University of North Carolina Press, 1998); Michael Hoberman, *New Israel / New England: Jews and Puritans in Early America* (Amherst: University of Massachusetts Press, 2011); Shalev, *American Zion.*

17. The terms "Zion" for the church, "the cause of Zion" for evangelical reform, and "friends of Zion" for reform's supporters were especially common in missionary periodicals and tracts. See, e.g., *Connecticut Evangelical Magazine,*

and Religious Intelligencer 1 (June 1800–July 1801): 7–12, 21–30, 136–42, 286–87; "Hancock Female Tract Society" *Panoplist, or, the Christian's Armory* 3, no. 4 (September 1807): 189–190, American Historical Periodicals from the American Antiquarian Society, Gale Cengage; Pastor, "Survey of New England Churches" *Panoplist* 2, no. 11 (April 1807): 503–512, American Historical Periodicals from the American Antiquarian Society, Gale Cengage; Ethan Smith, *Daughters of Zion Excelling. A Sermon Preached to the Ladies of the Cent Institutions, in Hopkinton, New-Hampshire August 18, 1814* (Concord, NH: George Hough, 1814); General Association of Massachusetts, "Report," *Panoplist and Missionary Magazine* 11 (second series), no. 8 (August 1815): 373–77, ProQuest: American Periodicals Series II.

18. Sylvester Johnson, *African American Religions, 1500–2000*, 2–4, 399–405; John P. Bowes, *Land Too Good for Indians: Northern Indian Removal* (Norman: University of Oklahoma Press, 2016), 18–49.

19. Sigourney, *Traits of the Aborigines of America*, 7–8. Boudinot should not be confused with the younger, and now more famous, Cherokee newspaper editor and political leader of the same name. Elias Boudinot, the Cherokee editor, born Gallegina Uwati, took the older man's name as a gesture of gratitude for funding his education at a missionary boarding school in Connecticut. Elias Boudinot [Gallegina Uwati], *Cherokee Editor: The Writings of Elias Boudinot*, ed. Theda Perdue (Athens: University of Georgia Press, 1996); John Demos, *The Heathen School: A Story of Hope and Betrayal in the Age of the Early Republic* (New York: Alfred A. Knopf, 2014).

20. Elias Boudinot, *The Life, Public Services, Addresses, and Letters of Elias Boudinot, LL. D., President of the Continental Congress*, ed. Jane J. Boudinot (New York: Houghton, Mifflin & Co., 1896); George Adams Boyd, *Elias Boudinot: Patriot and Statesman* (Princeton, NJ: Princeton University Press, 1952); Susanna Linsley, "Saving the Jews: Religious Toleration and the American Society for Meliorating the Condition of the Jews," *Journal of the Early Republic* 34, no. 4 (Winter 2014): 625–51; Fea, *The Bible Cause*, 19–29.

21. Elias Boudinot, *A Star in the West; or, A Humble Attempt to Discover the Long Lost Ten Tribes of Israel, Preparatory to Their Return to Their Beloved City, Jerusalem* (Trenton: D. Fenton, S. Hutchinson and J. Dunham, 1816), 41–45, 73, 81–82, 279–301.

22. Elias Boudinot, "A Star in the West," *Jewish Expositor and Friend of Israel*, January 1820, 3 passim; "Indian Civilization," *Church Record*, July 20, 1822, ProQuest: American Periodicals; "Ten Tribes," *Jewish Intelligencer: A Monthly Publication* 1, no. 10 (May 1837). See also the summary of the diffusion of this idea in the early republic in Megan C. L. Howey "'The Question Which Has Puzzled, and Still Puzzles': How American Indian Authors Challenged Dominant Discourse about Native American Origins in the Nineteenth Century," *American Indian Quarterly* 34, no. 4 (Fall 2010): 435–74.

23. See the frontispiece of Josiah Priest, *American Antiquities and Discoveries in the West*, 5th ed. (Albany, NY: Hoffman and White, 1835). Josephine Guy and Ian Small, *The Routledge Concise History of Nineteenth Century Literature* (London: Routledge, 2011), 204. Josiah Priest, *The Wonders of Nature and Prov-*

idence, Displayed: Compiled from Authentic Sources, Both Ancient and Modern, Giving an Account of Various and Strange Phenomena Existing in Nature, of Travels, Adventures, Singular Providences, &c. . . . (Albany, NY: J. Priest, 1825).

24. Boudinot, *A Star in the West*, 1816, 114.

25. Leigh Eric Schmidt, *Hearing Things: Religion, Illusion, and the American Enlightenment* (Cambridge, MA: Harvard University Press, 2000).

26. Boudinot, *A Star in the West*, 189–90.

27. Boudinot, *A Star in the West*, 229–30.

28. Boudinot likely read Adair's work in manuscript as early as 1775. Elias Boudinot, "Commonplace Book" (1803), 160ff., Stimson Collection of Elias Boudinot, Princeton University Rare Books and Special Collections.

29. James Adair, *The History of the American Indians*, ed. Kathryn E. Holland Braund (1775; repr., Tuscaloosa: University of Alabama Press, 2005), 166–68, 363–65.

30. Adair, *The History of the American Indians*, n. 485.

31. John Payne and D.S. [Daniel Sabin] Butrick, *The Payne-Butrick Papers, Volumes 1,2,3*, ed. William L. Anderson, Jane L. Brown, and Anne F. Rogers (Lincoln: University of Nebraska Press, 2010), 45.

32. Thomas Robbins, *A View of All Religions; and the Religious Ceremonies of All Nations at the Present Day*, 3rd ed. (Hartford, CT: Oliver D. Cooke & Sons, 1824), II: 162; "From the New York Sun: The Jews and American Aborigines," *Connecticut Courant*, October 7, 1837, Readex: Early American Newspapers.

33. Genesis 3:15

34. "Epitome of Lowman's Hebrew Ritual," *Panoplist and Missionary Magazine* 3, no. 3 (August 1810): 86–90.

35. Ambrose Serle, *Horae Solitariae; or, Essays upon Some Remarkable Names and Titles of Jesus Christ, Occurring in the Old Testament*, 1st American, from the 2nd London ed. (Philadelphia: Patterson and Cochran, 1799).

36. Boudinot, *A Star in the West*, 193.

37. Z. "Religious Communications: On Christian Zeal," *Panoplist* 3, no. 1 (June 1807): 8–13, ProQuest American Periodicals Series II.

38. See Laura M. Stevens' discussion of pity in earlier British missions, Laura Stevens, *The Poor Indians: British Missionaries, Native Americans, and Colonial Sensibility* (Philadelphia: University of Pennsylvania Press, 2004). These quotations are from student essays on ethics written by Joseph Patterson, a Presbyterian pastor, in the early nineteenth century. "Joseph Patterson Notebooks" (1803–1883), Blandina Diedrich Collection, William L. Clements Library, The University of Michigan.

39. Sophia Sawyer to Linda Raymond Ward Kingsbury, May 24, 1824, Sophia Sawyer Papers, Duane Norman Diedrich Collection, William L. Clements Library, The University of Michigan.

40. Morse, *The American Universal Geography*, 76–77.

41. Leviticus 16: 1–34, 23:26–32, Numbers 29: 7–11. I use the English translation "the Day of Atonement" because the holiday by that name described in the Bible is distinct from the rabbinic Jewish holiday of Yom Kippur (lit. "day of atonement").

42. Charles Hudson, *Elements of Southeastern Indian Religion* (Leiden, Netherlands: E.J. Brill, 1984); Mary C. Churchill, "The Oppositional Paradigm of Purity versus Pollution in Charles Hudson's: 'The Southeastern Indians,'" *American Indian Quarterly* 20, no. 3/4 (July 1, 1996): 563–93; Charles Hudson, "Reply to Mary Churchill," *American Indian Quarterly* 24, no. 3 (July 1, 2000): 494–502.

43. Leviticus 16: 1–18.

44. Boudinot, *A Star in the West*, 221.

45. Ethan Smith, *View of the Hebrews*, 2nd ed. (1825; repr., Provo, UT: Religious Studies Center, Brigham Young University, 1996), 73–74.

46. Boudinot, *A Star in the West*, 215–16.

47. Stevens, *The Poor Indians*, 20–22.

48. T. Charlton Henry, *A Plea for the West: A Sermon Preached before the Missionary Society of the Synod of South-Carolina and Georgia in Augusta, November 21, 1824* (Charleston, SC: W.M. Riley, 1824).

49. "Millennial" and "millennialism" here refer to the belief in a thousand-year period of peace accompanying the return of Jesus. There has been substantial disagreement among Christian groups about the timing and literal reality of the millennium. In general, Protestant reformers in the early United States anticipated that this millennium would be a thousand-year reign of a perfected Christian society, after which Jesus would return. Tuveson, *Redeemer Nation*; Ruth Bloch, *Visionary Republic: Millennial Themes in American Thought, 1756–1800* (Cambridge: Cambridge University Press, 1985); Gin Lum, *Damned Nation*.

50. Jacob Lindley, Joseph Moore, and Oliver Paxton, "Expedition to Detroit, 1793," *Michigan Pioneer and Historical Society Collections* 17 (1890): 597.

51. Unfortunately, Lindley did not record the reaction of his host, the prominent fur trader John Askin, to his argument. Askin had his first three children, at least some of whom would have been present at dinner, with an enslaved Indigenous woman whom he called Manette or Monette. The term used for her in the existing records, *sauvage panis*, could indicate that she was Pawnee, but *panis* was a generic enough term that it is impossible to be certain. Brett Rushforth, "'A Little Flesh We Offer You': The Origins of Indian Slavery in New France," in *American Encounters: Natives and Newcomers from European Contact to Indian Removal, 1500–1850*, ed. Peter Mancall and James Merrell, 2nd ed. (New York: Routledge, 2007), 455–82. David R. Farrell, "Askin, John," in *Dictionary of Canadian Biography*, vol. 5 (Toronto, ON: University of Toronto/Université Laval, 1983).

52. Boudinot, *A Star in the West*, 309.

53. Harriet Livermore, *The Harp of Israel: To Meet the Loud Echo in the Wilds of America* (Philadelphia: J. Rakestraw, 1835), 171. The phrase intentionally echoes Numbers 24:9.

54. Morgan, "American Slavery, American Freedom"; Joyce Appleby, *Inheriting the Revolution: The First Generation of Americans* (Cambridge, MA: Harvard University Press, 2000); Harry Watson, *Liberty and Power: The Politics of Jacksonian America* (New York: Hill and Wang, 2006); Peter Onuf, "Imperial-

ism and Nationalism in the Early American Republic"; Johnson, *African American Religions, 1500–2000*, 1–12.

55. Daniel Vickers, "Competency and Competition: Economic Culture in Early America," *William and Mary Quarterly* 47, no. 1 (January, 1990): 3–29; Hietala, *Manifest Design: American Exceptionalism and Empire*, 55, 170–72; Alan Taylor, *The Divided Ground: Indians, Settlers and the Northern Borderland of the American Revolution* (New York: Alfred A. Knopf, 2006); Bowes, *Land Too Good for Indians: Northern Indian Removal*; Karp, *This Vast Southern Empire*; Nancy Isenberg, *White Trash: The 400-Year Untold History of Class in America* (New York: Viking, 2016), 64–134.

56. Washington Irving, "Traits of Indian Character," *Analectic Magazine* 3 (February 1814): 145–56, American Historical Periodicals from the American Antiquarian Society, Gale Cengage. See also Boudinot, *A Star in the West*, xvii–xviii. The quotation "the roar is up . . ." is from John Milton's *Comus*, a 1634 masque often reprinted throughout the eighteenth century.

57. Eustace, *Passion Is the Gale*.

58. Haselby's characterization of this northeastern style of Christian nationalism as "anti-racist" misses the hierarchy that White evangelicals still imagined between themselves and non-White people. Haselby, *The Origins of American Religious Nationalism*, 1–20.

59. Guyatt, *Providence and the Invention of the United States, 1607–1876*, 173–74.

60. Boudinot, *A Star in the West*, 300.

61. As quoted in ibid., 294–95. In the Authorized Version, the verse opens "Woe to the land of whirring wings along the rivers of Cush" before continuing in the same vein as Boudinot's. It is possible that Boudinot's interpretation of this passage also drew on John McDonald, *Isaiah's Message to the American Nation, a New Translation of Isaiah, Chapter XVIII with Notes Critical and Explanatory, A Remarkable Prophecy, Respecting the Restoration of the Jews Aided by the American Nation; with An Universal Summons to the Battle of Armageddon, and a Description of That Solemn Scene* (Albany, NY: E. & E. Hosford, 1814). McDonald's is the earliest work I have found that identifies the United States with Faber's nation "spreading the shadow of thy wings" and deduces that America must restore the Jews to Israel.

62. Boudinot, "Commonplace Book," II:28.

63. Boudinot, *A Star in the West*, 297–98.

64. Charles Crawford, *An Essay on the Propagation of the Gospel*, 2nd ed. (James Humphreys, 1801), 26–29.

65. Smith, *View of the Hebrews*, 199, 202.

66. Nicholas Guyatt, *Bind Us Apart*.

Chapter 2. The Remnant of Joseph

1. The largest church tracing its roots to the ministry of Joseph Smith, the Church of Jesus Christ of Latter-day Saints, recently rejected the use of the term

"Mormon." I use the terms "Mormon" and "Mormon movement" because they are the best I can find that include all those who embraced the Book of Mormon as scripture, whether or not they belonged to the subset of the movement that became the Church of Jesus Christ of Latter-day Saints. Unfortunately, even to choose the preferred term "Latter-day saint" would reinforce this church's view of itself as the sole legitimate inheritor of Smith's movement, since "Latter Day Saint" is preferred in the Community of Christ (formerly the Reorganized Church of Jesus Christ of Latter Day Saints), the second-largest contemporary church stemming from Smith's teachings. For the theological reasoning behind the Church of Jesus Christ of Latter-day Saints' decision, see Russell M. Nelson, "The Correct Name of the Church," a talk given at the General Conference of the Church of Jesus Christ of Latter-day Saints, Salt Lake City, UT, September 2018, https://www.churchofjesuschrist.org/study/general -conference/2018/10/the-correct-name-of-the-church?lang=eng.

2. Fawn Brodie, *No Man Knows My History: The Life of Joseph Smith*, 2nd ed. (New York: Alfred A. Knopf, 1971), 208–10; Glen Leonard, *Nauvoo: A Place of Peace, a People of Promise* (Salt Lake City, UT: Brigham Young University Press, 2002); Bushman, *Joseph Smith*, 322–41.

3. Thomas Burdick to JS, "Letter," August 28, 1840, Joseph Smith's Letterbook 2, 174–76, Joseph Smith Papers. Early Mormons often had irregular educations, and many of the early documents contain numerous misspellings and grammatical mistakes. To cut down on the number of times I insert [sic], I silently correct some spelling errors that were obvious slips of the pen or of the transcriber's fingers—such as "theri" for "their"—and occasionally emend or insert in brackets common words such as pronouns, auxiliary verbs, and conjunctions that were omitted or misspelled in the original.

4. In the period from 1830 to 1847 covered in this chapter, Mormons regarded "Lamanites" and "Indians" as synonyms and identified places described in the Book of Mormon with locations in North America. Subsequent generations, however, have located the events of the Book of Mormon elsewhere. Today, Mormons who explicitly identify a modern population of people with Lamanites more often name Indigenous peoples of the Pacific or Central and South America. John-Charles Duffy, "The Use of 'Lamanite' in Official LDS Discourse," *Journal of Mormon History* 34, no. 1 (Winter 2008): 118–67. In addition, some Mormons with Indigenous ancestry from the Pacific or the Americas now claim Lamanite identity and ascribe a positive meaning to it that is often absent from White Mormons' discussion of the issue. See Thayne, "The Blood of Father Lehi: Indigenous Americans and the Book of Mormon."

5. 3 Nephi 21:12. The prophecy is also given in 3 Nephi 20:14–20. Both passages echo Micah 5:7–8.

6. Burdick to JS, "Letter," August 28, 1840.

7. Lori Elaine Taylor estimates that about a dozen Indigenous people became Mormons before 1847. Lori Elaine Taylor, "Elder Nigeajasha and Other Mormon Indians Moving Westward," *John Whitmer Historical Association Journal* 24 (2004): 112–13. See also G. St. John Stott, "New Jerusalem Aban-

doned: The Failure to Carry Mormonism to the Delaware," *Journal of American Studies* 21, no. 1 (April 1987): 71–85; Ronald W. Walker, "Seeking the 'Remnant': The Native American during the Joseph Smith Period," *Journal of Mormon History* 19, no. 1 (April 1, 1993): 1–33; Taylor, "Telling Stories About Mormons and Indians," 138–54, 161–302.

8. Terryl Givens, *By the Hand of Mormon: The American Scripture That Launched a New World Religion* (New York: Oxford University Press, 2002); Bushman, *Joseph Smith*; Maffly-Kipp, "Introduction."

9. Book of Mormon, Jacob 1: 13–14

10. Grant Hardy, *Understanding the Book of Mormon: A Reader's Guide* (New York: Oxford University Press, 2010), 3–30.

11. Givens, *By the Hand of Mormon*, 90–91; Duffy, "The Use of 'Lamanite' in Official LDS Discourse."

12. The phrase "a history of the origin of the Indians" comes from an early Mormon mission, see Dan Vogel, ed., *Early Mormon Documents* (Salt Lake City, UT: Signature Books, 1996), 1: 419. "A record of the aborigines of America" comes from an idealized missionary dialogue printed in *Times and Seasons* in 1841. "Dialogue on Mormonism II," *Times and Seasons*, July 15, 1841, Mormon Publications: 19th and 20th Centuries, Brigham Young University, Harold B. Lee Library Digital Collections. "A full account . . ." comes from the autobiography of Phineas Howe Young, reprinted in Vogel, ed., *Early Mormon Documents*, 3: 353. Young wrote his autobiography in 1863, but the incident in question occurred in 1830.

13. Brodie, *No Man Knows My History: The Life of Joseph Smith*; Vogel, *Indian Origins and the Book of Mormon*; Givens, *By the Hand of Mormon*; Bushman, *Joseph Smith*.

14. On these complexities, see Maffly-Kipp, "Introduction"; Hardy, *Understanding the Book of Mormon*.

15. Doctrine and Covenants 57; Grant Underwood, *The Millenarian World of Early Mormonism* (Urbana: University of Illinois Press, 1993), 40–41, 80–83; Givens, *By the Hand of Mormon*, 69–71; Bushman, *Joseph Smith*, 387–88, 511–12.

16. Joseph Smith, "A Book of Commandments, for the Government of the Church of Christ, Organized According to Law, on the 6th of April, 1830," 1833, 68, 129, Joseph Smith Papers, https://www.josephsmithpapers.org/paper-summary/book-of-commandments-1833/1.

17. Bowes, *Land Too Good for Indians*.

18. Henry Caswall, *The City of the Mormons; or, Three Days at Nauvoo, in 1842*, 2nd ed. (London: J. G. F. & J. Rivington, 1843), 10–12.

19. Book of Mormon, 2 Nephi 10:18–19

20. Mauss, *All Abraham's Children*, 50–55, 268–69; Fenella Cannell, "The Blood of Abraham: Mormon Redemptive Physicality and American Idioms of Kinship," *Journal of the Royal Anthropological Institute* 19, no. 1 (May 2013): 77–94; Coviello, *Make Yourselves Gods*, 52–88, 193–200.

21. Bushman, *Joseph Smith*, 564–89; Joseph Smith, "A Book of Commandments & Revelations of the Lord given to Joseph the Seer & Others by the Inspiration of God & gift & power of the Holy Ghost which Beareth Re[c]ord of

the Father & Son & Holy Ghost which is one God Infinite & eternal World without end Amen [Revelation Book 1]," March 1831, 191, Joseph Smith Papers, https://www.josephsmithpapers.org/paper-summary/revelation-book-1/179. Cf. Doctrine and Covenants 103.

22. Joseph Smith, Willard Richards, and Thomas Bullock, "History, 1838–1856, Volume A-1 [23 December 1805–30 August 1834]," 1843, 482–83, Joseph Smith Papers, https://www.josephsmithpapers.org/paper-summary/history-1838–1856-volume-a-1-23-december-1805–30-august-1834/1.

23. Doctrine and Covenants 57

24. Smith, Richards, and Bullock, "History, 1838–1856, Volume A-1," 482–83.

25. Book of Mormon, Mosiah 9:12–10:12, 2 Nephi 5:21

26. Farmer, On Zion's Mount, 58.

27. One writer in the missionary publication The Panoplist, for example, argued that Christian education lightened skin because skin color came from environment more than descent. "I have seen a young Indian woman, who had been educated in the manner, in which young women . . . are educated among ourselves. Her father was one of the darkest colored Aborigines: yet the daughter was as fair, as a considerable number of persons of her own sex, who have descended from English ancestors." "Lectures on the Evidences of Divine Revelation, No. XVI," Panoplist and Missionary Magazine 9, no. 2 (July 1813): 50–56, American Historical Periodicals from the American Antiquarian Society, Gale Cengage.

28. Conn, History's Shadow; Christopher Heaney, "A Peru of Their Own: English Grave-Opening and Indian Sovereignty in Early America," William and Mary Quarterly 73, no. 4 (October 2016): 609–46.

29. There is a rich literature on Mormonism and race. See, especially, Mauss, All Abraham's Children; Cannell, "The Blood of Abraham"; Reeve, Religion of a Different Color; Coviello, Make Yourselves Gods; Mueller, Race and the Making of the Mormon People.

30. Because I focus on the question of what early Mormons did with their sacred history, I leave open the question of what the Book of Mormon itself does or may be read to do in the context of American racism. For explorations of this second question, see Bushman, Joseph Smith, 94–95; Jared Hickman, "The Book of Mormon as Amerindian Apocalypse," American Literatures 86, no. 3 (September 2014): 429–61; Coviello, Make Yourselves Gods 135–170.

31. M[atthew] S. C[lapp], "Mormonism," Painesville [Ohio] Telegraph 2, no. 35 (February 15, 1831), http://www.sidneyrigdon.com/dbroadhu/OH/painte12.htm. My interpretation of early Mormon Lamanite exercises draws on Christopher C. Smith, "Playing Lamanite: Ecstatic Performance of American Indian Roles in Early Mormon Ohio," Journal of Mormon History 41, no. 3 (2015): 131–66.

32. Smith, "Playing Lamanite."

33. On revivalism in America, see John Wigger, Taking Heaven by Storm: Methodism and the Rise of Popular Christianity in America (New York: Oxford University Press, 1998); Leigh Eric Schmidt, Holy Fairs: Scotland and the Making of

American Revivalism, 2nd ed. (Grand Rapids, MI: William B. Eerdmans, 2001). On revival as a scripted or performed act, see John Corrigan, *Business of the Heart: Religion and Emotion in the Nineteenth Century* (Berkeley: University of California Press, 2001); Eitler and Scheer, "Emotionengeschichte Als Körpergeschichte."

34. This section draws on my article, Dougherty, "None Can Deliver: Imagining Lamanites and Feeling Mormon, 1837–1847."

35. Smith, "Playing Lamanite," 158–62; Reeve, *Religion of a Different Color*, 60. Such spiritual gifts were a key concern for early Mormons. See Underwood, *The Millenarian World of Early Mormonism*.

36. Parley P. Pratt, *A Voice of Warning and Instruction to All People: Containing a Declaration of the Faith and Doctrine of the Church of the Latter-Day Saints, Commonly Called Mormons* (New York: W. Standford, 1837), 180.

37. Pratt, *A Voice of Warning and Instruction*, 186.

38. Pratt, *A Voice of Warning and Instruction*, 190–91.

39. Pratt, *A Voice of Warning and Instruction*, 191.

40. Lauren Berlant, "Cruel Optimism," in *The Affect Theory Reader*, ed. Melissa Gregg and Gregory J. Seigworth (Durham, NC: Duke University Press, 2010). See also Dougherty, "None Can Deliver: Imagining Lamanites and Feeling Mormon, 1837–1847."

41. Stephen LeSueur, *The 1838 Mormon War in Missouri* (Columbia: University of Missouri Press, 1987); T. Ward Frampton, "'Some Savage Tribe': Race, Legal Violence, and the Mormon War of 1838," *Journal of Mormon History* 40, no. 1 (Winter 2014): 175–207.

42. Elizabeth Haven Barlow, "Elizabeth Haven Barlow, Quincy [IL], to Elizabeth Howe Bullard, Holliston [MA], Feb. 24, 1839," in *Women's Voices: An Untold History of the Latter- Day Saints*, ed. Kenneth W. Godfrey, Audrey M. Godfrey, and Jill Mulvay Derr (Salt Lake City: Deseret Book Company, 1982), 110–11. On my identification of these "Indians," see Francis A. Chardon, *Chardon's Journal at Fort Clark, 1834–1839; Descriptive of Life on the Upper Missouri; of a Fur Trader's Experiences among the Mandans, Gros Ventres and Their Neighbors; of the Ravages of the Small-Pox Epidemic of 1837* (Pierre, SD, 1932); Roy Meyer, *The Village Indians of the Upper Missouri: The Mandans, Hidatsas, and Arikaras* (Lincoln: University of Nebraska Press, 1977); Elizabeth Fenn, *Encounters at the Heart of the World: A History of the Mandan People* (New York: Hill and Wang, 2014).

43. Eliza R. Snow, *The Personal Writings of Eliza Roxcy Snow*, ed. Maureen Ursenbach Beecher (Logan: Utah State University Press, 2000), 176.

44. This did not go unnoticed. For decades, accusations that Mormons intended to collude with Indigenous people to destroy White settlers were part of anti-Mormon discourses questioning their racial fitness for citizenship. Reeve, *Religion of a Different Color*, 52–74.

45. Matthew J. Grow et al., eds., "Volume Introduction: The Council of Fifty in Nauvoo, Illinois," in *Council of Fifty, Minutes, March 1844–January 1846*, Joseph Smith Papers, Administrative Records (Salt Lake City, UT: The Church Historian's Press, 2016), xl–xlv; Benjamin E. Park, "Joseph Smith's Kingdom

of God: The Council of Fifty and the Mormon Challenge to American Democratic Politics," *Church History* 87, no. 4 (December 2018): 1029–55.

46. Matthew J. Grow et al., eds., *Council of Fifty, Minutes, March 1844–January 1846*, Joseph Smith Papers, Administrative Records (Salt Lake City, UT: The Church Historian's Press, 2016), 275–76.

47. Grow et al., *Council of Fifty*, 283–84.

48. Benedict Anderson, *Imagined Communities*, rev. ed. (New York: Verso, 2006), 5; David Morgan, "Emotion and Imagination in the Ritual Entanglement of Religion, Sport, and Nationalism," in *Feeling Religion*, ed. John Corrigan (Durham, NC: Duke University Press, 2017), 222–41.

49. Grow et al., *Council of Fifty*, 396, 421, 431–32, 593.

50. Grow et al., *Council of Fifty*, 283.

51. Grow et al., *Council of Fifty*, 289.

52. Grow et al., *Council of Fifty*, 275–76.

53. Joseph Smith, Willard Richards, and Thomas Bullock, "History, 1838–1856, Volume C-1 Addenda," 1841, 10–11, Joseph Smith Papers, https://www.josephsmithpapers.org/paper-summary/history-1838–1856-volume-c-1-addenda/11#facts.

54. Richard White, *The Middle Ground: Indians, Empires, and Republics in the Great Lakes Region, 1650–1815* (Cambridge: Cambridge University Press, 1991); Colin Calloway, *New Worlds for All: Indians, Europeans, and the Remaking of Early America*, 2nd ed. (Baltimore: Johns Hopkins University Press, 2013), 72, 119–35, 215–16.

55. Taylor, "Telling Stories About Mormons and Indians," 197–212.

56. Grow et al., *Council of Fifty*, 306.

57. Grow et al., *Council of Fifty*, 323–24, 461–62; Taylor, "Telling Stories About Mormons and Indians," 245–52.

58. Grow et al., *Council of Fifty*, 356.

59. Grow et al., *Council of Fifty*, 303.

60. Taylor, "Telling Stories About Mormons and Indians," 261–67; Farmer, *On Zion's Mount*, 58–60.

61. On the relationship between competition for resources and tensions between Great Basin peoples and Mormon settlers during this period, see Farmer, *On Zion's Mount*, 62–77.

62. Grow et al., *Council of Fifty*, 189–215.

63. Farmer, *On Zion's Mount*, 92–100.

64. The process summarized here was not completed until the 1890 abandonment of plural marriage. See Coviello, *Make Yourselves Gods*, 171–214.

65. Taylor, "Elder Nigeajasha and Other Mormon Indians Moving Westward," 113; Mueller, *Race and the Making of the Mormon People*, 125. Taylor identifies Herring and his brother Joseph as Mohawks, whereas Mueller identifies the brothers as men of mixed Shawnee and White descent.

66. Daniel Spencer, a member of the Council who met with Dana that summer, claimed he told him that "the Cherokees had given permission for any number of our people to settle by them, and offered to lend us any assistance they could either to locate or to go West to explore." I have not found any mention of

this offer in Cherokee Nation records, and Spencer may have been confused. Dana was in contact with the Cherokee leader John Brown, who had formerly led the "Old Settler" Cherokees who voluntarily relocated to the Indian Territory before the majority of the Cherokee were forced westward on the infamous Trail of Tears in 1838. After 1838, the Old Settlers reintegrated into the new Cherokee Nation, though not always smoothly. Brown had lost his leadership position by 1845, and so may have extended such an offer in the hopes that an alliance with the Mormons would increase his standing in the Nation. Grow et al., *Council of Fifty*, 468–71.

67. Dunham and Dana planned for their mission to be to the Oneida but turned to the Lenape after the Oneidas, who settled in what is now Kansas, left almost immediately because the conditions were too harsh. Taylor, "Elder Nigeajasha and Other Mormon Indians Moving Westward."

68. Hyde was trying to convince Young that he should remain in Iowa rather than visit Salt Lake City, so he was possibly exaggerating the reach of "Indian Cutlerism" to avoid a long trip that might undermine his interests in Iowa. Orson Hyde to Brigham Young, April 27, 1850, Brigham Young office files, 1832–1878 (bulk 1844–1877); General Correspondence, Incoming, 1840–1877; Letters from Church Leaders and Others, 1840–1877; Orson Hyde, 1850–1851, Church History Library, https://catalog.churchofjesuschrist.org/assets?id=0e7f9f2c-478a-4995-af57-70863b90f230&crate=0&index=1.

69. Richard E. Bennett, "Lamanism, Lymanism and Cornfields," *Journal of Mormon History* 13 (1986): 44–59; Danny L Jorgensen, "Building the Kingdom of God: Alpheus Cutler and the Second Mormon Mission to the Indians, 1846–1853," *Kansas History* 15, no. 3 (Autumn 1992): 192–209; Danny L Jorgensen, "Conflict in the Camps of Israel: The 1853 Cutlerite Schism," *Journal of Mormon History* 21, no. 1 (1995): 25–64; Taylor, "Elder Nigeajasha and Other Mormon Indians Moving Westward"; Grow et al., *Council of Fifty*, 593.

70. Missions to Indigenous people continued for some time but came over time to hew closer to dominant White American pessimism about "Indians." See Mueller, *Race and the Making of the Mormon People*, 153–80.

Chapter 3. Our Common Father

1. Gura, *The Life of William Apess, Pequot*, 129.

2. James Gordon Bennett, "A Rabbi in the Rostrum," *Herald* [New York], February 14, 1837, Nineteenth Century U.S. Newspapers, Gale Cengage; Mordecai M. Noah to Robert H. Pruyn, Esq., March 20, 1837, Mordecai Manuel Noah, papers, P-75, box 1, folder 5, American Jewish Historical Society, New York; Mordecai M. Noah, *Discourse on the Evidences of the American Indians Being the Descendants of the Lost Tribes of Israel: Delivered before the Mercantile Library Association, Clinton Hall* (New York: James Van Norden, 1837).

3. James Gordon Bennett, "Rabbi Noah at a Discount," *Herald* [New York], March 8, 1837, Nineteenth Century U.S. Newspapers, Gale Cengage. Gura, *The Life of William Apess, Pequot*, 123–31; Daniel Radus, "Apess's Eulogy

on Tour: Kinship and the Transnational History of Native New England," *Studies in American Indian Literatures* 28, no. 3 (Fall 2016): 81–110. On Metacom, see Pulsipher, *Subjects unto the Same King.* On Sganyodaiyo, see Handsome Lake and Arthur Caswell Parker, *The Code of Handsome Lake, the Seneca Prophet* (Albany, NY: University of the State of New York, 1913); Wallace, *The Death and Rebirth of the Seneca.*

4. Waldstreicher, *In the Midst of Perpetual Fetes*; Watson, *Liberty and Power*; Griffin, *American Leviathan*, 241–71; Adam Dahl, *Empire of the People: Settler Colonialism and the Foundations of Modern Democratic Thought* (Lawrence: University Press of Kansas, 2018).

5. Egal Feldman, *Dual Destinies: The Jewish Encounter with Protestant America* (Urbana: University of Illinois Press, 1990); Frederic Jaher, *A Scapegoat in the New Wilderness: The Origins and Rise of Anti-Semitism in America* (Cambridge, MA: Harvard University Press, 1994); Noel Ignatiev, *How the Irish Became White* (New York: Routledge, 1995); Matthew Jacobson, *Whiteness of a Different Color: European Immigrants and the Alchemy of Race* (Cambridge, MA: Harvard University Press, 1998); Eric Goldstein, *The Price of Whiteness: Jews, Race, and American Identity* (Princeton, NJ: Princeton University Press, 2006); Tracy Fessenden, *Culture and Redemption: Religion, the Secular, and American Literature* (Princeton, NJ: Princeton University Press, 2007).

6. Kevin Bruyneel theorized this "third space" between local and national powers as a fruitful site for the creation of Indigenous sovereignty. See Kevin Bruyneel, *The Third Space of Sovereignty: The Postcolonial Politics of U.S.–Indigenous Relations* (Minneapolis: University of Minnesota Press, 2007). On local and federal power in expansion, see Andrew Cayton and Peter S. Onuf, *The Midwest and the Nation: Rethinking the History of an American Region* (Bloomington: Indiana University Press, 1990); Taylor, *The Divided Ground*; Andrew Shankman, "Conflict for a Continent: Land, Labor, and the State in the First American Republic," in *The World of the Revolutionary American Republic: Land, Labor, and the Conflict for a Continent*, ed. Andrew Shankman, Routledge Worlds (New York: Routledge, 2014), 1–24; Onuf, "Imperialism and Nationalism in the Early American Republic"; Saler, *The Settlers' Empire*; Bowes, *Land Too Good for Indians*; Lori J. Daggar, "The Mission Complex: Economic Development, 'Civilization,' and Empire in the Early Republic," *Journal of the Early Republic* 36, no. 3 (September 9, 2016): 467–91.

7. Malcom H. Stern, "The 1820s: American Jewry Comes of Age," in *A Bicentennial Festschrift for Jacob Rader Marcus*, ed. Bertram Wallace Korn (New York: KTAV Publishing, 1976); Naomi W. Cohen, *Encounter with Emancipation: The German Jews in the United States, 1830–1914* (Philadelphia: Jewish Publication Society of America, 1984); Feldman, *Dual Destinies*; Lance J. Sussman, *Isaac Leeser and the Making of American Judaism* (Detroit, MI: Wayne State University Press, 1995); Jonathan Sarna, *American Judaism: A History* (New Haven, CT: Yale University Press, 2004); William Pencak, *Jews & Gentiles in Early America: 1654–1800* (Ann Arbor: University of Michigan Press, 2005); Goldstein, *The Price of Whiteness*; Hoberman, *New Israel / New England.*

8. Jonathan Sarna, *Jacksonian Jew: The Two Worlds of Mordecai Noah* (New York: Holmes & Meier, 1981), 1–5.

9. Sarna, *Jacksonian Jew*, 5–6, 35–59, 77–96, 111–13; Appleby, *Inheriting the Revolution*. On American Jews, anti-Semitism, and the Democratic party, see Jaher, *A Scapegoat in the New Wilderness*; Pencak, *Jews & Gentiles in Early America*, 75–77. On religious affiliation and voting patterns more generally, see Swieringa, "Ethnoreligious Political Behavior in the Early Nineteenth Century," 145–68.

10. My description of whiteness and class politics in the early United States relies on Alexander Saxton, *The Rise and Fall of the White Republic: Class Politics and Mass Culture in Nineteenth-Century America* (New York: Verso, 1990); Ignatiev, *How the Irish Became White*; Jacobson, *Whiteness of a Different Color*; Appleby, *Inheriting the Revolution*, 135–42, 159–60, 262–66. On the co-constitution of religion and race in the United States, see Karen Brodkin, *How Jews Became White Folks and What That Says about Race in America* (New Brunswick, NJ: Rutgers University Press, 1998); Johnson, *The Myth of Ham in Nineteenth-Century American Christianity*; Colin Kidd, *The Forging of Races: Race and Scripture in the Protestant Atlantic World, 1600–2000* (Cambridge: Cambridge University Press, 2006); Goldstein, *The Price of Whiteness*; Edward Blum et al., "Forum on Whiteness," *Religion and American Culture: A Journal of Interpretation* 19, no. 1 (Winter 2009): 1–35; Edward Blum and Paul Harvey, *The Color of Christ: The Son of God & the Saga of Race in America* (Chapel Hill: University of North Carolina Press, 2012); Joshua Paddison, *American Heathens: Religion, Race, and Reconstruction in California* (Berkeley: University of California Press, 2012); Johnson, *African American Religions, 1500–2000*; Wenger, *Religious Freedom*; Paul Harvey, *Bounds of Their Habitation: Race and Religion in American History* (Lanham, MD: Rowman & Littlefield, 2017); Jodi Eichler-Levine, "American Judaism and Race," in *The Oxford Handbook of Religion and Race in American History*, ed. Kathryn Gin Lum and Paul Harvey (New York: Oxford University Press, 2018).

11. Beth S. Wenger, *History Lessons: The Creation of American Jewish Heritage* (Princeton, NJ: Princeton University Press, 2010), 37–41; Shalev, *American Zion*.

12. Michael Schuldiner and Daniel J. Kleinfeld, eds., "The Ararat Proclamation and Speech, The Buffalo Patriot Vol. VIII Buffalo, Tuesday September 20, 1825," in *The Selected Writings of Mordecai Noah* (Westport, CT: Greenwood Press, 1999), 106.

13. Mordecai M. Noah, "Signed Petition by M.M. Noah for Insolvency, Accomplished and Signed by Noah, Countersigned by Richard Riker," March 5, 1824, New York, Mordecai Manuel Noah, papers, P-75, box 1, folder 2, American Jewish Historical Society, New York; Mordecai M. Noah to Peter B. Porter, "New York," August 17, 1824, HH-11, Peter B. Porter Papers, Buffalo and Erie County Historical Society, Buffalo, NY.

14. Louis Ruchames, "Mordecai Manuel Noah and Early American Zionism," *American Jewish Historical Quarterly* 64, no. 3 (March 1975): 195–223;

Sarna, *Jacksonian Jew*, 61–75; Cohen, *Encounter with Emancipation*, 291; Sussman, *Isaac Leeser and the Making of American Judaism*, 144.

15. Schuldiner and Kleinfeld, "The Ararat Proclamation," 109.

16. Schuldiner and Kleinfeld, "The Ararat Proclamation," 107, 109. This tax would have been $1 in U.S. currency as well, since the Coinage Act of 1792 pegged the value of the U.S. dollar to the Spanish dollar.

17. Historians disagree both over how serious a project Ararat was and over how independent Noah believed it should be from the authority of the United States. Following Eran Shalev, I view Noah's ambiguity on this point as strategic. He likely wanted to see how much independence he could win for Ararat rather than commit himself to one position. See Eran Shalev, "'Revive, Renew, and Reestablish': Mordecai Noah's Ararat and the Limits of Biblical Imagination in the Early American Republic," *American Jewish Archives Journal* 62, no. 1 (2010): 1–20. Other arguments for Ararat as a serious political proposal appear in Sarna, *Jacksonian Jew*, 61–65; Feldman, *Dual Destinies*, 61–62. The most convincing arguments that Noah did not mean Ararat as a serious proposal have argued that it was an assertion of Jewish identity meant to impress and convince but not necessarily to found a polity. These interpretations, however, underestimate both the chaotic state of American expansion, which would have made a semi-independent Jewish state in North America seem more possible, and the extent of Noah's investment in the project. S. Joshua Kohn, "Mordecai Manuel Noah's Ararat Project and the Missionaries," *American Jewish Historical Quarterly* 55, no. 2 (December 1, 1965); Rubinstein, *Members of the Tribe*, 18; Linsley, "Saving the Jews."

18. Waldstreicher, *In the Midst of Perpetual Fetes*; Peter Coviello, "Agonizing Affection: Affect and Nation in Early America," *Early American Literature* 37, no. 3 (2002): 439–68; Anderson, *Imagined Communities*; Scheer, "Are Emotions a Kind of Practice (and Is That What Makes Them Have a History)?"; Morgan, "Emotion and Imagination in the Ritual Entanglement of Religion, Sport, and Nationalism."

19. Noah to Porter, "New York," August 17, 1824.

20. Noah would likely have understood the resonances of Masonic ceremonies, since he became a third degree, or Master Mason, in New York City's Independent Royal Arch Lodge No. 2 on March 25, 1825. R.W. William Duncan, *A History of Independent Royal Arch Lodge No. 2 F&AM of the State of New York* (New York, 1904), 274. Samuel Oppenheim, "The Jews and Masonry in the United States Before 1810," *Publications of the American Jewish Historical Society*, 19 (January 1, 1910), 1–94. The lodge records are not clear about Noah's degree, but since he is listed as a full member he was probably raised to the Master Mason degree that granted full membership in the lodge on that date. Despite its name, Independent Royal Arch Lodge No. 2 did not confer the Royal Arch degrees. Sarna, *Jacksonian Jew*, 186, n. 17.

21. Nathan R. Perl-Rosenthal, "The 'Divine Right of Republics': Hebraic Republicanism and the Debate over Kingless Government in Revolutionary America," *William and Mary Quarterly*, 3rd ser., 66, no. 3 (July 2009): 535–64; Wenger, *History Lessons*, 37–41; Shalev, *American Zion*.

22. "Regeneration of the Jews," *New-York National Advocate*, January 17, 1826: 1, Readex: America's Historical Newspapers. The original letter appeared in the *Journal des Débats*. Noah republished the letter in the *New-York National Advocate*, of which he was then the editor, in part to frame European rabbis' opposition to his plan as "efforts of the old governments" holding back Jewish immigration to America and in part out of the sense that any publicity was good publicity.

23. Noah wrote in 1833 to the New York comptroller asking if he owned land on Grand Island, and his confusion has sometimes been taken as evidence that he never bought any land there. However, his contemporary Lewis F. Allen claimed that the gas lighting magnate Samuel Leggett bought Noah two and a half thousand acres on Grand Island. If this were true, Noah might have been confused as to whether Leggett had transferred the title to him or retained it himself and would have had reason to investigate when Allen bought Leggett's holdings on the island that same year. Mordecai M. Noah to A.C. Flagg, November 19, 1833, Mordecai Manuel Noah, papers, P-75, box 1, folder 4, American Jewish Historical Society, New York; Lewis F. Allen, "The Story of the Tablet of the City of Ararat," in *The Book of the Museum*, by Frank H. Severance, vol. 25, Publications of the Buffalo Historical Society (Buffalo, NY: Buffalo Historical Society, 1921), 113–22, 134.

24. Schuldiner and Kleinfeld, "The Ararat Proclamation," 109.

25. Sarna, *Jacksonian Jew*, 110–14; Rubinstein, *Members of the Tribe*, 34.

26. Schuldiner and Kleinfeld, "The Ararat Proclamation," 110, 122–23.

27. William Hutchison, *Errand to the World: American Protestant Thought and Foreign Missions* (Chicago: University of Chicago Press, 1987); Conroy-Krutz, *Christian Imperialism*.

28. This reading builds on earlier analyses of Noah's Jewish nationalism in Rubinstein, *Members of the Tribe*, 27, 34.

29. Koffman, *The Jews' Indian*, 1–5.

30. Rubinstein, *Members of the Tribe*; Imhoff, "Wild Tribes and Ancient Semites"; Koffman, *The Jews' Indian*.

31. Noah to Porter, "New York," August 17, 1824. The number twenty-three is established in Mishnah Sanhedrin 1:6, although Noah may also have been thinking of the larger Grand Sanhedrin in Paris that met under Napoleon in 1808. Abraham was the nephew of Gershom Mendes Seixas, the respected and influential cantor of New York's Congregation Shearith Israel. Ruchames, "Mordecai Manuel Noah and Early American Zionism." See also Allen, "The Story of the Tablet of the City of Ararat"; "Genealogy" (n.d.), Seixas Family Papers, box 1, folder 4, American Jewish Historical Society, New York.

32. Sarna, *Jacksonian Jew*, 72–75.

33. Allen, "The Story of the Tablet of the City of Ararat," 135.

34. John Prentiss, "Variety," *New Hampshire Sentinel*, November 18, 1825, Readex: America's Historical Newspapers.

35. Allen, "The Story of the Tablet of the City of Ararat," 119.

36. Feldman, *Dual Destinies;* Linsley, "Saving the Jews."

37. Schuldiner and Kleinfeld, "The Ararat Proclamation," 122–23.

38. Noah, *Discourse on the Evidences of the American Indians Being the Descendants of the Lost Tribes of Israel*, 28.

39. Alex Zakaras, "Nature, Religion, and the Market in Jacksonian Political Thought," *Journal of the Early Republic* 39, no. 1 (Spring 2019); Reginald Horsman, "The Dimensions of an 'Empire for Liberty': Expansionism and Republicanism, 1775–1825," *Journal of the Early Republic* 9, no. 1 (Spring 1989).

40. Robert Berkhofer, *The White Man's Indian: Images of the American Indian, from Columbus to the Present* (New York: Vintage Books, 1979); Philip Deloria, *Playing Indian* (New Haven, CT: Yale University Press, 1998), 38–70.

41. Noah, *Discourse on the Evidences of the American Indians Being the Descendants of the Lost Tribes of Israel*, 8.

42. Bryan C. Rindfleisch, "'What It Means to Be a Man': Contested Masculinity in the Early Republic and Antebellum America," *History Compass* 10, no. 11 (November 2012): 852–65; Nicole Eustace, *1812: War and the Passions of Patriotism*. (Philadelphia: University of Pennsylvania Press, 2012).

43. Sander Gilman, *The Jew's Body* (New York: Routledge, 1991); Daniel Boyarin, *Unheroic Conduct: The Rise of Heterosexuality and the Invention of the Jewish Man* (Berkeley: University of California Press, 1997); Sarah Imhoff, *Masculinity and the Making of American Judaism* (Bloomington: Indiana University Press, 2017).

44. Jenna Supp-Montgomery, "Affect and the Study of Religion," *Religion Compass* 9, no. 10 (2015): 335–45; Morgan, "Emotion and Imagination in the Ritual Entanglement of Religion, Sport, and Nationalism."

45. Jean O'Brien, *Dispossession by Degrees: Indian Land and Identity in Natick, Massachusetts, 1650–1790* (Cambridge: Cambridge University Press, 1997); Lisa Brooks, *The Common Pot: The Recovery of Native Space in the Northeast* (Minneapolis: University of Minnesota Press, 2008); Jean O'Brien, *Firsting and Lasting: Writing Indians out of Existence in New England* (Minneapolis: University of Minnesota Press, 2010); Nancy Shoemaker, "Mr. Tashtego: Native American Whalemen in Antebellum New England," *Journal of the Early Republic* 33, no. 1 (Spring 2013): 109–32.

46. Barry O'Connell, "Introduction," in *On Our Own Ground: The Complete Writings of William Apess, a Pequot* (Amherst: University of Massachusetts Press, 1992), xiii–lxxix; Jace Weaver, *That the People Might Live: Native American Literatures and Native American Community* (New York: Oxford University Press, 1997); Wyss, *Writing Indians*; Maureen Konkle, *Writing Indian Nations: Native Intellectuals and the Politics of Historiography, 1827–1863* (Chapel Hill: University of North Carolina Press, 2004); Robert Warrior, *The People and the Word: Reading Native Nonfiction* (Minneapolis: University of Minnesota Press, 2005); Brooks, *The Common Pot*, 163–97; O'Brien, *Firsting and Lasting*, 180–90. Apess's most obvious predecessor is Samson Occum, the eighteenth-century Mohegan minister and author. See Samson Occom, *Samson Occom: Collected Writings from a Founder of Native American Literature*, ed. Joanna Brooks (New York: University Press, 2006).

47. Linford Fisher, *The Indian Great Awakening: Religion and the Shaping of Native Cultures in Early America* (New York: Oxford University Press, 2012); Lin-

ford Fisher, "An Indian Bible and A Brass Hawk: Land, Sachemship Disputes, and Power in the Conversion of Ben Uncas II," *Journal of Social History* 47, no. 2 (Winter 2013): 319–43; David Silverman, *Red Brethren: The Brothertown and Stockbridge Indians and the Problem of Race in Early America* (Ithaca, NY: Cornell University Press, 2010); Steven W. Hackel and Hilary Wyss, "Hendrick Apaumut: Christian-Mahican Prophet," in *Native Americans, Christianity, and the Reshaping of the American Religious Landscape*, ed. Joel W. Martin and Mark A. Nicholas (Chapel Hill: University of North Carolina Press, 2010).

48. Apess's exact ecclesiastical rank is not entirely clear. Carl Benn argues that Apess was likely a lay preacher, not an ordained minister. The distinction was that lay preachers could give sermons but not perform marriages or lead communion services. Carl Benn, ed., *Native Memoirs from the War of 1812: Black Hawk and William Apess* (Baltimore: Johns Hopkins University Press, 2014), 88, 154–55 n. 19.

49. During these four years, Apess published two editions of his autobiography, *A Son of the Forest* (1829, 1831); a sermon, *The Increase of the Kingdom of Christ* (1831), which he published along with an essay entitled "The Indians: The Ten Lost Tribes;" and *The Experiences of Five Christian Indians of the Pequot Tribe* (1833), which included an essay entitled "An Indian's Looking-Glass for the White Man." *A Son of the Forest*, "The Indians," and "An Indian's Looking-Glass" all explicitly referenced Israelite Indian stories. William Apess, *On Our Own Ground: The Complete Writings of William Apess, a Pequot*, ed. Barry O'Connell (Amherst: University of Massachusetts Press, 1992).

50. O'Connell, "Introduction," xlvii; Wyss, *Writing Indians*, 156–57, 161–63.

51. William Jr. added the second "s" to his last name during his publishing career, perhaps to suggest that it was to be pronounced with two syllables. Most scholars have followed Barry O'Connell's pioneering work in spelling his parents' surname as "Apes" and his as "Apess." O'Connell, "Introduction," xxvii–xxx; Benn, *Native Memoirs from the War of 1812*, 82–84; Gura, *The Life of William Apess, Pequot*, 3–6.

52. Ashbo lived near enough to the Furman family—to whom Apess was first indentured—to refer to them as "neighbors," and it is difficult to imagine he would not have visited his nephew during the seven years he was indentured there. Furthermore, Apess probably retained at least some familiarity with the Pequot language later in life, a fact that seems likelier if he conversed in that language during his early childhood. O'Connell, "Introduction," xxiv–xxxi; Gura, *The Life of William Apess, Pequot*, 3–12, n.44 p.11.

53. William Apess, "A Son of the Forest," in *On Our Own Ground: The Complete Writings of William Apess, a Pequot*, ed. Barry O'Connell, rev. ed. (1831; repr., Amherst: The University of Massachusetts Press, 1992), 12.

54. Apess, "A Son of the Forest," 10.

55. Apess, "A Son of the Forest," 1. On the memorialization of "Indian wars" in nineteenth-century New England, see O'Brien, *Firsting and Lasting*. The literature around Indian wars or "border warfare" is also discussed in chapter 5.

56. Apess, "A Son of the Forest," 10.

57. Some Black Americans during this period wrote "race histories" to assemble the scraps of African history available in a majority-White culture into a usable past. Johnson, *The Myth of Ham in Nineteenth-Century American Christianity*; Maffly-Kipp, *Setting down the Sacred Past*. One such race history, written by a man of mixed Black and Mohegan or Pequot descent, explicitly invoked Israelite Indian stories: *Light and Truth* by Robert B. Lewis. Lewis's work used Israelite Indian stories to cast Indigenous people as righteous, suffering Christians. Lewis, *Light and Truth*.

58. Apess, "A Son of the Forest," 10.

59. It is unclear why Apess believed that he could be certain about Adam's color. It is possible that he was citing an oral tradition or that he based this reading on a section of Boudinot's *A Star in the West*, in which the older man discussed reports of Indigenous peoples' "color" alongside reports of their beliefs that they were the first people. Boudinot, *A Star in the West*, 137–38.

60. Irving, "Traits of Indian Character."

61. Apess, "A Son of the Forest," 62.

62. Apess, "A Son of the Forest," 67.

63. Jeremy Cohen, *Living Letters of the Law: Ideas of the Jew in Medieval Christianity* (Berkeley: University of California Press, 1999); Boyarin, *The Unconverted Self*.

64. Apess, "A Son of the Forest," 74. Apess errs by referring to these tribes as the "lost tribes of Judah." The group of people known as the "lost tribes of Israel" were supposedly from the northern kingdom of the divided monarchy, called Israel, rather than from the southern kingdom, called Judah.

65. Brooks, *The Common Pot*, 163–97; O'Brien, *Firsting and Lasting*, 180–90.

66. Here I build on earlier examinations of Apess's use of what the authors call "Jewish Indian" or "Lost Tribe" narratives in the works of Sandra Gustafson and Rochelle Raineri Zuck. Gustafson argues that Apess used narratives about Israelites to construct a sense of Native community and contextualizes this argument among similar uses of the term "Israelite" by Joseph Smith and Mordecai Noah. Zuck, meanwhile, argues that Apess's use of Lost Tribes narratives constitutes an instance of indigenous "survivance"—a speech act meant to demonstrate that indigenous people continue to live and flourish despite colonialism. These are valuable points, but in the context of contemporary arguments about land and nationalism in which Israelite Indian narratives were involved, I read Apess's claims as stronger assertions of Native political independence and right to use the land of the Northeast. Sandra Gustafson, "Nations of Israelites: Prophecy and Cultural Autonomy in the Writings of William Apess," *Religion and Literature* 26, no. 1 (Spring 1994): 31–53; Rochelle Raineri Zuck, "William Apess, the 'Lost Tribes,' and Indigenous Survivance," *Studies in American Indian Literatures* 25, no. 1 (Spring 2013): 1–26.

67. On conversion narratives as a genre, see D. Bruce Hindmarsh, *The Evangelical Conversion Narrative: Spiritual Autobiography in Early Modern England* (New York: Oxford University Press, 2005); Lincoln Mullen, *The Chance of Salvation: A History of Conversion in America* (Cambridge, MA: Harvard University Press, 2017).

68. William Apess, "The Increase of the Kingdom of Christ: A Sermon," in *On Our Own Ground: The Complete Writings of William Apess, a Pequot,* ed. Barry O'Connell (1831; repr., Amherst: University of Massachusetts Press, 1992), 106.

69. Apess, "The Increase of the Kingdom of Christ: A Sermon," 114.

70. Gustafson, "Nations of Israelites."

71. Apess, "The Increase of the Kingdom of Christ: A Sermon," 106.

72. Apess, "The Increase of the Kingdom of Christ: A Sermon," 107.

73. Apess, "A Son of the Forest," 34.

74. Brooks, *The Common Pot*; O'Brien, *Dispossession by Degrees.*

75. Brooks, *The Common Pot*; Mark Rifkin, "Shadows of Mashantucket: William Apess and the Representation of Pequot Place," *American Literature* 84, no. 4 (December 1, 2012): 692–93.

76. Apess, "A Son of the Forest," 34.

77. Apess, "The Increase of the Kingdom of Christ: A Sermon," 107.

78. Apess, "The Increase of the Kingdom of Christ: A Sermon," 107.

79. Stevens, *The Poor Indians.*

80. On emotion and self-making in a slightly later series of conversions, see Corrigan, *Business of the Heart.* On Methodist emotionalism, see David Hempton, *Methodism: Empire of the Spirit* (New Haven, CT: Yale University Press, 2005), 32–54.

81. On the transition in emotional styles in the United States between the Revolution and the War of 1812, see Eustace, *Passion Is the Gale*; Eustace, *1812.*

82. Hatch, *The Democratization of American Christianity*; Corrigan, *Business of the Heart,* 104–27; Gin Lum, *Damned Nation,* 43–83.

83. Apess, "The Increase of the Kingdom of Christ: A Sermon," 107.

84. Apess, "The Increase of the Kingdom of Christ: A Sermon," 114–15.

85. Barry O'Connell, for example, reads the passage this way in O'Connell, "Introduction," lxxi.

86. Joseph Wolff, *Narrative of a Mission to Bokhara in the Years 1843–1845, to Ascertain the Fate of Colonel Stoddart and Captain Conolly,* vol. 1 (London: Harrison & Co., 1845), 64–65. See also the discussion of this source in Tudor Parfitt, *Black Jews in Africa and the Americas* (Cambridge, MA: Harvard University Press, 2013), 72, 191–92 n. 11. Simon, who was married to another Jewish convert to evangelical Christianity, published *The Hope of Israel* in 1829, which went on to become one of the most influential pro-Israelite Indian texts in Britain.

87. Wolff, *Narrative of a Mission to Bokhara in the Years 1843–1845,* 65.

88. Mohicans should not be confused with Mohegans. Both originally spoke Algonquian languages, but Mohican traditional territory lies in the Hudson River Valley in what is now western Massachusetts, southwestern Vermont, and eastern New York, while Mohegan traditional territory is centered on the Thames River Valley in what is now southeastern Connecticut. The Stockbridge-Munsee Community in Shawano County, Wisconsin, and the Mohegan Tribe in southeastern Connecticut, respectively, now represent some members of these groups to the federal government. David J Silverman, "The Curse of God: An Idea and Its Origins among the Indians of New York's Revolutionary Frontier," *William and Mary Quarterly* 66, no. 3 (July 2009): 495–534.

89. Peter Jones, *History of the Ojebway Indians with Special Reference to Their Conversion to Christianity* (London: A.W. Bennett, 1861), 37–38; Howey "The Question Which Has Puzzled, and Still Puzzles."

90. Brooks, *The Common Pot*; Fisher, *The Indian Great Awakening*; Christine M. Delucia, *Memory Lands: King Philip's War and the Place of Violence in the Northeast* (New Haven, CT: Yale University Press, 2018).

91. O'Connell notes that "An Indian's Looking-Glass" was omitted from the 1837 reprint of *Experiences of Five Christian Indians,* which was Apess's last publication along with a second edition of *Eulogy on King Philip,* and replaced with a shorter, less racially charged paragraph. It is doubtful that his abandonment of Israelite Indian narratives alone would have led to the deletion of the whole section rather than an offending paragraph, but it may have contributed to an otherwise difficult-to-understand editorial decision. Barry O'Connell, "Textual Afterword," in *On Our Own Ground: The Complete Writings of William Apess, a Pequot* (Amherst: University of Massachusetts Press, 1992), 311–24.

92. William Apess, "Eulogy on King Philip, as Pronounced at the Odeon, in Federal Street, Boston," in *On Our Own Ground: The Complete Writings of William Apess, a Pequot,* ed. Barry O'Connell (1836; repr., Amherst: University of Massachusetts Press, 1992); Radus, "Apess's Eulogy on Tour."

Chapter 4. The Original Customs of Our Nation

1. The American Board of Commissioners for Foreign Missions was a joint operation of the Presbyterian, Congregational, and Dutch Reformed churches. The ministers in the Cherokee Nation were mostly Congregationalists from New England, but the Union Presbytery of eastern Tennessee oversaw the churches. William McLoughlin, *Cherokees and Missionaries, 1789–1839* (New Haven, CT: Yale University Press, 1984), 102–6, 151–54, 164–67.

2. The Carmel church was originally known as Taloney and appears under that name in some records. Butrick, "Butrick Journal, May 26 to Sept 22, 1838," July 2, 1838, 18.3.3 v. 4 (sec. 6) Cherokee Mission, Miscellaneous, ABC 1–91, by permission of the Houghton Library, Harvard University; *Map of Georgia* (Philadelphia: Anthony Finley, 1830); C. C. Royce, *Map of the Former Territorial Limits of the Cherokee "Nation of" Indians* (Smithsonian Institution Bureau of Ethnology, 1884), Library of Congress, Geography and Map Division, Washington, DC, https://www.loc.gov/resource/g3861e.np000155/?r=-0.104,0.06,0.766,0.381,0.

3. Butrick, "Butrick Journal, May 26 to Sept 22, 1838," June 7, 1838.

4. Numbers 23, 24.

5. Butrick, "Butrick Journal, May 26 to Sept 22, 1838," June 7, 1838.

6. Arthur W. Evans, "A History of the Presbyterian Church in the Cherokee Nation," n.d., 6, box 4, Arthur W. Evans Collection, Western History Collections, University of Oklahoma Libraries; Payne and Butrick, *The Payne-Butrick Papers, Volumes 1,2,3,* xx–xxii.

7. John Payne and D.S. [Daniel Sabin] Butrick, *The Payne-Butrick Papers*, *Volumes 4,5,6*, ed. William L. Anderson, Jane L. Brown, and Anne F. Rogers (Lincoln: University of Nebraska Press, 2010), 15.

8. Payne and Butrick, *The Payne-Butrick Papers*, *Volumes 1,2,3*, xviii–xix. Butrick's manuscripts now exist in four versions held in two separate collections. The earliest versions of Butrick's work appear in the American Board of Commissioners for Foreign Missions Papers archive at Harvard University. Alongside Butrick's diary and letters, this collection has an undated manuscript entitled "Jews & Indians" that contains some of the results of his interviews, arranged to stress what he saw as parallels between ancient Israelites and Cherokees. Some of the material in this manuscript may have been collected before Ross gave Butrick permission to work in 1835. Three successive revisions of the original "Jews & Indians" manuscript appear in the John Howard Payne papers at the Newberry Library in Chicago and are published as *The Payne-Butrick Papers* by the University of Nebraska Press. Butrick's manuscripts in the John Howard Payne papers cover the same topics as the "Jews & Indians" manuscript in three successive forms: a body of letters Butrick sent to Payne on Cherokee history and culture, a systematic draft edited by Butrick entitled "Indian Antiquities," and a draft Payne edited for publication entitled "Cherokees Vol. 1." Payne also published a very short summary of Butrick's findings as "The Ancient Cherokee Traditions and Religious Rites," *American Quarterly Register and Magazine* 3, no. 2 (December 1849): 444–50. This chapter mainly relies on the "Indian Antiquities" manuscript that was the last version edited by Butrick.

9. Payne and Butrick, 211. Thomas Smith is referred to both by that name and as Shield Eater or A-ska-lo-gi-ski in the manuscripts. Throughout the rest of this chapter, I refer to Thomas Smith as "Shield Eater" to avoid confusion with Thomas Nutsawi, Ethan Smith, or Joseph Smith.

10. Payne and Butrick, *The Payne-Butrick Papers*, *Volumes 1,2,3*, 213.

11. Payne and Butrick, *The Payne-Butrick Papers*, *Volumes 1,2,3*, 210.

12. Payne and Butrick, *The Payne-Butrick Papers*, *Volumes 1,2,3*, 208.

13. Payne and Butrick, *The Payne-Butrick Papers*, *Volumes 4,5,6*, 86–87. It is possible that Israelite Indian stories, specifically, may have come to the Nation through the Cherokee author, editor, and statesman Gallegina Uwati. He was educated at the American Board's Foreign Mission School in Connecticut and on the way northward spent time with Elias Boudinot in New Jersey. He took the older man's name in tribute. I have been unable to find evidence that the younger Elias Boudinot supported Israelite Indian ideas, however. Boudinot [Gallegina Uwati], *Cherokee Editor*, 6.

14. There were 167 recorded Cherokee members of American Board churches in 1835, when the population of the Cherokee Nation was 22,000. In the same year, there were 700 Cherokee members of Methodist churches and 244 Cherokee members of Baptist churches. The Moravian mission claimed 65 converts when it closed in 1833. These numbers count only those whom the missionaries formally recognized as converted—regardless of how they thought

of themselves—and may double count some Cherokees who joined more than one church. With those flaws in mind, William McLoughlin estimates that 10–12 per cent of Cherokees were church members by 1838. William McLoughlin, *Cherokee Renascence in the New Republic* (Princeton, NJ: Princeton University Press, 1986), 382; Russell Thornton, "The Demography of the Trail of Tears Period: A New Estimate of Cherokee Population Losses," in *Cherokee Removal: Before and After*, ed. William Anderson, John R. Finger, and Douglas C. Wilms (Athens: University of Georgia Press, 1991), 78.

15. The "Indian Antiquities" manuscript names seventeen Cherokees as sources: Thomas Nutsawi, Corn Tassel, Tarapin Head [sic], Nettle, Thomas Smith, or Shield Eater, Raven, Isaac Short Arrow, Three Killer, Mrs. Chism [Chisholm?], Deer in the Water, "George Hicks's Grandmother," Zachariah, Samuel Candey (or Candy), Johnson Pridget, Thomas Pridget, Andrew Sanders, or Snake, and Caty Vann. Only two of these, Corn Tassel and Tarapin Head, were, as far as I have found, entirely unconnected with the American Board churches. Eleven (64.7 percent) were members, and an additional four (23.5 percent) had close kin who were members. Nutsawi, Johnson Pridget, Thomas Pridget, and Zachariah were members of Carmel church; Deer in the Water was a member of Candy's Creek church; Nettle, and likely Three Killer, were members of the Haweis church; and Shield Eater, Isaac Short Arrow, Andrew Sanders, and probably Raven were part of American Board churches, but I have not yet traced them to a specific congregation. Butrick's journal refers to a "Br. Raven," who is presumably the same man whom Butrick used as a source, but the identification is uncertain because "Raven" was a war title that multiple Cherokee men could have held at the time. George Hicks's Grandmother, Samuel Candey, Caty Vann, and possibly Mrs. Chisholm had immediate family who were church members. I have determined church membership, where possible, based on biographical notes in *The Payne-Butrick Papers* and using the index of Kutsche's *A Guide to Cherokee Documents* to find American Board letters that mention the people in question. Payne and Butrick, *The Payne-Butrick Papers*, Volumes 1,2,3, 293–333; Paul Kutsche, *A Guide to Cherokee Documents in the Northeastern United States* (Metuchen, NJ: Scarecrow Press, 1986).

16. McLoughlin, *Cherokees and Missionaries, 1789–1839*, 132–33; McLoughlin, *Cherokee Renascence in the New Republic*, 277–78, 294; Theda Perdue, *Cherokee Women: Gender and Culture Change, 1700–1835* (Lincoln: University of Nebraska Press, 1999), 41–59, 159–184; Circe Sturm, *Blood Politics: Race, Culture, and Identity in the Cherokee Nation of Oklahoma* (Berkeley: University of California Press, 2002), 30–31, 36–39; Tiya Miles, *Ties That Bind: The Story of an Afro-Cherokee Family in Slavery and Freedom* (Berkeley: University of California Press, 2005); Tyler Boulware, *Deconstructing the Cherokee Nation: Town, Region, and Nation among Eighteenth-Century Cherokees* (Gainesville: University Press of Florida, 2011).

17. Perdue, *Cherokee Women*; Sturm, *Blood Politics*. On American Board approaches to missions and "civilization," see Hutchison, *Errand to the World*, 43–46, 62–78; Conroy-Krutz, *Christian Imperialism*.

18. On Indigenous intellectuals, see Weaver, *That the People Might Live*; Konkle, *Writing Indian Nations*; Kiara Vigil, *Indigenous Intellectuals: Sovereignty, Citizenship, and the American Imagination, 1880–1930* (Cambridge: Cambridge University Press, 2015).

19. William McLoughlin argues that the incorporation of Bible stories with Indigenous narratives demonstrates that Cherokee thinkers understood the Bible to be the universal history of humanity and believed that reading themselves into its narratives would put them in a stronger position in American society. I read Cherokees as telling Israelite Indian narratives in this period to claim stories from the Bible as the possessions of their people, not universally available stories. McLoughlin's interpretation, furthermore, naturalizes the idea that Christianity is a "universal" religion. The idea that Christianity is universal, while Indigenous peoples' religions are "national" or "particular" is a theological assertion that, in the context of scholarship on comparative religions, naturalized colonial relationships. William McLoughlin, "Fractured Myths: The Cherokees' Use of Christianity," in *The Cherokees and Christianity, 1794–1870: Essays on Acculturation and Cultural Persistence*, ed. Walter H. Conser Jr. (Athens: University of Georgia Press, 1994), 152–87. On "universal" versus "national" religions, see Masuzawa, *The Invention of World Religions*.

20. Circe Sturm argues that modern Cherokees continue to create usable histories and identities by demarcating certain activities as traditional ones that affirm their survival as a people. That some of these activities, such as attendance at Cherokee Baptist services, have a shorter history than others, such as the Green Corn Ceremony, does not change the fact that members of the Cherokee Nation of Oklahoma recognize both as ways of being Cherokee. Sturm, *Blood Politics*, 126–29.

21. On mediation in missionary records, see Chidester, *Empire of Religion*, 5–11.

22. Alexander Longe, "The Nation of Indians Called Charrikees," 1698, Thomas Gilcrease Library and Archive, Helmerich Center for American Research.

23. Walter Adair Duncan, "Cherokee Antiquities—'The Buttrick Collections,'" *Cherokee Advocate*, April 25, 1884.

24. Payne and Butrick, *The Payne-Butrick Papers, Volumes 1,2,3*, 317–18, 320, 322, 325–26; Butrick, "Butrick Journal, May 26 to Sept 22, 1838," July 25, 1838. Butrick was also a pastor at Carmel for part of 1831 but fled to Candey's Creek station after Georgia expelled White missionaries to Indigenous people who did not swear a loyalty oath to the state. Georgia did not recognize the territorial claims of the Cherokee Nation and so regarded Carmel as within its borders. Candey's Creek was in land claimed by Tennessee, so Butrick was safe from arrest there. Daniel S. Butrick, "Butrick Journal 1825–1827," April 10, 1826, 18.3.3 v. 4 Cherokee Mission, Miscellaneous, Butrick Journal, ABC 1–91, by permission of the Houghton Library, Harvard University; The Prudential Committee, "Mission Among the Cherokees," *Annual Report of the American Board of Commissioners for Foreign Missions* 22 (1831): 59–76; McLoughlin, *Cherokee Renascence in the New Republic*.

25. Many of his relatives and descendants remained in the church at Dwight Mission, and today the burying ground is filled with Sanders markers. Joyce B. Phillips and Paul Gary Phillips, eds., *The Brainerd Journal: A Mission to the Cherokees, 1817–1823, Indians of the Southeast* (Lincoln: University of Nebraska Press, 1998), 538–39; Sarah Tuttle, *Letters and Conversations on the Cherokee Mission* (Boston: Massachusetts Sunday School Union, 1830), 116–17; "Report of Dwight Mission Church, 1822–1862" (1980), Microfiche Collection, John Vaughan Library Special Collections, Northeastern State University.

26. Nancy Shoemaker, "How Indians Got to Be Red," *American Historical Review* 102, no. 3 (June 1, 1997): 625–44.

27. "A Memorandum of Cherokee Traditions" (July 4, 1837), Folder 224A, John Ross Papers, Thomas Gilcrease Library and Archive, Helmerich Center for American Research.

28. There are several reasons to think Sanders could read English. His father was a Continental Army deserter who married a Cherokee woman, named Susannah, of the Bird clan and likely made sure that he could read English. A Sanders household in the Etowah River district—which was likely Andrew's since his family was from the vicinity of Taloney, which was near the Etowah River in what is now Cherokee County, Georgia—was listed as having several members literate in English in the 1835 Cherokee census. Sanders later served as a member of the National Committee for the Skin Bayou District in what is now Sequoyah County, Oklahoma, a position that would have been easier if he had English literacy. The only one of the interviewed intellectuals whose literacy we know about, Nutsawi, was literate only in Cherokee, not in English, and so could have read only portions of the New Testament. Therefore, he could not have been familiar with the arrangement of these stories in the text of the Bible, only with their use in sermons and their incorporation into Cherokee oral histories. James W. Tyner, *Those Who Cried the 16,000: A Record of the Individual Cherokee Listed in the United States Official Census of the Cherokee Nation Conducted in 1835* (Norman, OK: Chi-ga-u, 1974), 34; John Ross, *The Papers of Chief John Ross*, ed. Gary E. Moulton (Norman: University of Oklahoma Press, 1985), II: 162–63; Payne and Butrick, *The Payne-Butrick Papers, Volumes 1,2,3*, 317–18, 320, 322, 325–26; Butrick, "Butrick Journal, May 26 to Sept 22, 1838," July 25, 1838; McLoughlin, "Fractured Myths: The Cherokees' Use of Christianity," 156.

29. "A Memorandum of Cherokee Traditions" (July 4, 1837), Folder 224A, John Ross Papers, Thomas Gilcrease Library and Archive, Helmerich Center for American Research.

30. Payne and Butrick, *The Payne-Butrick Papers, Volumes 4,5,6*, 5–6.

31. John Howard Payne to George Watterson, December 2, 1840, Grant Foreman Papers, box 13, folder 10b, Thomas Gilcrease Library and Archive, Helmerich Center for American Research.

32. Cephas Washburn, *Reminisces of the Indians* (Richmond, VA: Presbyterian Committee of Publication, 1869), 174, 177–78, 215.

33. Butrick, "Butrick Journal, May 26 to Sept 22, 1838," August 1838. The name "Ulunyi" for what was called in English Turnip Town or Turnipmine

Town appears in James Mooney, *Historical Sketch of the Cherokee* (1900; repr., New Brunswick, NJ: Transaction Publishers, 2009), 106.

34. Christopher Teuton, *Cherokee Stories of the Turtle Island Liars' Club: Dakasi Elohi Anigagoga Junilawisdii (Turtle, Earth, the Liars, Meeting Place)* (Chapel Hill: University of North Carolina Press, 2012), 4–8, 33–35, 146–51. On the importance of stories in Indigenous thought, see also Thomas King, *The Truth about Stories: A Native Narrative* (Minneapolis: University of Minnesota Press, 2005); Daniel Justice, *Our Fire Survives the Storm: A Cherokee Literary History* (Minneapolis: University of Minnesota Press, 2006).

35. Perdue, *Cherokee Women*; Miles, *Ties That Bind*.

36. McLoughlin, *Cherokee Renascence in the New Republic*, 446; Theda Perdue and Michael D. Green, *The Cherokee Nation and the Trail of Tears* (New York: Viking, 2007); Joel W. Martin, "Crisscrossing Projects of Sovereignty and Conversion: Cherokee Christians and New England Missionaries during the 1820s," in *Native Americans, Christianity, and the Reshaping of the American Religious Landscape*, ed. Joel W. Martin and Mark A. Nicholas (Chapel Hill: University of North Carolina Press, 2010); Conroy-Krutz, *Christian Imperialism*, 130–50.

37. Crawford, *An Essay on the Propagation of the Gospel*, 28–29.

38. Daniel S. Butrick, "Saturday [June?]," 1838, in "Butrick Journal, May 26 to Sept 22, 1838."

39. Payne and Butrick, *The Payne-Butrick Papers, Volumes 1,2,3*, 210.

40. Payne and Butrick, *The Payne-Butrick Papers, Volumes 1,2,3*, 211.

41. Teuton, *Cherokee Stories of the Turtle Island Liars' Club*, 76–78.

42. Payne and Butrick, *The Payne-Butrick Papers, Volumes 1,2,3*, 210–11.

43. Payne and Butrick, *The Payne-Butrick Papers, Volumes 1,2,3*, 211.

44. Calloway, *New Worlds for All*, 118–35.

45. Although the text here reads "Indians," elsewhere Nutsawi depicts both Abraham and Moses as Cherokee men who authorized or originated Cherokee religious traditions. It is thus likely that these stories were told with the Cherokee foremost in mind. Butrick renders the Cherokee version of the name "Abraham" as "E-ga-ha-yi" or "Aquāhäyi," and "Moses" as Wosi or Wâsi.

46. Payne and Butrick, *The Payne-Butrick Papers, Volumes 1,2,3*, 211.

47. Payne and Butrick, *The Payne-Butrick Papers, Volumes 1,2,3*, 211.

48. This contrasts strongly, for example, with the metaphorical use of about the promised land, Canaan, and Israel by Black American Christians during this period. David W. Kling, "A Contested Legacy: Interpreting, Debating, and Translating the Bible in America," in *American Christianities: A History of Dominance and Diversity*, ed. Catherine A. Brekus and W. Clark Gilpin (Chapel Hill: University of North Carolina Press, 2011).

49. Payne and Butrick, *The Payne-Butrick Papers, Volumes 1,2,3*, 211.

50. Butrick, "Saturday [June?]."

51. Daniel S. Butrick, "Butrick Journal, 1830–1832," November 25, 1831, 18.3.3 v. 4 (sec. 4) Cherokee Mission, Miscellaneous, ABC 1–91, by permission of the Houghton Library, Harvard University.

52. Payne and Butrick, *The Payne-Butrick Papers, Volumes 4,5,6*, 109, 205. Cf. Payne and Butrick, *The Payne-Butrick Papers, Volumes 1,2,3*, 210–11.

53. Like most American Board missionaries, Butrick held strongly to the Trinitarian position. When the American Board sent him a copy of a sermon preached by a minister with Unitarian sympathies, he burned it because "I could not feel willing to keep in the house a sermon preached by a tongue employed in denying the sacred Trinity."Daniel S. Butrick, "Butrick Journal, Jan 11, 1832– Dec (?) 1832," n.d. 1832, 18.3.3 v. 4 (sec. 5) Cherokee Mission, Miscellaneous, ABC 1–91, by permission of the Houghton Library, Harvard University. On the idea that the Israelites were Trinitarian in theology, see Serle, *Horae Solitariae*.

54. Payne and Butrick, *The Payne-Butrick Papers, Volumes 1,2,3*, 208.

55. I preserve the textual notations made in the edited version of the Payne-Butrick papers, where struck through text indicates a crossing out and ˇcaratsˇ indicate inserted text. Payne and Butrick, *The Payne-Butrick Papers, Volumes 1,2,3*, 208.

56. McLoughlin, *Cherokees and Missionaries, 1789–1839*; Martin, "Criss-crossing Projects of Sovereignty and Conversion."

57. Payne and Butrick, *The Payne-Butrick Papers, Volumes 1,2,3*, 12.

58. Exodus 19–20 and 31 describe the initial appearance of God and the creation of the first set of tablets. Exodus 33–34 describe God appearing a second time to Moses and the creation of a second set of tablets, since Moses destroyed the first. A second version of this story, occurring at Mount Horeb rather than Sinai, appears in Deuteronomy 4 and 10.

59. Payne and Butrick, *The Payne-Butrick Papers, Volumes 1,2,3*, 212.

60. Charles Hudson, *The Southeastern Indians* (Knoxville: University of Tennessee Press, 1978), 166–69, 355–58.

61. Payne and Butrick, *The Payne-Butrick Papers, Volumes 1,2,3*, 12, 35.

62. Daniel S. Butrick, "[A Cherokee Missionary on Jews and Indians]" n.d., 18.3.3 v. 3 (part 1, sec. A), ABC 1–91, by permission of the Houghton Library, Harvard University.

63. Payne and Butrick, *The Payne-Butrick Papers, Volumes 1,2,3*, 211.

64. Payne and Butrick, *The Payne-Butrick Papers, Volumes 1,2,3*, 216.

65. McLoughlin, *Cherokee Renascence in the New Republic*, 351–400.

66. See, for example, the below discussion of Butrick's sermon on traditional healing. Butrick, "Butrick Journal, 1830–1832," 1830.

67. Butrick, "Butrick Journal, May 26 to Sept 22, 1838," August 1838. After removal, Butrick claimed at one point that up to sixty Cherokees were learning to be exhorters. However, other records corroborate only two: Epenetus and Jesse Barrow. Epenetus eventually became licensed as an exhorter, but it is unclear if Jesse Barrow did. Samuel A. Worcester, "Records of the Session of New Echota Church Constituted Aug 1 1830" (to 1857 1830), box 1, Arthur W. Evans Collection, Western History Collections, University of Oklahoma Librar-ies; Cassandra Sawyer Lockwood, "Diary" (1835 1833), Roberta Robey Col-lection, Western History Collections, University of Oklahoma Libraries; Daniel S. Butrick to S.B. Treat, January 19, 1851, Stephen Foreman Papers, Western History Collections, University of Oklahoma Libraries. Cherokee laity,

rather than missionaries, often composed the hymns sung in American Board churches. For example, a Cherokee woman named Lydia Keys Taylor recalled in the early twentieth century that her grandmother, a member of the American Board's Brainerd mission, composed a hymn in Cherokee after it came to her in a dream. James R. Carselowey, "An Interview with Lydia Keys Taylor," November 10, 1937, Indian-Pioneer Papers, Western History Collections, University of Oklahoma Libraries.

68. Foreman preached in both English and Cherokee, but Huss seems to have preferred Cherokee. The American Board even accepted his ordination sermon in Cherokee. In fact, he might have been only literate in that language. An encomium on him after his death mentioned that he had a full command of that portion of the Bible that had been translated into Cherokee by his death, and he signed his name in the Sequoyan syllabary in the constitution of the Association of Ministers in the Cherokee Nation, formed on October 3, 1840. The influential historian of the Cherokee, William McLoughlin, mistakenly believed that neither Huss nor Foreman had churches of their own after the 1838 forced migration. This was true for Foreman, who was a regular pastor at Park Hill but not the sole pastor, but Huss seems to have been the sole pastor at Honey Creek church. Roughly two-thirds of the members of Honey Creek church were Cherokees, and the remaining third were Black people, likely enslaved or formerly enslaved people who would have likely known Cherokee. Worcester, "Records of the Session of New Echota Church Constituted Aug 1 1830," 339 and passim; William Chamberlin, "Extracts from a Letter of Mr. Chamberlin, Dated at Willstown, April 29 1831," *Missionary Herald* 27, no. 8 (August 1831): 247–48; John Huss, "Ordination of Mr. John Huss," *Missionary Herald* 30, no. 3 (March 1834): 89–101, American Historical Periodicals from the American Antiquarian Society, Gale Cengage; Samuel A. Worcester, "Cherokees," *Missionary Herald* 54, no. 11 (November 1858): 357. For McLoughlin's argument, see McLoughlin, *Cherokees and Missionaries, 1789–1839*, 339.

69. McLoughlin, *Cherokee Renascence in the New Republic*; Julie Reed, *Serving the Nation: Cherokee Sovereignty and Social Welfare, 1800–1907* (Norman: University of Oklahoma Press, 2016); William McLoughlin, "Two Boston Missionaries," in *The Cherokees and Christianity, 1794–1870: Essays on Acculturation and Cultural Persistence*, ed. Walter H. Conser Jr. (Athens: University of Georgia Press, 1994), 50–90.

70. Daniel S. Butrick, "Butrick Journal, 1833," December 1833, 18.3.3 v. 4 (sec. 5) Cherokee Mission, Miscellaneous, ABC 1–91, by permission of the Houghton Library, Harvard University.

71. Payne and Butrick, *The Payne-Butrick Papers, Volumes 4,5,6*, 104.

72. Morse, *The American Universal Geography*, 76–77.

73. Butrick, "Butrick Journal, 1830–1832," 1830; Hudson, *The Southeastern Indians*, 352–65. Hudson's descriptions of traditional healing rely on the idea that beings and forces are sorted into oppositional groups. This has been challenged as depending too much on Mary Douglas's thought. Churchill, "The Oppositional Paradigm of Purity versus Pollution in Charles Hudson's: 'The Southeastern Indians.'" Hudson, "Reply to Mary Churchill." See also Mary

Douglas, *Purity and Danger: An Analysis of Concepts of Pollution and Taboo* (London: Routledge, 1966).

74. Butrick, "Butrick Journal, May 26 to Sept 22, 1838," August 1838.

75. Payne and Butrick, *The Payne-Butrick Papers, Volumes 4,5,6,* 167–68.

76. Payne and Butrick, *The Payne-Butrick Papers, Volumes 1,2,3,* 240.

77. Perdue, *Cherokee Women,* 148, 180; McLoughlin, *Cherokee Renascence in the New Republic,* 333.

78. Payne and Butrick, *The Payne-Butrick Papers, Volumes 4,5,6,* 218–19; James Mooney, *Myths of the Cherokee* (Washington, DC: Government Printing Office, 1902), 311–15.

79. Hudson, *The Southeastern Indians,* 174–83; Payne and Butrick, *The Payne-Butrick Papers, Volumes 4,5,6,* 208.

80. Daniel S. Butrick, "Butrick Journal Oct. 4 1838, to May, 1839," October 4, 1838, 18.3.3 v. 4 (sec. 7) Cherokee Mission, Miscellaneous, ABC 1–91, by permission of the Houghton Library, Harvard University. Samuel A. Worcester, "Wednes[Day] Oct 31 [1838]," 1857 1830, "Records of the Session of New Echota Church Constituted Aug 1 1830," box 1, Arthur W. Evans Collection, Western History Collections, University of Oklahoma Libraries; Evans, "A History of the Presbyterian Church in the Cherokee Nation," 187.

81. Worcester, "Records of the Session of New Echota Church Constituted Aug 1 1830"; Minta Ross Foreman, "Reverend Stephen Foreman, Cherokee Missionary," *Chronicles of Oklahoma* 18, no. 3 (September 1940): 229–42; Oscar Payne and Betty Payne, *Dwight: A Brief History of Old Dwight Cherokee Mission, 1820–1953* (Tulsa, OK: Dwight Presbyterian Mission, 1954); "Report of Dwight Mission Church, 1822–1862."

82. Evans, "A History of the Presbyterian Church in the Cherokee Nation"; Joseph Leiper to Sarah McCarrell Welling, Rebecca McCarrell, and Juliet McCarrell, June 7, 1890, Kathleen Leiper Faux Collection, F43, Western History Collections, University of Oklahoma Libraries; W. M. Hamilton to Joseph McCarrell Leiper, December 6, 1897, Kathleen Leiper Faux Collection, F61, Western History Collections, University of Oklahoma Libraries; Reed, *Serving the Nation.*

Chapter 5. The Indian War Is Only Begun

1. David Wyrick, "Hebrew Inscriptions Alleged to Have Been Dug up in Ohio, U.S.A.," 1860, David Wyrick Collection, William L. Clements Library, University of Michigan.

2. Wyrick, "Hebrew Inscriptions"; Bradley T. Lepper and Jeffrey Gill, "The Newark Holy Stones: The Social Context of an Enduring Scientific Forgery," Ohio Archaeological Council Fall Meeting, Newark, OH, November 1, 2008, https://www.ohioarchaeology.org/39-resources/research/articles-and-abs tracts-2008/279-the-newark-qholy-stonesq-the-social-context-of-an-enduring -scientific-forgery; Kenneth L. Feder et al., "Lessons Learned from Lost Civilizations," in *Lost City, Found Pyramid: Understanding Alternative Archaeologies*

and Pseudoscientific Practices, ed. David S. Anderson and Jeb J. Card (Tuscaloosa: University of Alabama Press, 2016), 167–84.

3. Farmer, *On Zion's Mount*; Thayne, "The Blood of Father Lehi."

4. Rubinstein, *Members of the Tribe*; Imhoff, "Wild Tribes and Ancient Semites"; Koffman, *The Jews' Indian*.

5. The most complete such bibliography extant is an unpublished manuscript: Walter Hart Blumenthal, "In Old America—The Ten Lost Tribes of Israel," 1931, MS-229, Jacob Rader Marcus Center of the American Jewish Archives. Blumenthal, an early twentieth century scholar, compiled this massive summary of works mentioning the ten lost tribes of Israel spanning more than five hundred years and multiple continents. A small portion of this bibliography was published as Blumenthal, *In Old America: Random Chapters on the Early Aborigines*. Special thanks go to David Koffman of York University for bringing Blumenthal's manuscript to my attention. Another useful work, containing an extensive bibliography and a bibliographic essay focused on works that informed Joseph Smith's intellectual world, is Vogel, *Indian Origins and the Book of Mormon*.

6. Conn, *History's Shadow*.

7. Bloch, *Visionary Republic*; Abzug, *Cosmos Crumbling*; Guyatt, *Providence and the Invention of the United States, 1607–1876*. Guyatt's work distinguishes several forms of providentialism. Here, I discuss what he calls "national providentialism," or the idea that God guides the destinies of nations, in general terms, while acknowledging that the subtypes of national providentialism he identifies represent usefully distinct strains of thought.

8. None of these policies went uncontested, however, often by White Catholics who were in the strongest position to do so. See, for example, Robert A. Orsi, *Between Heaven and Earth: The Religious Worlds People Make and the Scholars Who Study Them* (Princeton, NJ: Princeton University Press, 2005); Fessenden, *Culture and Redemption*; Graber, *The Gods of Indian Country*. On the interrelated questions of secularism and religious freedom in the United States specifically, see Winnifred Fallers Sullivan, *The Impossibility of Religious Freedom* (Princeton, NJ: Princeton University Press, 2005); Fessenden, *Culture and Redemption*; Jakobsen and Pellegrini, *Secularisms*; Elizabeth Shakman Hurd, *The Politics of Secularism in International Relations* (Princeton, NJ: University Press, 2008); Modern, *Secularism in Antebellum America*; Wenger, *Religious Freedom*; Coviello, *Make Yourselves Gods*, 23–50. These works on the United States engage with a larger conversation about modernity and secularism. Key texts in that conversation include Talal Asad, *Formations of the Secular: Christianity, Islam, Modernity* (Stanford, CA: Stanford University Press, 2003); Charles Taylor, *A Secular Age* (Cambridge, MA: Harvard University Press, 2007); Saba Mahmood, *Religious Difference in a Secular Age: A Minority Report* (Princeton, NJ: Princeton University Press, 2016). For a recent review and appraisal of this larger conversation, see Udi Greenberg and Daniel Steinmetz-Jenkins, eds., "Roundtable: What Comes after the Critique of Secularism?" *Journal of the American Academy of Religion* 88, no. 1 (March 2020): 1–91.

9. Tisa Wenger, *We Have a Religion: The 1920s Pueblo Indian Dance Controversy and American Religious Freedom* (Chapel Hill: University of North Carolina

Press, 2009); Johnson, *African American Religions, 1500–2000*; Reeve, *Religion of a Different Color*; Coviello, *Make Yourselves Gods*, 45–47.

10. Fessenden, *Culture and Redemption*.

11. Conroy-Krutz, *Christian Imperialism*, 130–50, 208–9; Curtis, *Holy Humanitarians*, 111–12, 119–20, 129–31, 284–89.

12. Henry, *A Plea for the West*.

13. Edward Brerewood, *Enquiries Touching the Diversity of Languages and Religions, through the Chief Parts of the World* (1614; repr., London: SM, JM, and HH, 1674), 114–17.

14. Samuel George Morton and George Combe, *Crania Americana; or, A Comparative View of the Skulls of Various Aboriginal Nations of North and South America. To Which Is Prefixed an Essay on the Varieties of the Human Species* (Philadelphia: J. Dobson; London: Simpkin, Marshall & Co., 1839), 30.

15. Mark Noll, *The Scandal of the Evangelical Mind* (Grand Rapids, MI.: W.B. Eerdmans, 1995), 59–108; Modern, *Secularism in Antebellum America*, 1–48.

16. Smith, *View of the Hebrews*. A later evangelical investigator, Epaphras Jones, re-investigated the Pittsfield tefillin using similar methods. Epaphras Jones, *On the Ten Tribes of Israel and the Aborigines of America &c &c* (New Albany, IN: Collins & Green, 1831). The tefillin case seems to have been destroyed and the papers it contained lost at the Massachusetts Historical Society.

17. Ira Hill, *Antiquities of America Explained* (Hagerstown, MD: William D. Bell, 1831), 30–54.

18. The most famous text written to combat this idea was Thomas Jefferson's 1785 *Notes on the State of Virginia*. See John Van Atta, *Securing the West: Politics, Public Lands, and the Fate of the Old Republic, 1785–1850* (Baltimore: Johns Hopkins University Press, 2014), 170–204; Kariann Akemi Yokota, *Unbecoming British: How Revolutionary America Became a Postcolonial Nation* (New York: Oxford University Press, 2011), 156–64, 213–25.

19. Hill, *Antiquities of America Explained*, 90–95.

20. Hill, *Antiquities of America Explained*, 109, 115–18.

21. Broader American practices around archaeology and grave digging, similarly, asserted White settlers' control over both the past and the land of North America. Conn, *History's Shadow*, 116–53. Heaney, "A Peru of Their Own."

22. Priest, *American Antiquities and Discoveries in the West*, 98, 160, 198–99.

23. Priest, *American Antiquities and Discoveries in the West*, 96.

24. Henry Rowe Schoolcraft, *Archives of Aboriginal Knowledge. Containing All the Original Paper Laid before Congress Respecting the History, Antiquities, Language, Ethnology, Pictography, Rites, Superstitions, and Mythology of the Indian Tribes of the United States.*, vol. 5 (Philadelphia: J.B. Lippencott & Co., 1860), 87.

25. Schoolcraft, *Archives of Aboriginal Knowledge*, 86.

26. Schoolcraft, *Archives of Aboriginal Knowledge*, 688.

27. Boudinot, *A Star in the West*.

28. On "competency" and Jacksonian policies, see Daniel Vickers, "Competency and Competition: Economic Culture in Early America," *William and Mary Quarterly* 47, no. 1 (January 1990): 3–29; Andrew Shankman, "Conflict

for a Continent." On land, see Hietala, *Manifest Design*; Van Atta, *Securing the West*; Bowes, *Land Too Good for Indians*.

29. Haselby, *The Origins of American Religious Nationalism*; Zakaras, "Nature, Religion, and the Market in Jacksonian Political Thought."

30. A robust body of scholarship describes and interprets this change in American literature. Starting points include Richard Slotkin, *Regeneration through Violence; the Mythology of the American Frontier, 1600–1860* (Middletown, CT: Wesleyan University Press, 1973); Richard Drinnon, *Facing West: The Metaphysics of Indian-Hating and Empire Building* (Minneapolis: University of Minnesota Press, 1980); Pearce, *Savagism and Civilization*; O'Brien, *Firsting and Lasting*.

31. Hietala, *Manifest Design*, 173–214, 255–72; Watson, *Liberty and Power*, 109–12; Guyatt, *Providence and the Invention of the United States, 1607–1876*, 173–74; Zakaras, "Nature, Religion, and the Market in Jacksonian Political Thought."

32. John Lardas Modern argues that spirituality and evangelical Protestantism were essentially compatible in their endorsement of an overarching secular order in Modern, *Secularism in Antebellum America*, 119–82. This genealogy of spirituality underemphasizes the role of Americans of color, gender and sexual minorities, and others who imagined spirituality in divergent ways. Molly McGarry, *Ghosts of Futures Past: Spiritualism and the Cultural Politics of Nineteenth-Century America*, electronic resource (Berkeley: University of California Press, 2008); Leigh Eric Schmidt, *Heaven's Bride: The Unprintable Life of Ida C. Craddock, American Mystic, Scholar, Sexologist, Martyr, and Madwoman* (New York: Basic Books, 2010); Leigh Eric Schmidt, *Restless Souls: The Making of American Spirituality*, 2nd ed. (Berkeley: University of California Press, 2012); Emily Suzanne Clark, *A Luminous Brotherhood: Afro-Creole Spiritualism in Nineteenth-Century New Orleans* (Chapel Hill: University of North Carolina Press, 2016).

33. On tracking diffuse religious feelings and the ways that these feelings canalize thought, see Jakobsen and Pellegrini, "Introduction: Times Like These"; Modern, *Secularism in Antebellum America*. The contours I sketch of conversations about religious nationalism owe much to Sam Haselby's analysis. However, unlike Haselby, I do not see American religious nationalism as consisting of basically two strands that reached their synthesis in the age of Jackson and disagree that frontier revivalism was basically apolitical. New forms of revivalist Protestantism undergirded secular approaches to land by calling on individuals to trust their "commonsense" impressions of the world and of the Bible, which seemed in turn to confirm the naturalness of expansion. Although they often posed as apolitical, therefore, revivalist Protestants in fact helped to shift the boundaries of what could be thought or felt about expansion. Haselby, *The Origins of American Religious Nationalism*, 194, 203, 241–58, 268, 315.

34. "The March of Empire towards the West," *Connecticut Courant*, August 26, 1837, Readex: America's Historical Newspapers.

35. Joseph Pritts, *Incidents of Border Life, Illustrative of the Times and Condition of the First Settlements in Parts of the Middle and Western States* (Chambersburg, PA: Joseph Pritts, 1839), 491.

36. John Dix, "The Ten-Regiment Bill," *Congressional Globe*, n.s., 18, no. 16 (January 27, 1848): 256.

37. Zakaras, "Nature, Religion, and the Market in Jacksonian Political Thought."

38. George Edward Ellis, *Our Good Land, and Its Good Institutions. A Discourse Delivered in Harvard Church, Charlestown, on Thanksgiving Day, November 30, 1854* (Boston: Crosby, Nichols, & Co., 1854), 14–17.

39. Horace Eaton, *The Land We Live In: A Sermon Preached Thanksgiving Day, Nov 23, 1848* (New York: Leavitt Trow & Co., 1848), 5–8.

40. Horsman, *Race and Manifest Destiny*; Johannsen, "The Meaning of Manifest Destiny"; Hietala, *Manifest Design*.

41. John L. O'Sullivan, "The True Title," *Morning News*, December 27, 1845. Quoted in Julius W. Pratt, "The Origin of 'Manifest Destiny,'" *American Historical Review* 32, no. 4 (July 1927): 795–98. See also Johannsen, "The Meaning of Manifest Destiny"; Robert J. Miller, "The Doctrine of Discovery, Manifest Destiny, and American Indians," in *Why You Can't Teach United States History without American Indians*, ed. Susan Sleeper-Smith et al. (Chapel Hill: University of North Carolina Press, 2015), 87–100.

42. Tuveson, *Redeemer Nation*; Richard Slotkin, *The Fatal Environment: The Myth of the Frontier in the Age of Industrialization, 1800–1890* (Norman: University of Oklahoma Press, 1998); Woodworth, *Manifest Destinies: America's Westward Expansion and the Road to the Civil War*. Many of these accounts depend on the early, and more nuanced, exploration of "manifest destiny" and chosen-ness in Weinberg, *Manifest Destiny*.

43. Henry Smith, *Virgin Land: The American West as Symbol and Myth* (Cambridge, MA: Harvard University Press, 1970); Drinnon, *Facing West*; Slotkin, *The Fatal Environment*, 21–26, 530–32.

44. Eustace, *1812*.

45. My argument about the rhetorical uses of lower-class White anger draws on Griffin, *American Leviathan*.

46. Alexander S. Withers, *Chronicles of Border Warfare, or a History of the Settlement by Whites, of North-Western Virginia: And of the Indian Wars and Masscres, In That Section of the State; with Reflections, Anecdotes, &c.* (Clarksburg, VA: Joseph Israel, 1831), 156–57.

47. Withers, *Chronicles of Border Warfare*, 217–18.

48. James Eldridge Quinlan, *Tom Quick, the Indian Slayer: And the Pioneers of Minisink and Wawarsink* (Monticello, NY: DeVoe and Quinlan, 1851), 240.

49. Charles S. Daveis, *An Address Delivered on the Commemoration at Fryeburg, May 19, 1825* (Portland, ME: James Adams Jr., 1825), 3–5.

50. John Grenier, *The First Way of War: American War Making on the Frontier, 1607–1814* (Cambridge: Cambridge University Press, 2005), 50–52.

51. Gail H. Bickford, "Lovewell's Fight, 1725–1958," *American Quarterly* 10, no. 3 (1958): 358–66.

52. Daniel Clarke Sanders, *A History of the Indian Wars with the First Settlers of the United States to the Commencement of the Late War* (Rochester, NY: Edwin Scrantom, 1828), 100.

53. On King Philip's War, see Lepore, *The Name of War*; Pulsipher, *Subjects unto the Same King.*

54. O'Brien, *Firsting and Lasting.*

55. Daveis, *An Address Delivered on the Commemoration at Fryeburg, May 19, 1825*, 32–33.

Conclusion

1. Leah Sottile, "Bundyville," *Longreads*, May 2018, https://longreads.com/bundyville/; Anthony McCann, *Shadowlands: Fear and Freedom at the Oregon Standoff* (New York: Bloomsbury, 2019), 42–59; James Pogue, *Chosen Country: A Rebellion in the West* (New York: Henry Holt, 2018).

2. Crooked River Currents View, "Harney County Town Hall #1 Dec 15, 2015," YouTube, December 17, 2015, https://www.youtube.com/watch?v=3qcr93G0InA; McCann, *Shadowlands: Fear and Freedom at the Oregon Standoff*, 47–57.

3. McCann, *Shadowlands: Fear and Freedom at the Oregon Standoff*, 41–42; Pogue, *Chosen Country*, 116–25, 279–89.

4. McCann, *Shadowlands: Fear and Freedom at the Oregon Standoff*, xx, 119–33.

5. LaVoy Finicum, "Liberty Revolution ~ Neglected Paiute Artifacts and a Message to the Native Americans," YouTube, January 25, 2016, https://www.youtube.com/watch?v=cQfKOOG8MHY&list=PLWLhyHWZv171Gq96iEg1 UEeVoScfIf1Pj. The same video is quoted, with slight differences from my transcript, in McCann, *Shadowlands: Fear and Freedom at the Oregon Standoff*, 180.

Bibliography

Archives

American Jewish Historical Society. New York, NY.
  Mordecai Manuel Noah, papers
  Seixas Family Papers
Buffalo and Erie County Historical Society. Buffalo, NY.
  Peter B. Porter Papers
Church History Library, the Church of Jesus Christ of Latter-day Saints. Salt Lake City, UT.
  Brigham Young office files, 1832–1878
Harold B. Lee Library Digital Collections, Brigham Young University. Provo, UT.
  Mormon Publications: 19th and 20th Centuries
Houghton Library, Harvard University. Cambridge, MA.
  American Board of Commissioners for Foreign Mission Papers
Jacob Rader Marcus Center of the American Jewish Archives, Cincinnati, OH.
John Vaughan Library Special Collections, Northeastern State University. Tulsa, OK.
Joseph Smith Papers. http://josephsmithpapers.org/.
  History, 1838–1856 (Manuscript History of the Church)
  Joseph Smith Letterbooks
Library of Congress. Washington, DC.
  Geography and Map Division
  Prints and Photographs Division
Princeton University Rare Books and Special Collections. Princeton, NJ.
  Stimson Collection of Elias Boudinot
Thomas Gilcrease Library and Archive, Helmerich Center for American Research. Tulsa, OK.
  Grant Foreman Papers
  John Ross Papers
Western History Collections, University of Oklahoma Libraries. Norman, OK.

Arthur W. Evans Collection
Indian-Pioneer Papers
Kathleen Leiper Faux Collection
Roberta Robey Collection
Stephen Foreman Papers
William L. Clements Library, University of Michigan. Ann Arbor, MI.
Blandina Diedrich Collection
Duane Norman Diedrich Collection, Sophia Sawyer Papers
David Wyrick Collection

Published Primary Sources

Abbot, Abiel. *Traits of Resemblance in the People of the United States of America to Ancient Israel. In a Sermon, Delivered at Haverhill, on the Twenty-Eighth of November, 1799, the Day of Anniversary Thanksgiving. By Abiel Abbot, Pastor of the First Church in Haverhill.* MA: from the press of Moore & Stebbins. Published for the subscribers, 1799.

Adair, James. *The History of the American Indians.* 1775. Edited by Kathryn E. Holland Braund. Reprint, Tuscaloosa: University of Alabama Press, 2005.

Allen, Lewis F. "The Story of the Tablet of the City of Ararat." In *The Book of the Museum.* Edited by Frank H. Severance, 113–44. Publications of the Buffalo Historical Society. 25. Buffalo, NY: Buffalo Historical Society, 1921.

Apess, William. "A Son of the Forest." Revised edition, 1831. In *On Our Own Ground: The Complete Writings of William Apess, a Pequot.* Edited by Barry O'Connell, 1–98. Amherst: University of Massachusetts Press, 1992.

———. "Eulogy on King Philip, as Pronounced at the Odeon, in Federal Street, Boston." 1836. In *On Our Own Ground: The Complete Writings of William Apess, a Pequot.* Edited by Barry O'Connell, 275–310. Amherst: University of Massachusetts Press, 1992.

———. "The Increase of the Kingdom of Christ: A Sermon." 1831. In *On Our Own Ground: The Complete Writings of William Apess, a Pequot.* Edited by Barry O'Connell, 101–15. Amherst: University of Massachusetts Press, 1992.

———. "Indian Nullification of the Unconstitutional Laws of Massachusetts Relative to the Marshpee Tribe; or, The Pretended Riot Explained." 1835. In *On Our Own Ground: The Complete Writings of William Apess, a Pequot.* Edited by Barry O'Connell, 163–275. Amherst: University of Massachusetts Press, 1992.

———. *On Our Own Ground: The Complete Writings of William Apess, a Pequot.* Edited by Barry O'Connell. Amherst: University of Massachusetts Press, 1992.

"The Ararat Proclamation and Speech, The Buffalo Patriot Vol. VIII Buffalo, Tuesday September 20, 1825." In *The Selected Writings of Mordecai Noah.* Edited by Michael Schuldiner and Daniel J. Kleinfeld, 105–24. Westport, CT: Greenwood Press, 1999.

Ben Israel, Menasseh. *The Hope of Israel.* 1650. Edited by Henry Méchoulan and Gérard Nahon. New York: Oxford University Press, 1987.

Bennett, James Gordon. "A Rabbi in the Rostrum." *Herald* [New York]. February 14, 1837. Nineteenth Century U.S. Newspapers, Gale Cengage.
———. "Rabbi Noah at a Discount." *Herald* [New York]. March 8, 1837. Nineteenth Century U.S. Newspapers, Gale Cengage.
Blumenthal, Walter Hart. *In Old America: Random Chapters on the Early Aborigines*. New York: Walton Book Company, 1931.
Boudinot, Elias. *The Life, Public Services, Addresses, and Letters of Elias Boudinot, LL. D., President of the Continental Congress*. Edited by Jane J. Boudinot. New York: Houghton, Mifflin & Co., 1896.
———. "A Star in the West." *Jewish Expositor and Friend of Israel*, January 1820, 3 passim.
———. *A Star in the West; or, A Humble Attempt to Discover the Long Lost Ten Tribes of Israel, Preparatory to Their Return to Their Beloved City, Jerusalem*. Trenton: D. Fenton, S. Hutchinson and J. Dunham, 1816.
Boudinot, Elias [Gallegina Uwati]. *Cherokee Editor: The Writings of Elias Boudinot*. Edited by Theda Perdue. Athens: University of Georgia Press, 1996.
Brerewood, Edward. *Enquiries Touching the Diversity of Languages and Religions, through the Chief Parts of the World*. 1614. Reprint, London: SM, JM, and HH, 1674.
Caswall, Henry. *The City of the Mormons; or, Three Days at Nauvoo, in 1842*. 2nd ed. London: J.G.F. & J. Rivington, 1843.
Chamberlin, William. "Extracts from a Letter of Mr. Chamberlin, Dated at Willstown, April 29 1831." *Missionary Herald* 27, no. 8 (August 1831): 247–48.
Chardon, Francis A. *Chardon's Journal at Fort Clark, 1834–1839; Descriptive of Life on the Upper Missouri; of a Fur Trader's Experiences among the Mandans, Gros Ventres and Their Neighbors; of the Ravages of the Small-Pox Epidemic of 1837*. Pierre, SD, 1932.
C[lapp], M[atthew] S. "Mormonism." *Painesville* [Ohio] *Telegraph* 2, no. 35 (February 15, 1831). Readex: America's Historical Newspapers.
Connecticut Evangelical Magazine, and Religious Intelligencer 1 (June 1800–July 1801).
Crawford, Charles. *An Essay on the Propagation of the Gospel*. 2nd ed. James Humphreys, 1801.
Crooked River Currents View. "Harney County Town Hall #1 Dec 15, 2015." YouTube, December 17, 2015. https://www.youtube.com/watch?v=3qcr93G0InA.
Daveis, Charles S. *An Address Delivered on the Commemoration at Fryeburg, May 19, 1825*. Portland, ME: James Adams Jr., 1825.
"Dialogue on Mormonism II." *Times and Seasons*, July 15, 1841. Mormon Publications: 19th and 20th Centuries, Brigham Young University, Harold B. Lee Library Digital Collections.
Dix, John. "The Ten-Regiment Bill." *Congressional Globe*, n.s., 18, no. 16 (January 27, 1848): 250–56.
Duncan, R.W. William. *A History of Independent Royal Arch Lodge No. 2 F&AM of the State of New York*. New York, 1904.

Duncan, Walter Adair. "Cherokee Antiquities—'The Buttrick Collections.'" *Cherokee Advocate*, April 25, 1884.

Durán, Diego. *Historia de Las Indias de Nueva España e Islas de La Tierra Firme.* 2 vols. 1581. Edited by Angel María Garibay K. [Kintana]. Mexico [DF]: Editorial Porrúa, 1967.

Dwight, Timothy. *Conquest of Canäan.* [Hartford, CT]: printed by Elisha Babcock, 1785.

Eaton, Horace. *The Land We Live In: A Sermon Preached Thanksgiving Day, Nov 23, 1848.* New York: Leavitt Trow & Co., 1848.

Ellis, George Edward. *Our Good Land, and Its Good Institutions: A Discourse Delivered in Harvard Church, Charlestown, on Thanksgiving Day, November 30, 1854.* Boston: Crosby, Nichols, & Co., 1854.

"Epitome of Lowman's Hebrew Ritual." *Panoplist and Missionary Magazine* 3, no. 3 (August 1810): 86–90. American Historical Periodicals from the American Antiquarian Society, Gale Cengage.

Finicum, LaVoy. "Liberty Revolution ~ Neglected Paiute Artifacts and a Message to the Native Americans." YouTube, January 25, 2016. https://www.youtube.com/watch?v=cQfKOOG8MHY&list=PLWLhyHWZv171Gq96iEg1UEeVoScfIf1Pj.

"From the New York Sun: The Jews and American Aborigines," *Connecticut Courant*, October 7, 1837. Readex: Early American Newspapers.

García, Gregorio. *Origen de Los Indios de El Nuevo Mundo, e Indias Occidentales.* 1607. Reprint, Madrid: F. Martinez Abad, 1729.

General Association of Massachusetts. "Report." *Panoplist and Missionary Magazine* 11, 2nd ser., no. 8 (August 1815): 373–77. ProQuest: American Periodicals Series II.

Grow, Matthew J., Ronald K. Esplin, Mark Ashurst-McGee, Gerrit J. Dirkmaat, and Jeffrey D. Mahas, eds. *Council of Fifty, Minutes, March 1844-January 1846.* Joseph Smith Papers, Administrative Records. Salt Lake City, UT: Church Historian's Press, 2016.

"Hancock Female Tract Society." *Panoplist, or, the Christian's Armory* 3, no. 4 (September 1807): 189–90. American Historical Periodicals from the American Antiquarian Society, Gale Cengage.

Henry, T. Charlton. *A Plea for the West: A Sermon Preached before the Missionary Society of the Synod of South-Carolina and Georgia in Augusta, November 21, 1824.* Charleston, SC: W.M. Riley, 1824.

Huss, John. "Ordination of Mr. John Huss." *Missionary Herald* 30, no. 3 (March 1834): 89–101. American Historical Periodicals from the American Antiquarian Society, Gale Cengage.

"Indian Civilization." *Church Record*, July 20, 1822. ProQuest: American Periodicals.

Irving, Washington. "Traits of Indian Character." *Analectic Magazine* 3 (February 1814): 145–56. American Historical Periodicals from the American Antiquarian Society, Gale Cengage.

Jones, Epaphras. *On the Ten Tribes of Israel and the Aborigines of America &c &c.* New Albany, IN: Collins & Green, 1831.

Jones, Peter. *History of the Ojebway Indians with Special Reference to Their Conversion to Christianity.* London: A.W. Bennett, 1861.

"Lectures on the Evidences of Divine Revelation, No. XVI." *Panoplist and Missionary Magazine* 9, no. 2 (July 1813): 50–56. American Historical Periodicals from the American Antiquarian Society, Gale Cengage.

Lewis, Robert Benjamin. *Light and Truth; Collected from the Bible and Ancient and Modern History, Containing the Universal History of the Colored and the Indian Race, from the Creation of the World to the Present Time.* Boston: A Committee of Colored Gentlemen, 1844.

Lindley, Jacob, Joseph Moore, and Oliver Paxton. "Expedition to Detroit, 1793." *Michigan Pioneer and Historical Society Collections* 17 (1890): 565–632.

Livermore, Harriet. *The Harp of Israel: To Meet the Loud Echo in the Wilds of America.* Philadelphia: J. Rakestraw, 1835.

Map of Georgia. Philadelphia: Anthony Finley, 1830.

"The March of Empire towards the West." *Connecticut Courant,* August 26, 1837. Readex: America's Historical Newspapers.

McDonald, John. *Isaiah's Message to the American Nation, a New Translation of Isaiah, Chapter XVIII with Notes Critical and Explanatory, A Remarkable Prophecy, Respecting the Restoration of the Jews Aided by the American Nation; with An Universal Summons to the Battle of Armageddon, and a Description of That Solemn Scene.* Albany, NY: E. & E. Hosford, 1814.

Mooney, James. *Historical Sketch of the Cherokee.* 1900. Reprint, New Brunswick, NJ: Transaction, 2009.

———. *Myths of the Cherokee.* Washington, DC: Government Printing Office, 1902.

Morse, Jedidiah. *The American Geography: Or, a View of the Present Situation of the United States of America.* Elizabethtown, NJ: Shepard Kollock, 1789.

———. *The American Universal Geography; or, A View of the Present State of All the Kingdoms, States and Colonies in the Known World.* 7th ed. 2 vols. Charlestown: G. Clarke, 1819.

Morton, Samuel George, and George Combe. *Crania Americana; or, A Comparative View of the Skulls of Various Aboriginal Nations of North and South America. To Which Is Prefixed an Essay on the Varieties of the Human Species.* Philadelphia: J. Dobson; London: Simpkin, Marshall & Co., 1839.

Noah, Mordecai M. *Discourse on the Evidences of the American Indians Being the Descendants of the Lost Tribes of Israel: Delivered before the Mercantile Library Association, Clinton Hall.* New York: James Van Norden, 1837.

Occom, Samson. *Samson Occom: Collected Writings from a Founder of Native American Literature.* Edited by Joanna Brooks. New York: University Press, 2006.

O'Sullivan, John L. "The True Title." *Morning News,* December 27, 1845.

Parish, Elijah. *A New System of Modern Geography, or, A General Description of All the Considerable Countries in the World.* Newburyport, MA, 1810.

Pastor. "Survey of New England Churches." *Panoplist* 2, no. 11 (April 1807): 503–12. American Historical Periodicals from the American Antiquarian Society, Gale Cengage.

Payne, John. "The Ancient Cherokee Traditions and Religious Rites." *American Quarterly Register and Magazine* 3, no. 2 (December 1849): 444–50.

Payne, John, and D.S. [Daniel Sabin] Butrick. *The Payne–Butrick Papers, Volumes 1,2,3.* Edited by William L. Anderson, Jane L. Brown, and Anne F. Rogers. Lincoln: University of Nebraska Press, 2010.

———. *The Payne–Butrick Papers, Volumes 4,5,6.* Edited by William L. Anderson, Jane L. Brown, and Anne F. Rogers. Lincoln: University of Nebraska Press, 2010.

Payne, Oscar, and Betty Payne. *Dwight: A Brief History of Old Dwight Cherokee Mission 1820–1953.* Tulsa, OK: Dwight Presbyterian Mission, 1954.

Philadelphian. "Descendants of Israel." *Philadelphia Recorder,* July 8, 1826. ProQuest: American Periodicals.

Pratt, Parley P. *A Voice of Warning and Instruction to All People: Containing a Declaration of the Faith and Doctrine of the Church of the Latter-Day Saints, Commonly Called Mormons.* New York: W. Standford, 1837.

Prentiss, John. "Variety." *New Hampshire Sentinel,* November 18, 1825.

Priest, Josiah. *American Antiquities and Discoveries in the West.* 5th ed. Albany: Hoffman and White, 1835.

———. *The Wonders of Nature and Providence, Displayed: Compiled from Authentic Sources, Both Ancient and Modern, Giving an Account of Various and Strange Phenomena Existing in Nature, of Travels, Adventures, Singular Providences, &c. . . .* Albany: J. Priest, 1825.

Pritts, Joseph. *Incidents of Border Life, Illustrative of the Times and Condition of the First Settlements in Parts of the Middle and Western States.* Chambersburg, PA: Joseph Pritts, 1839.

Probate Court (Hartford, Connecticut). "Probate Records," September 5, 1851. Connecticut, Wills and Probate Records, 1609–1999. Ancestry.com.

"The Progress of Knowledge." *Western Recorder,* January 19, 1830. ProQuest: American Periodicals Series II.

The Prudential Committee. "Mission Among the Cherokees." *Annual Report of the American Board of Commissioners for Foreign Missions* 22 (1831): 59–76.

Quinlan, James Eldridge. *Tom Quick, the Indian Slayer: And the Pioneers of Minisink and Wawarsink.* Monticello, NY: DeVoe and Quinlan, 1851.

"Regeneration of the Jews," *New-York National Advocate* [New York], January 17, 1826: 1. Readex: America's Historical Newspapers.

Ross, John, *The Papers of Chief John Ross.* Edited by Gary Moulton. 2 vols. Norman: University of Oklahoma Press, 1985.

Schoolcraft, Henry Rowe. *Archives of Aboriginal Knowledge. Containing All the Original Paper Laid before Congress Respecting the History, Antiquities, Language, Ethnology, Pictography, Rites, Superstitions, and Mythology of the Indian Tribes of the United States.* Vol. 5. Philadelphia: J.B. Lippencott & Co., 1860.

Serle, Ambrose. *Horae Solitariae; or, Essays upon Some Remarkable Names and Titles of Jesus Christ, Occurring in the Old Testament.* First American edition, from the second London edition. Philadelphia: Patterson and Cochran, 1799.

Sigourney, Lydia Howard. *Traits of the Aborigines of America: A Poem.* Cambridge, MA: University Press, 1822.

Smith, Ethan. *Daughters of Zion Excelling. A Sermon Preached to the Ladies of the Cent Institutions, in Hopkinton, New-Hampshire August 18, 1814.* Concord, NH: George Hough, 1814.

———. *View of the Hebrews.* 2nd ed. 1825. Reprint. Provo, UT: Religious Studies Center, Brigham Young University, 1996.

Snow, Eliza R. *The Personal Writings of Eliza Roxcy Snow.* Edited by Maureen Ursenbach Beecher. Logan: Utah State University Press, 2000.

"Ten Tribes." *Jewish Intelligencer: A Monthly Publication* 1, no. 10 (May 1837).

Tuttle, Sarah. *Letters and Conversations on the Cherokee Mission.* Boston: Massachusetts Sunday School Union, 1830.

Washburn, Cephas. *Reminisces of the Indians.* Richmond, VA: Presbyterian Committee of Publication, 1869.

Withers, Alexander S. *Chronicles of Border Warfare, or a History of the Settlement by Whites, of North-Western Virginia: And Of the Indian Wars and Masscres, In That Section of the State; with Reflections, Anecdotes, &c.* Clarksburg, VA: Joseph Israel, 1831.

Wolff, Joseph. *Narrative of a Mission to Bokhara in the Years 1843–1845, to Ascertain the Fate of Colonel Stoddart and Captain Conolly.* 2 vols. London: Harrison & Co., 1845.

Woodruff, Ephraim T. *A Sermon Delivered Before the Ecclesiastical Society in Williamsfield and Wayne, Ashtabula County, Ohio; On the 4th of July, 1826: In Celebration of the Jubilee of the Independence of the United States of America.* Warren, OH: Hapgood and Quinby, 1826.

Worcester, Samuel A. "Cherokees." *Missionary Herald* 54, no. 11 (November 1858): 357.

Z. "Religious Communications: On Christian Zeal," *Panoplist* 3, no. 1 (June 1807): 8–13. ProQuest: American Periodicals Series II.

Secondary Sources

Abzug, Robert. *Cosmos Crumbling: American Reform and the Religious Imagination.* New York: Oxford University Press, 1994.

Ahmed, Sara. "Affective Economies." *Social Text* 22, no. 2 (Summer 2004): 117–39.

———. *The Cultural Politics of Emotion.* New York: Routledge, 2004.

Anderson, Benedict. *Imagined Communities.* Revised edition. New York: Verso, 2006.

Appleby, Joyce. *Inheriting the Revolution: The First Generation of Americans.* Cambridge, MA: Harvard University Press, 2000.

Asad, Talal. *Formations of the Secular: Christianity, Islam, Modernity.* Stanford, CA: Stanford University Press, 2003.

Balik, Shelby. *Rally the Scattered Believers: Northern New England's Religious Geography.* Bloomington: Indiana University Press, 2014.

Bartlett, Robert. "Medieval and Modern Concepts of Race and Ethnicity." *Journal of Medieval and Early Modern Studies* 31, no. 1 (2001): 39–56.

Bebbington, David. *Evangelicalism in Modern Britain: A History from the 1730s to the 1980s*. Winchester, MA: Allen & Unwin, 1989.

Ben-Dor Benite, Zvi. *The Ten Lost Tribes: A World History*. New York: Oxford University Press, 2009.

Benn, Carl, ed. *Native Memoirs from the War of 1812: Black Hawk and William Apess*. Baltimore: Johns Hopkins University Press, 2014.

Bennett, Richard E. "Lamanism, Lymanism and Cornfields." *Journal of Mormon History* 13 (1987 1986): 44–59.

Berkhofer, Robert. *The White Man's Indian: Images of the American Indian, from Columbus to the Present*. New York: Vintage Books, 1979.

Berlant, Lauren. "Cruel Optimism." In *The Affect Theory Reader*. Edited by Melissa Gregg and Gregory J. Seigworth, 93–117. Durham, NC: Duke University Press, 2010.

Bickford, Gail H. "Lovewell's Fight, 1725–1958." *American Quarterly* 10, no. 3 (1958): 358–66.

Blackhawk, Ned. *Violence over the Land: Indians and Empires in the Early American West*. Cambridge, MA: Harvard University Press, 2006.

Bloch, Ruth. *Visionary Republic: Millennial Themes in American Thought 1756–1800*. Cambridge: Cambridge University Press, 1985.

Blum, Edward, Tracy Fessenden, Prema Kurien, and Judith Weisenfeld. "Forum on Whiteness." *Religion and American Culture: A Journal of Interpretation* 19, no. 1 (Winter 2009): 1–35.

Blum, Edward, and Paul Harvey. *The Color of Christ: The Son of God & the Saga of Race in America*. Chapel Hill: University of North Carolina Press, 2012.

Bonomi, Patricia U. *Under the Cope of Heaven: Religion, Society and Politics in Colonial America*. Updated edition. New York: Oxford University Press, 2003.

Boulware, Tyler. *Deconstructing the Cherokee Nation: Town, Region, and Nation among Eighteenth-Century Cherokees*. Gainesville: University Press of Florida, 2011.

Bourdieu, Pierre. *Outline of a Theory of Practice*. Cambridge: Cambridge University Press, 1977.

Bowes, John P. *Land Too Good for Indians: Northern Indian Removal*. Norman: University of Oklahoma Press, 2016.

Boyarin, Daniel. *Unheroic Conduct: The Rise of Heterosexuality and the Invention of the Jewish Man*. Berkeley: University of California Press, 1997.

Boyarin, Jonathan. *The Unconverted Self: Jews, Indians, and the Identity of Christian Europe*. Chicago: University of Chicago Press, 2009.

Boyd, George Adams. *Elias Boudinot: Patriot and Statesman*. Princeton, NJ: Princeton University Press, 1952.

Brodie, Fawn. *No Man Knows My History: The Life of Joseph Smith*. 2nd ed. New York: Alfred A. Knopf, 1971.

Brodkin, Karen. *How Jews Became White Folks and What That Says about Race in America*. New Brunswick, NJ: Rutgers University Press, 1998.

Brooke, John. *The Refiner's Fire: The Making of Mormon Cosmology, 1644–1844*. Cambridge: Cambridge University Press, 1994.

Brooks, Lisa. *The Common Pot: The Recovery of Native Space in the Northeast.* Minneapolis: University of Minnesota Press, 2008.

Bruyneel, Kevin. *The Third Space of Sovereignty: The Postcolonial Politics of U.S.–Indigenous Relations.* Minneapolis: University of Minnesota Press, 2007.

Burbank, Jane, and Frederick Cooper. *Empires in World History: Power and the Politics of Difference.* Princeton, NJ: Princeton University Press, 2010.

Burns, Kathryn. "Unfixing Race." In *Rereading the Black Legend: The Discourse of Religious and Racial Difference in the Renaissance Empires.* Edited by Margaret R. Greer, Walter Mignolo, and Maureen Quilligan, 188–204. Chicago: University of Chicago Press, 2007.

Bushman, Richard. *Joseph Smith: Rough Stone Rolling.* New York: Alfred A. Knopf, 2005.

Butler, Jon. *Awash in a Sea of Faith: Christianizing the American People.* Cambridge, MA: Harvard University Press, 1990.

Calloway, Colin. *New Worlds for All: Indians, Europeans, and the Remaking of Early America.* 2nd ed. Baltimore: Johns Hopkins University Press, 2013.

Cannell, Fenella. "The Blood of Abraham: Mormon Redemptive Physicality and American Idioms of Kinship." *Journal of the Royal Anthropological Institute* 19, no. 1 (May 2013): 77–94.

Cave, Alfred. *Prophets of the Great Spirit: Native American Revitalization Movements in Eastern North America.* Lincoln: University of Nebraska Press, 2006.

Cayton, Andrew, and Peter S. Onuf. *The Midwest and the Nation: Rethinking the History of an American Region.* Bloomington: Indiana University Press, 1990.

Cherry, Conrad. *God's New Israel: Religious Interpretations of American Destiny.* Revised and updated edition. Chapel Hill: University of North Carolina Press, 1998.

Chidester, David. *Empire of Religion: Imperialism and Comparative Religion.* Chicago: University of Chicago Press, 2014.

Churchill, Mary C. "The Oppositional Paradigm of Purity versus Pollution in Charles Hudson's: 'The Southeastern Indians.'" *American Indian Quarterly* 20, no. 3/4 (July 1, 1996): 563–93.

Clark, Emily Suzanne. *A Luminous Brotherhood: Afro-Creole Spiritualism in Nineteenth-Century New Orleans.* Chapel Hill: University of North Carolina Press, 2016.

Cogley, Richard W. "The Ancestry of the American Indians: Thomas Thorowgood's Iewes in America (1650) and Jews in America (1660)." *English Literary Renaissance* 35, no. 2 (March 1, 2005): 304–30.

———. "'Some Other Kinde of Being and Condition': The Controversy in Mid-Seventeenth-Century England over the Peopling of Ancient America." *Journal of the History of Ideas* 68, no. 1 (January 2007): 35–56.

Cohen, Jeremy. *Living Letters of the Law: Ideas of the Jew in Medieval Christianity.* Berkeley: University of California Press, 1999.

Cohen, Naomi W. *Encounter with Emancipation: The German Jews in the United States, 1830–1914.* Philadelphia: Jewish Publication Society of America, 1984.

Conn, Steven. *History's Shadow: Native Americans and Historical Consciousness in the Nineteenth Century.* Chicago: University of Chicago Press, 2004.

Conroy-Krutz, Emily. *Christian Imperialism: Converting the World in the Early American Republic.* Ithaca, NY: Cornell University Press, 2015.

Corrigan, John. *Business of the Heart: Religion and Emotion in the Nineteenth Century.* Berkeley: University of California Press, 2001.

Coviello, Peter. "Agonizing Affection: Affect and Nation in Early America." *Early American Literature* 37, no. 3 (2002): 439–68.

———. *Make Yourselves Gods: Mormons and the Unfinished Business of American Secularism.* Chicago: University of Chicago Press, 2019.

Curtis, Heather D. *Holy Humanitarians: American Evangelicals and Global Aid.* Cambridge, MA: Harvard University Press, 2018.

Daggar, Lori J. "The Mission Complex: Economic Development, 'Civilization,' and Empire in the Early Republic." *Journal of the Early Republic* 36, no. 3 (September 9, 2016): 467–91.

Dahl, Adam. *Empire of the People: Settler Colonialism and the Foundations of Modern Democratic Thought.* Lawrence: University Press of Kansas, 2018.

Deloria, Philip. *Playing Indian.* New Haven, CT: Yale University Press, 1998.

Delucia, Christine M. *Memory Lands: King Philip's War and the Place of Violence in the Northeast.* New Haven, CT: Yale University Press, 2018.

Demos, John. *The Heathen School: A Story of Hope and Betrayal in the Age of the Early Republic.* New York: Alfred A. Knopf, 2014.

Dennis, Matthew. *Seneca Possessed: Indians, Witchcraft, and Power in the Early American Republic.* Philadelphia: University of Pennsylvania Press, 2010.

Díaz, María Elena. "Conjuring Identities: Race, Nativeness, Local Citizenship, and Royal Slavery on the Imperial Frontier (Revisiting El Cobre, Cuba)." In *Imperial Subjects: Race and Identity in Colonial Latin America.* Edited by Andrew B. Fisher and Matthew D. O'Hara, 197–224. Durham, NC: Duke University Press, 2009.

Donawerth, Jane, ed. *Rhetorical Theory by Women before 1900: An Anthology.* Lanham, MD: Rowman & Littlefield, 2002.

Dougherty, Matthew W. "New Scholarship in Religion and United States Empire." *Religion Compass* 13, no. 5 (May 2019).

———. "None Can Deliver: Imagining Lamanites and Feeling Mormon, 1837–1847." *Journal of Mormon History* 43, no. 3 (2017): 22–45.

Douglas, Mary. *Purity and Danger: An Analysis of Concepts of Pollution and Taboo.* London: Routledge, 1966.

Dowd, Gregory. *A Spirited Resistance: The North American Indian Struggle for Unity, 1745–1815.* Baltimore: Johns Hopkins University Press, 1992.

Drinnon, Richard. *Facing West: The Metaphysics of Indian-Hating and Empire Building.* Minneapolis: University of Minnesota Press, 1980.

Duffy, John-Charles. "The Use of 'Lamanite' in Official LDS Discourse." *Journal of Mormon History* 34, no. 1 (Winter 2008): 118–67.

DuVal, Kathleen. *Independence Lost: Lives on the Edge of the American Revolution.* New York: Random House, 2015.

Edmunds, R. David. *Tecumseh and the Quest for Indian Leadership.* 2nd ed. New York: Pearson Longman, 2007.

Eichler-Levine, Jodi. "American Judaism and Race." In *The Oxford Handbook of Religion and Race in American History*. Edited by Kathryn Gin Lum and Paul Harvey, 191–204. New York: Oxford University Press, 2018.

Eitler, Pascal, and Monique Scheer. "Emotionengeschichte Als Körpergeschichte. Eine Heuristische Perspektive Auf Religiose Konversionen Im 19. Und 20. Jarhundert." *Geschichte Und Gesellschaft* 35, no. 2 (June 2009): 282–313.

Eustace, Nicole. *1812: War and the Passions of Patriotism*. Philadelphia: University of Pennsylvania Press, 2012.

———. *Passion Is the Gale: Emotion, Power, and the Coming of the American Revolution*. Chapel Hill: University of North Carolina Press, 2008.

Eustace, Nicole, Eugenia Lean, Julie Livingston, Jan Plamper, William M. Reddy, and Barbara H. Rosenwein. "AHR Conversation: The Historical Study of Emotions." *American Historical Review* 117, no. 5 (December 2012): 1486–1531.

Farmer, Jared. *On Zion's Mount: Mormons, Indians, and the American Landscape*. Cambridge, MA: Harvard University Press, 2008.

Farrell, David R. "Askin, John." In *Dictionary of Canadian Biography*. Vol. 5. Toronto: University of Toronto/Université Laval, 2003. http://www.biographi.ca/en/bio/askin_john_5E.html.

Fea, John. *The Bible Cause: A History of the American Bible Society*. New York: Oxford University Press, 2016.

Feder, Kenneth L., Terry Barnhart, Deborah A. Bolnick, and Bradley T. Lepper. "Lessons Learned from Lost Civilizations." In *Lost City, Found Pyramid: Understanding Alternative Archaeologies and Pseudoscientific Practices*. Edited by David S. Anderson and Jeb J. Card, 167–84. Tuscaloosa: University of Alabama Press, 2016.

Feldman, Egal. *Dual Destinies: The Jewish Encounter with Protestant America*. Urbana: University of Illinois Press, 1990.

Fenn, Elizabeth. *Encounters at the Heart of the World: A History of the Mandan People*. New York: Hill and Wang, 2014.

Fessenden, Tracy. *Culture and Redemption: Religion, the Secular, and American Literature*. Princeton, NJ: Princeton University Press, 2007.

Fisher, Linford. "An Indian Bible and A Brass Hawk: Land, Sachemship Disputes, and Power in the Conversion of Ben Uncas II." *Journal of Social History* 47, no. 2 (Winter 2013): 319–43.

———. *The Indian Great Awakening: Religion and the Shaping of Native Cultures in Early America*. New York: Oxford University Press, 2012.

Fitz, Caitlin. *Our Sister Republics: The United States in an Age of American Revolutions*. New York: W.W. Norton, 2016.

Foreman, Minta Ross. "Reverend Stephen Foreman, Cherokee Missionary." *Chronicles of Oklahoma* 18, no. 3 (September 1940): 229–42.

Frampton, T. Ward. "'Some Savage Tribe': Race, Legal Violence, and the Mormon War of 1838." *Journal of Mormon History* 40, no. 1 (Winter 2014): 175–207.

Gilman, Sander. *The Jew's Body.* New York: Routledge, 1991.

Gin Lum, Kathryn. *Damned Nation: Hell in America from the Revolution to Reconstruction.* New York: Oxford University Press, 2014.

Givens, Terryl. *By the Hand of Mormon: The American Scripture That Launched a New World Religion.* New York: Oxford University Press, 2002.

Goetz, Rebecca. *The Baptism of Early Virginia: How Christianity Created Race.* Baltimore: Johns Hopkins University Press, 2012.

Goldstein, Eric. *The Price of Whiteness: Jews, Race, and American Identity.* Princeton, NJ: Princeton University Press, 2006.

Graber, Jennifer. *The Gods of Indian Country: Religion and the Struggle for the American West.* New York: Oxford University Press, 2018.

Greenberg, Udi, and Daniel Steinmetz-Jenkins, eds. "Roundtable: What Comes After the Critique of Secularism?" *Journal of the American Academy of Religion* 88, no. 1 (March 2020): 1–91.

Gregg, Melissa, and Gregory J. Seigworth. "Introduction: An Inventory of Shimmers." In *The Affect Theory Reader.* Edited by Melissa Gregg and Gregory J. Seigworth, 1–28. Durham, NC: Duke University Press, 2010.

Grenier, John. *The First Way of War: American War Making on the Frontier, 1607–1814.* Cambridge: Cambridge University Press, 2005.

Griffin, Patrick. *American Leviathan: Empire, Nation, and Revolutionary Frontier.* New York: Hill and Wang, 2007.

Gura, Philip. *The Life of William Apess, Pequot.* Chapel Hill: University of North Carolina Press, 2015.

Gustafson, Sandra. "Nations of Israelites: Prophecy and Cultural Autonomy in the Writings of William Apess." *Religion and Literature* 26, no. 1 (Spring 1994): 31–53.

Guy, Josephine, and Ian Small. *The Routledge Concise History of Nineteenth Century Literature.* London: Routledge, 2011.

Guyatt, Nicholas. *Bind Us Apart: How Enlightened Americans Invented Racial Segregation.* New York: Basic Books, 2016.

———. *Providence and the Invention of the United States, 1607–1876.* New York: Cambridge University Press, 2007.

Hackel, Steven W., and Hilary Wyss. "Hendrick Apaumut: Christian-Mahican Prophet." In *Native Americans, Christianity, and the Reshaping of the American Religious Landscape.* Edited by Joel W. Martin and Mark A. Nicholas, 225–49. Chapel Hill: University of North Carolina Press, 2010.

Hall, David. *A Reforming People: Puritanism and the Transformation of Public Life in New England.* New York: Alfred A. Knopf, 2011.

Hämäläinen, Pekka. *The Comanche Empire.* New Haven, CT: Yale University Press, 2008.

Handsome Lake and Arthur Caswell Parker. *The Code of Handsome Lake, the Seneca Prophet.* Albany: University of the State of New York, 1913.

Hardy, Grant. *Understanding the Book of Mormon: A Reader's Guide.* New York: Oxford University Press, 2010.

Harvey, Paul. *Bounds of Their Habitation: Race and Religion in American History.* Lanham, MD: Rowman & Littlefield, 2017.

Haselby, Sam. *The Origins of American Religious Nationalism*. New York: Oxford University Press, 2015.

Hatch, Nathan. *The Democratization of American Christianity*. New Haven, CT: Yale University Press, 1989.

Hazard, Sonia. "Evangelical Encounters: The American Tract Society and the Rituals of Print Distribution in Antebellum America." *Journal of the American Academy of Religion* 87, no. 4 (December 2019).

Heaney, Christopher. "A Peru of Their Own: English Grave-Opening and Indian Sovereignty in Early America." *William and Mary Quarterly* 73, no. 4 (October 2016): 609–46.

Hempton, David. *Methodism: Empire of the Spirit*. New Haven, CT: Yale University Press, 2005.

Heyrman, Christine. *Southern Cross: The Beginnings of the Bible Belt*. Chapel Hill: University of North Carolina Press, 1998.

Hickman, Jared. "The Book of Mormon as Amerindian Apocalypse." *American Literatures* 86, no. 3 (September 2014): 429–61.

Hietala, Thomas. *Manifest Design: American Exceptionalism and Empire*. Revised edition. Ithaca, NY: Cornell University Press, 2003.

Hill, Ira. *Antiquities of America Explained*. Hagerstown, MD: William D. Bell, 1831.

Hindmarsh, D. Bruce. *The Evangelical Conversion Narrative: Spiritual Autobiography in Early Modern England*. New York: Oxford University Press, 2005.

Hixson, Walter. *American Settler Colonialism: A History*. New York: Palgrave Macmillan, 2013.

Hoberman, Michael. *New Israel / New England: Jews and Puritans in Early America*. Amherst: University of Massachusetts Press, 2011.

Horsman, Reginald. "The Dimensions of an 'Empire for Liberty': Expansionism and Republicanism, 1775–1825." *Journal of the Early Republic* 9, no. 1 (Spring 1989).

———. *Race and Manifest Destiny: The Origins of American Racial Anglo-Saxonism*. Cambridge, MA: Harvard University Press, 1981.

Howe, Daniel Walker. "Religion and Politics in the Antebellum North." In *Religion and American Politics: From the Colonial Period to the Present*. Edited by Mark A. Noll and Luke Harlow, 121–44. 2nd ed. New York: Oxford University Press, 2007.

Howey, Megan C.L. "'The Question Which Has Puzzled, and Still Puzzles': How American Indian Authors Challenged Dominant Discourse about Native American Origins in the Nineteenth Century." *American Indian Quarterly* 34, no. 4 (Fall 2010): 435–74.

Hoxie, Frederick E. "Retrieving the Red Continent: Settler Colonialism and the History of American Indians in the US." *Ethnic and Racial Studies* 31, no. 6 (September 1, 2008): 1153–67.

Huddleston, Lee. *Origins of the American Indians; European Concepts, 1492–1729*. Austin: University of Texas Press, 1967.

Hudson, Charles. *Elements of Southeastern Indian Religion*. Leiden, Netherlands: E.J. Brill, 1984.

————. "Reply to Mary Churchill." *American Indian Quarterly* 24, no. 3 (July 1, 2000): 494–502.

————. *The Southeastern Indians*. Knoxville: University of Tennessee Press, 1978.

Hurd, Elizabeth Shakman. *The Politics of Secularism in International Relations*. Princeton, NJ: Princeton University Press, 2008.

Hutchison, William. *Errand to the World: American Protestant Thought and Foreign Missions*. Chicago: University of Chicago Press, 1987.

Ignatiev, Noel. *How the Irish Became White*. New York: Routledge, 1995.

Imhoff, Sarah. *Masculinity and the Making of American Judaism*. Bloomington: Indiana University Press, 2017.

————. "Wild Tribes and Ancient Semites: Israelite-Indian Identification in the American West." *Culture and Religion* 15, no. 2 (2014): 227–49.

Isenberg, Nancy. *White Trash: The 400-Year Untold History of Class in America*. New York: Viking, 2016.

Jacobson, Matthew. *Whiteness of a Different Color: European Immigrants and the Alchemy of Race*. Cambridge, MA: Harvard University Press, 1998.

Jaher, Frederic. *A Scapegoat in the New Wilderness: The Origins and Rise of Anti-Semitism in America*. Cambridge, MA: Harvard University Press, 1994.

Jakobsen, Janet, and Ann Pellegrini. "Introduction: Times Like These." In *Secularisms*. Edited by Janet Jakobsen and Ann Pellegrini, 1–35. Durham, NC: Duke University Press, 2008.

————, eds. *Secularisms*. Durham, NC: Duke University Press, 2008.

Johannsen, Robert Walter. "Introduction" and "The Meaning of Manifest Destiny." In *Manifest Destiny and Empire: American Antebellum Expansionism*. Edited by Christopher Charles Morris and Sam Walter Haynes, 1–7. College Station: Texas A&M University Press, 1997.

Johnson, Sylvester. *African American Religions, 1500–2000: Colonialism, Democracy, and Freedom*. New York: Cambridge University Press, 2015.

————. *The Myth of Ham in Nineteenth-Century American Christianity: Race, Heathens, and the People of God*. New York: Palgrave Macmillan, 2004.

Jordan, Winthrop. *White over Black: American Attitudes towards the Negro, 1550–1812*. Baltimore: Penguin Books, 1973.

Jorgensen, Danny L. "Building the Kingdom of God: Alpheus Cutler and the Second Mormon Mission to the Indians, 1846–1853." *Kansas History* 15, no. 3 (Autumn 1992): 192–209.

————. "Conflict in the Camps of Israel: The 1853 Cutlerite Schism." *Journal of Mormon History* 21, no. 1 (1995): 25–64.

Justice, Daniel. *Our Fire Survives the Storm: A Cherokee Literary History*. Minneapolis: University of Minnesota Press, 2006.

Karp, Matthew. *This Vast Southern Empire: Slaveholders at the Helm of American Foreign Policy*. Cambridge, MA: Harvard University Press, 2016.

Kidd, Colin. *The Forging of Races: Race and Scripture in the Protestant Atlantic World, 1600–2000*. Cambridge: Cambridge University Press, 2006.

King, Thomas. *The Truth about Stories: A Native Narrative*. Minneapolis: University of Minnesota Press, 2005.

Klassen, Pamela E. "Ritual." In *The Oxford Handbook of Religion and Emotion.* Edited by John Corrigan, 144–58. New York: Oxford University Press, 2007.

Kling, David W. "A Contested Legacy: Interpreting, Debating and Translating the Bible in America." In *American Christianities: A History of Dominance and Diversity.* Edited by Catherine A. Brekus and W. Clark Gilpin, 214–41. Chapel Hill: University of North Carolina Press, 2011.

Koffman, David S. *The Jews' Indian: Colonialism, Pluralism, and Belonging in America.* New Brunswick, NJ: Rutgers University Press, 2019.

Kohn, S. Joshua. "Mordecai Manuel Noah's Ararat Project and the Missionaries." *American Jewish Historical Quarterly* 55, no. 2 (December 1, 1965).

Konkle, Maureen. *Writing Indian Nations: Native Intellectuals and the Politics of Historiography, 1827–1863.* Chapel Hill: University of North Carolina Press, 2004.

Kramer, Paul A. "Power and Connection: Imperial Histories of the United States in the World." *American Historical Review* 116, no. 5 (December 2011): 1348–91.

Kutsche, Paul. *A Guide to Cherokee Documents in the Northeastern United States.* Metuchen, NJ: Scarecrow Press, 1986.

Leonard, Glen. *Nauvoo: A Place of Peace, a People of Promise.* Salt Lake City, Utah: Brigham Young University Press, 2002.

Lepore, Jill. *The Name of War: King Philip's War and the Origins of American Identity.* New York: Random House, 1998.

Lepper, Bradley T., and Jeffrey Gill. "The Newark Holy Stones: The Social Context of an Enduring Scientific Forgery." Presented at the Ohio Archaeological Council Fall Meeting, Newark, OH, November 1, 2008. https://www.ohioarchaeology.org/39-resources/research/articles-and-abstracts-2008/279-the-newark-qholy-stonesq-the-social-context-of-an-enduring-scientific-forgery.

LeSueur, Stephen. *The 1838 Mormon War in Missouri.* Columbia: University of Missouri Press, 1987.

Linsley, Susanna. "Saving the Jews: Religious Toleration and the American Society for Meliorating the Condition of the Jews." *Journal of the Early Republic* 34, no. 4 (Winter 2014): 625–51.

Maffly-Kipp, Laurie. "Introduction." In *The Book of Mormon.* Translated by Joseph Smith Jr., vii–xxviii. New York: Penguin Books, 2008.

———. *Setting down the Sacred Past: African-American Race Histories.* Cambridge, MA: Belknap Press of Harvard University Press, 2010.

Mahmood, Saba. *Religious Difference in a Secular Age: A Minority Report.* Princeton, NJ: Princeton University Press, 2016.

Marsden, George. *Understanding Fundamentalism and Evangelicalism.* Grand Rapids, MI: W.B. Eerdmans, 1991.

Martin, Joel W. "Crisscrossing Projects of Sovereignty and Conversion: Cherokee Christians and New England Missionaries During the 1820s." In *Native Americans, Christianity, and the Reshaping of the American Religious Landscape.* Edited by Joel W. Martin and Mark A. Nicholas, 67–92. Chapel Hill: University of North Carolina Press, 2010.

Martínez, María Elena. *Genealogical Fictions: Limpieza de Sangre, Religion, and Gender in Colonial Mexico*. Stanford, CA: Stanford University Press, 2008.

Massumi, Brian. "The Autonomy of Affect." *Cultural Critique*, no. 31 (1995): 83–109.

Masuzawa, Tomoko. *The Invention of World Religions, or, How European Universalism Was Preserved in the Language of Pluralism*. Chicago: University of Chicago Press, 2005.

Mauss, Armand. *All Abraham's Children: Changing Mormon Conceptions of Race and Lineage*. Urbana: University of Illinois Press, 2003.

McBride, Spencer. *Pulpit and Nation: Clergymen and the Politics of Revolutionary America*. Charlottesville: University of Virginia Press, 2016.

McCann, Anthony. *Shadowlands: Fear and Freedom at the Oregon Standoff*. New York: Bloomsbury, 2019.

McDonnell, Michael. *Masters of Empire: Great Lakes Indians and the Making of America*. New York: Hill and Wang, 2015.

McGarry, Molly. *Ghosts of Futures Past: Spiritualism and the Cultural Politics of Nineteenth-Century America*. Electronic resource. Berkeley: University of California Press, 2008.

McLoughlin, William. *Cherokee Renascence in the New Republic*. Princeton, NJ: Princeton University Press, 1986.

———. *Cherokees and Missionaries, 1789–1839*. New Haven, CT: Yale University Press, 1984.

———. "Fractured Myths: The Cherokees' Use of Christianity." In *The Cherokees and Christianity, 1794–1870: Essays on Acculturation and Cultural Persistence*. Edited by Walter H. Conser Jr. 152–87. Athens: University of Georgia Press, 1994.

———. "Two Boston Missionaries." In *The Cherokees and Christianity, 1794–1870: Essays on Acculturation and Cultural Persistence*. Edited by Walter H. Conser Jr., 50–90. Athens: University of Georgia Press, 1994.

Méchoulan, Henry, and Gérard Nahon, eds. *The Hope of Israel: The English Translation by Moses Wall*. Written by Menasseh Ben Israel. New York: Oxford University Press, 1987.

Meyer, Roy. *The Village Indians of the Upper Missouri: The Mandans, Hidatsas, and Arikaras*. Lincoln: University of Nebraska Press, 1977.

Miles, Tiya. *Ties That Bind: The Story of an Afro-Cherokee Family in Slavery and Freedom*. Berkeley: University of California Press, 2005.

Miller, Paul B. "'Benedito Sea A. Que No Me Hizo Indio Ni Negro': Ethnic Paradigms in Menasseh Ben Israel's Esperança de Israel." *Bulletin of Hispanic Studies* 89, no. 5 (September 2012): 473–82.

Miller, Robert J. "The Doctrine of Discovery, Manifest Destiny, and American Indians." In *Why You Can't Teach United States History without American Indians*. Edited by Susan Sleeper-Smith, Jean O'Brien, Nancy Shoemaker, and Scott Manning Stevens, 87–100. Chapel Hill: University of North Carolina Press, 2015.

Minkema, Kenneth P., and Harry Stout. "The Edwardsean Tradition and the Antislavery Debate, 1740–1865." *Journal of American History* 92, no. 1 (June 2005): 47–74.

Modern, John. *Secularism in Antebellum America: With Reference to Ghosts, Protestant Subcultures, Machines, and Their Metaphors; Featuring Discussions of Mass Media, Moby-Dick, Spirituality, Phrenology, Anthropology, Sing Sing State Penitentiary, and Sex with the New Motive Power.* Chicago: University of Chicago Press, 2011.

Morgan, David. "Emotion and Imagination in the Ritual Entanglement of Religion, Sport, and Nationalism." In *Feeling Religion.* Edited by John Corrigan, 222–41. Durham, NC: Duke University Press, 2017.

Morgan, Edmund. *Visible Saints: The History of a Puritan Idea.* New York: New York University Press, 1963.

Morgan, Edmund S. *American Slavery, American Freedom: The Ordeal of Colonial Virginia.* New York: Norton, 1975.

Mueller, Max Perry. *Race and the Making of the Mormon People.* Chapel Hill: University of North Carolina Press, 2017.

Mullen, Lincoln. *The Chance of Salvation: A History of Conversion in America.* Cambridge, MA: Harvard University Press, 2017.

Nelson, G. Blair. "Men before Adam!: American Debates over the Unity and Antiquity of Humanity." In *When Science & Christianity Meet.* Edited by David Lindberg and Ronald L. Numbers, 161–82. Chicago: University of Chicago Press, 2003.

Noll, Mark. *America's God: From Jonathan Edwards to Abraham Lincoln.* New York: Oxford University Press, 2002.

———. *The Scandal of the Evangelical Mind.* Grand Rapids, MI: W.B. Eerdmans, 1995.

O'Brien, Jean. *Dispossession by Degrees: Indian Land and Identity in Natick, Massachusetts, 1650–1790.* Cambridge: Cambridge University Press, 1997.

———. *Firsting and Lasting: Writing Indians out of Existence in New England.* Minneapolis: University of Minnesota Press, 2010.

O'Connell, Barry. "Introduction." In *On Our Own Ground: The Complete Writings of William Apess, a Pequot.* Amherst: University of Massachusetts Press, 1992.

———. "Textual Afterword." In *On Our Own Ground: The Complete Writings of William Apess, a Pequot,* 311–24. Amherst: University of Massachusetts Press, 1992.

Onuf, Peter. "Imperialism and Nationalism in the Early American Republic." In *Empire's Twin: U.S. Anti-Imperialism from the Founding Era to the Age of Terrorism.* Edited by Ian Tyrrell and Jay Sexton. Ithaca, NY: Cornell University Press, 2015.

Oppenheim, Samuel. "The Jews and Masonry in the United States Before 1810." *Publications of the American Jewish Historical Society* 19 (January 1, 1910), 1–94.

Orsi, Robert A. *Between Heaven and Earth: The Religious Worlds People Make and the Scholars Who Study Them.* Princeton, NJ: Princeton University Press, 2005.

Paddison, Joshua. *American Heathens: Religion, Race, and Reconstruction in California.* Berkeley: University of California Press, 2012.

Pagden, Anthony. *The Fall of Natural Man: The American Indian and the Origins of Comparative Ethnology.* New York: Cambridge University Press, 1982.

Parfitt, Tudor. *Black Jews in Africa and the Americas*. Cambridge, MA: Harvard University Press, 2013.

———. *The Lost Tribes of Israel*. London: Weidenfeld & Nicolson, 2002.

Park, Benjamin E. *American Nationalisms: Imagining Union in the Age of Revolutions, 1783–1833*. New York: Cambridge University Press, 2018.

———. "Joseph Smith's Kingdom of God: The Council of Fifty and the Mormon Challenge to American Democratic Politics." *Church History* 87, no. 4 (December 2018): 1029–55.

Pearce, Roy Harvey. *Savagism and Civilization*. Berkeley: University of California Press, 1988.

Pencak, William. *Jews & Gentiles in Early America: 1654–1800*. Ann Arbor: University of Michigan Press, 2005.

Perdue, Theda. *Cherokee Women: Gender and Culture Change, 1700–1835*. Lincoln: University of Nebraska Press, 1999.

Perdue, Theda, and Michael D. Green. *The Cherokee Nation and the Trail of Tears*. New York: Viking, 2007.

Perl-Rosenthal, Nathan R. "The 'Divine Right of Republics': Hebraic Republicanism and the Debate over Kingless Government in Revolutionary America." *William and Mary Quarterly*, 3rd ser., 66, no. 3 (July 2009): 535–64.

Phillips, Joyce B., and Paul Gary Phillips, eds. *The Brainerd Journal: A Mission to the Cherokees, 1817–1823*. Indians of the Southeast. Lincoln: University of Nebraska Press, 1998.

Plamper, Jan. *The History of Emotions an Introduction*. New York: Oxford University Press, 2015.

Pogue, James. *Chosen Country: A Rebellion in the West*. New York: Henry Holt, 2018.

Popkin, Richard H. "The Rise and Fall of the Jewish Indian Theory." In *Menasseh Ben Israel and His World*. Edited by Yosef Kaplan, Henry Méchoulan, and Richard H. Popkin, 63–82. Leiden, Netherlands: E.J. Brill, 1989.

Porterfield, Amanda. *Conceived in Doubt: Religion and Politics in the New American Nation*. Chicago: University of Chicago Press, 2012.

Pratt, Julius W. "The Origin of 'Manifest Destiny.'" *The American Historical Review* 32, no. 4 (July 1927): 795–98.

Pulsipher, Jenny. *Subjects unto the Same King: Indians, English, and the Contest for Authority in Colonial New England*. Philadelphia: University of Pennsylvania Press, 2005.

Radus, Daniel. "Apess's Eulogy on Tour: Kinship and the Transnational History of Native New England." *Studies in American Indian Literatures* 28, no. 3 (Fall 2016): 81–110.

Rappaport, Joanne. "'Asi Lo Paresçe Por Su Aspeto': Physiognomy and the Construction of Difference in Colonial Bogotá." *Hispanic American Historical Review* 91, no. 4 (November 2011): 601–31.

Reed, Julie. *Serving the Nation: Cherokee Sovereignty and Social Welfare, 1800–1907*. Norman: University of Oklahoma Press, 2016.

Reeve, W. Paul. *Religion of a Different Color: Race and the Mormon Struggle for Whiteness*. New York: Oxford University Press, 2015.

Rifkin, Mark. "Shadows of Mashantucket: William Apess and the Representation of Pequot Place." *American Literature* 84, no. 4 (December 1, 2012): 691–714.

Rindfleisch, Bryan C. "'What It Means to Be a Man': Contested Masculinity in the Early Republic and Antebellum America." *History Compass* 10, no. 11 (November 2012): 852–65.

Robbins, Thomas. *A View of All Religions; and the Religious Ceremonies of All Nations at the Present Day*. 3rd ed. Hartford, CT: Oliver D. Cooke & Sons, 1824.

Roediger, David. *The Wages of Whiteness: Race and the Making of the American Working Class*. New York: Verso, 1991.

Rosenwein, Barbara. *Emotional Communities in the Early Middle Ages*. Ithaca, NY: Cornell University Press, 2006.

Rubinstein, Rachel. *Members of the Tribe: Native America in the Jewish Imagination*. Detroit, MI: Wayne State University Press, 2010.

Ruchames, Louis. "Mordecai Manuel Noah and Early American Zionism." *American Jewish Historical Quarterly* 64, no. 3 (March 1975): 195–223.

Rushforth, Brett. "'A Little Flesh We Offer You': The Origins of Indian Slavery in New France." In *American Encounters: Natives and Newcomers from European Contact to Indian Removal, 1500–1850*. Edited by Peter Mancall and James Merrell. 2nd ed., 455–82. New York: Routledge, 2007.

Saler, Bethel. *The Settlers' Empire: Colonialism and State Formation in America's Old Northwest*. Philadelphia: University of Pennsylvania Press, 2015.

Sanders, Daniel Clarke. *A History of the Indian Wars with the First Settlers of the United States to the Commencement of the Late War*. Rochester, NY: Edwin Scrantom, 1828.

Sarna, Jonathan. *American Judaism: A History*. New Haven, CT: Yale University Press, 2004.

———. *Jacksonian Jew: The Two Worlds of Mordecai Noah*. New York: Holmes & Meier, 1981.

Sassi, Jonathan. *A Republic of Righteousness: The Public Christianity of the Post-Revolutionary New England Clergy*. New York: Oxford University Press, 2001.

Saxton, Alexander. *The Rise and Fall of the White Republic: Class Politics and Mass Culture in Nineteenth-Century America*. New York: Verso, 1990.

Schaefer, Donovan O. *Religious Affects: Animality, Evolution, and Power*. Durham, NC: Duke University Press, 2015.

Scheer, Monique. "Are Emotions a Kind of Practice (and Is That What Makes Them Have a History)? A Bourdieuian Approach to Understanding Emotion." *History and Theory* 51 (May 2012): 193–220.

Schmidt, Leigh Eric. *Hearing Things: Religion, Illusion, and the American Enlightenment*. Cambridge, MA: Harvard University Press, 2000.

———. *Heaven's Bride: The Unprintable Life of Ida C. Craddock, American Mystic, Scholar, Sexologist, Martyr, and Madwoman*. New York: Basic Books, 2010.

———. *Holy Fairs: Scotland and the Making of American Revivalism*. 2nd ed. Grand Rapids, MI: William B. Eerdmans, 2001.

———. *Restless Souls: The Making of American Spirituality*. 2nd ed. Berkeley: University of California Press, 2012.

Shalev, Eran. *American Zion: The Old Testament as a Political Text from the Revolution to the Civil War*. New Haven, CT: Yale University Press, 2013.

———. "'Revive, Renew, and Reestablish': Mordecai Noah's Ararat and the Limits of Biblical Imagination in the Early American Republic." *American Jewish Archives Journal* 62, no. 1 (2010): 1–20.

Shankman, Andrew. "Conflict for a Continent: Land, Labor, and the State in the First American Republic." In *The World of the Revolutionary American Republic: Land, Labor, and the Conflict for a Continent*. Edited by Andrew Shankman, 1–24. Routledge Worlds. New York: Routledge, 2014.

Shoemaker, Nancy. "How Indians Got to Be Red." *American Historical Review* 102, no. 3 (June 1, 1997): 625–44.

———. "Mr. Tashtego: Native American Whalemen in Antebellum New England." *Journal of the Early Republic* 33, no. 1 (Spring 2013): 109–32.

Silverblatt, Irene. *Modern Inquisitions: Peru and the Colonial Origins of the Civilized World*. Durham, NC: Duke University Press, 2004.

Silverman, David. *Red Brethren: The Brothertown and Stockbridge Indians and the Problem of Race in Early America*. Ithaca, NY: Cornell University Press, 2010.

Silverman, David J. "The Curse of God: An Idea and Its Origins among the Indians of New York's Revolutionary Frontier." *William and Mary Quarterly* 66, no. 3 (July 2009): 495–534.

Slotkin, Richard. *The Fatal Environment: The Myth of the Frontier in the Age of Industrialization, 1800–1890*. Norman: University of Oklahoma Press, 1998.

———. *Regeneration through Violence; the Mythology of the American Frontier, 1600–1860*. Middletown, CT: Wesleyan University Press, 1973.

Smith, Christopher C. "Playing Lamanite: Ecstatic Performance of American Indian Roles in Early Mormon Ohio." *Journal of Mormon History* 41, no. 3 (2015): 131–66.

Smith, Henry. *Virgin Land: The American West as Symbol and Myth*. Cambridge, MA: Harvard University Press, 1970.

Smith, Jonathan Z. "Religion, Religions, Religious." In *Relating Religion: Essays in the Study of Religion*. Edited by Jonathan Z. Smith, 179–96. Chicago: University of Chicago, 2004.

Sobel, Mechal. *The World They Made Together: Black and White Values in Eighteenth-Century Virginia*. Princeton, NJ: Princeton University Press, 1987.

Sottile, Leah. "Bundyville." *Longreads*, May 2018. https://longreads.com/bundyville/.

Stephanson, Anders. *Manifest Destiny: American Expansionism and the Empire of Right*. New York: Hill and Wang, 1995.

Stern, Malcom H. "The 1820s: American Jewry Comes of Age." In *A Bicentennial Festschrift for Jacob Rader Marcus*. Edited by Bertram Wallace Korn, 539–50. New York: KTAV, 1976.

Stevens, Laura. *The Poor Indians: British Missionaries, Native Americans, and Colonial Sensibility*. Philadelphia: University of Pennsylvania Press, 2004.

Stott, G. St. John. "New Jerusalem Abandoned: The Failure to Carry Mormonism to the Delaware." *Journal of American Studies* 21, no. 1 (April 1987): 71–85.

Sturm, Circe. *Blood Politics: Race, Culture, and Identity in the Cherokee Nation of Oklahoma.* Berkeley: University of California Press, 2002.

Sullivan, Winnifred Fallers. *The Impossibility of Religious Freedom.* Princeton, NJ: Princeton University Press, 2005.

Supp-Montgomery, Jenna. "Affect and the Study of Religion." *Religion Compass* 9, no. 10 (2015): 335–45.

Sussman, Lance J. *Isaac Leeser and the Making of American Judaism.* Detroit, MI: Wayne State University Press, 1995.

Sweringa, Robert P. "Ethnoreligious Political Behavior in the Early Nineteenth Century." In *Religion and American Politics: From the Colonial Period to the Present.* Edited by Mark Noll and Luke E. Harlow, 145–68. New York: Oxford University Press, 2007.

Taylor, Alan. *American Colonies.* New York: Viking, 2001.

———. *American Revolutions: A Continental History, 1750–1804.* New York: W.W. Norton, 2016.

———. *The Divided Ground: Indians, Settlers and the Northern Borderland of the American Revolution.* New York: Alfred A. Knopf, 2006.

Taylor, Charles. *A Secular Age.* Cambridge, MA: Harvard University Press, 2007.

Taylor, Lori Elaine. "Elder Nigeajasha and Other Mormon Indians Moving Westward." *John Whitmer Historical Association Journal* 24 (2004).

———. "Telling Stories about Mormons and Indians." PhD diss., State University of New York–Buffalo, 2000.

Teuton, Christopher. *Cherokee Stories of the Turtle Island Liars' Club: Dakasi Elohi Anigagoga Junilawisdii (Turtle, Earth, the Liars, Meeting Place).* Chapel Hill: University of North Carolina Press, 2012.

Thayne, Stanley J. "The Blood of Father Lehi: Indigenous Americans and the Book of Mormon." PhD diss., University of North Carolina–Chapel Hill, 2016.

Thornton, Russell. "The Demography of the Trail of Tears Period: A New Estimate of Cherokee Population Losses." In *Cherokee Removal: Before and After.* Edited by William Anderson, John R. Finger, and Douglas C. Wilms, 75–95. Athens: University of Georgia Press, 1991.

Tuveson, Ernest. *Redeemer Nation: The Idea of America's Millennial Role.* Chicago: University of Chicago Press, 1968.

Tyner, James W. *Those Who Cried the 16,000: A Record of the Individual Cherokee Listed in the United States Official Census of the Cherokee Nation Conducted in 1835.* Norman, OK: Chi-ga-u Inc., 1974.

Underwood, Grant. *The Millenarian World of Early Mormonism.* Urbana: University of Illinois Press, 1993.

Van Atta, John. *Securing the West: Politics, Public Lands, and the Fate of the Old Republic, 1785–1850.* Baltimore: Johns Hopkins University Press, 2014.

Vickers, Daniel. "Competency and Competition: Economic Culture in Early America." *William and Mary Quarterly* 47, no. 1 (January 1990): 3–29.

Vigil, Kiara. *Indigenous Intellectuals: Sovereignty, Citizenship, and the American Imagination, 1880–1930.* Cambridge: Cambridge University Press, 2015.

Vogel, Dan, ed. *Early Mormon Documents.* 5 vols. Salt Lake City, UT: Signature Books, 1996.

———. *Indian Origins and the Book of Mormon: Religious Solutions from Columbus to Joseph Smith.* Salt Lake City, UT: Signature Books, 1986.

Waldstreicher, David. *In the Midst of Perpetual Fetes: The Making of American Nationalism, 1776–1820.* Chapel Hill: University of North Carolina Press, 1997.

Walker, Ronald W. "Seeking the 'Remnant': The Native American during the Joseph Smith Period." *Journal of Mormon History* 19, no. 1 (April 1, 1993): 1–33.

Wallace, Anthony. *The Death and Rebirth of the Seneca.* New York: Alfred A. Knopf, 1970.

Warrior, Robert. *The People and the Word: Reading Native Nonfiction.* Minneapolis: University of Minnesota Press, 2005.

Watson, Harry. *Liberty and Power: The Politics of Jacksonian America.* New York: Hill and Wang, 2006.

Weaver, Jace. *That the People Might Live: Native American Literatures and Native American Community.* New York: Oxford University Press, 1997.

Weinberg, Albert. *Manifest Destiny: A Study of Nationalist Expansionism in American History.* Baltimore: Johns Hopkins University Press, 1935.

Wenger, Beth S. *History Lessons: The Creation of American Jewish Heritage.* Princeton, NJ: Princeton University Press, 2010.

Wenger, Tisa. *Religious Freedom: The Contested History of an American Ideal.* Chapel Hill: University of North Carolina Press, 2017.

———. *We Have a Religion: The 1920s Pueblo Indian Dance Controversy and American Religious Freedom.* Chapel Hill: University of North Carolina Press, 2009.

White, Richard. *The Middle Ground: Indians, Empires, and Republics in the Great Lakes Region, 1650–1815.* Cambridge: Cambridge University Press, 1991.

Wigger, John. *Taking Heaven by Storm: Methodism and the Rise of Popular Christianity in America.* New York: Oxford University Press, 1998.

Williams, Raymond. *Marxism and Literature.* Marxist Introductions. New York: Oxford University Press, 1977.

Wolf, Eric. *Europe and the People without History.* Berkeley: University of California Press, 2010.

Wolfe, Patrick. "Settler Colonialism and the Elimination of the Native." *Journal of Genocide Research* 8, no. 4 (December 2006): 387–409.

Wood, Gordon. *Empire of Liberty: A History of the Early Republic, 1789–1815.* New York: Oxford University Press, 2009.

Woodworth, Steven. *Manifest Destinies: America's Westward Expansion and the Road to the Civil War.* New York: Alfred A. Knopf, 2010.

Wulf, Karin. *Not All Wives: Women of Colonial Philadelphia.* Ithaca, NY: Cornell University Press, 2000.

Wyss, Hilary. *Writing Indians: Literacy, Christianity, and Native Community in Early America.* Amherst: University of Massachusetts Press, 2000.

Yokota, Kariann Akemi. *Unbecoming British: How Revolutionary America Became a Postcolonial Nation*. New York: Oxford University Press, 2011.

Zagarell, Sandra A. "Lydia Howard Huntley Sigourney (1791–1865)." In *The Heath Anthology of American Literature*. Edited by Paul Lauter. 5th ed. Vol. B. Boston: Houghton Mifflin College, 2005.

Zakaras, Alex. "Nature, Religion, and the Market in Jacksonian Political Thought." *Journal of the Early Republic* 39, no. 1 (Spring 2019).

Zuck, Rochelle Raineri. "William Apess, the 'Lost Tribes,' and Indigenous Survivance." *Studies in American Indian Literatures* 25, no. 1 (Spring 2013): 1–26.

Index

Abenaki, 150
Adair, James, 31–32, 50
affect. *See* emotions
Allen, Lewis F., 83, 183n23
American Antiquities (publication),
   29
*American Antiquities and
   Discoveries in the West* (Priest),
   139
American Board of
   Commissioners for Foreign
   Missions (American Board),
   100–104, 116–23, 127–28,
   188n1, 189nn13–14. *See also*
   Cherokee Nation; missionaries
American Universal Geography
   (Morse), 23, 35
Antiquities of America Explained
   (Hill), 137–38
Apache, 140
Apess, William: on Christianity
   and Indigenous nationhood,
   91–98; identity of, 18, 73–74,
   86, 185n48, 185n52; on
   Israelite Indians, 74–75, 86–91,
   186n59, 186n64, 186n66;
   names for, 72–73; on Noah's
   work, 86; works by, 73, 88, 90,
   91, 185n49, 188n91

Ararat, 77–81, 82, 83, 182nn16–17
archaeology, 130–31, 135, 137,
   198n21
Askin, John, 172n51
authority, 35–38. *See also* racial
   categorization of people

Balaam, 101
Baptist Church, 25, 26, 27, 121,
   189n14, 191n20
benevolence, 26, 33–35, 94, 147,
   153
Ben Israel, Menasseh, 3
Benite, Zvi Ben-Dor, 7
Black, as term and category, 12
Black Americans: Christianity of,
   193n48; deportation to Africa
   of, 9; enslavement of, 10;
   political rights of, 41; race
   histories by, 186n57; religious
   nationalism and, 5
Book of Mormon, 48, 50–51, 52,
   71. *See also* Mormons
Book of Numbers, 101
Boudinot, Elias (author), 28–32,
   37–38, 43–44, 129, 133. See also
   A Star in the West (Boudinot)
Boudinot, Elias (Cherokee
   editor), 170n19, 189n13